BLACK FRENCH WOMEN AND THE STRUGGLE FOR EQUALITY, 1848–2016

France Overseas: Studies in Empire and Decolonization

Series editors: A. J. B. Johnston, James D. Le Sueur, and Tyler Stovall

Black French Women and the Struggle for Equality, 1848–2016

EDITED AND WITH AN INTRODUCTION BY
FÉLIX GERMAIN AND SILYANE LARCHER

Foreword by T. Denean Sharpley-Whiting

UNIVERSITY OF NEBRASKA PRESS | LINCOLN AND LONDON

∞

Library of Congress Cataloging-in-Publication Data
Names: Germain, Félix F., editor. | Larcher, Silyane, editor.
| Sharpley-Whiting, T. Denean, writer of foreword.
Title: Black French women and the struggle for equality,
1848–2016 / edited and with an introduction by Félix Germain
and Silyane Larcher; foreword by T. Denean Sharpley-Whiting.
Description: Lincoln: University of Nebraska Press, [2018] |
Series: France overseas: studies in empire and decolonization
| Includes bibliographical references and index.
Identifiers: LCCN 2017056180
ISBN 9781496201270 (pbk.: alk. paper)
ISBN 9781496210357 (epub)
ISBN 9781496210364 (mobi)
ISBN 9781496210371 (pdf)
Subjects: LCSH: Women's rights—France. | Women,
Black—France—Social conditions. | Women, Black—Legal
status, laws, etc.—France. | France—Race relations.
Classification: LCC HQ1236.5.F8 B483
2018 | DDC 323.3/40944—dc23
LC record available at https://lccn.loc.gov/2017056180

Set in Garamond Premier by Mikala R Kolander.
Designed by N. Putens.

Contents

Foreword

T. DENEAN SHARPLEY-WHITING

That black French women and black women in French history, whether citizens or not, have been eclipsed in the gales of historical research on women and France is the corrective this volume, *Black French Women and the Struggle for Equality, 1848–2016*, intends to offer, as invisibility has come at the high cost of social justice. A French version of Gloria Hull, Patricia Bell-Scott, and Barbara Smith's *All the Women Are White, All the Blacks Are Men, but Some of Us Are Brave*, this volume attests that black women inhabit some of the most important sociopolitical and cultural moments and tensions around race, gender, sexuality, and class in modern French history. From Sarah Baartman, whose story of silences, pseudo-science, possible sex work, and agency continues to trouble and intrigue researchers; to Mayotte Capécia, the complicated writer, particularly with respect to darker working-class French Caribbean women, who became the *bête noire* of Frantz Fanon and his theories of lactification; to French Assembly politics with Gerty Archimède; to the negritude of Paulette and Jane Nardal, to name the more recognized figures in the volume, the reader will find, like the Age of Discovery, uncharted territories of black French women's radicalism, insurgency, politics, and prose on a global scale.

The collection of assembled scholars, from literary and cultural critics to historians, despite their disciplinary training, tends toward interdisciplinary frameworks to mine their subjects, for the lives of black French women require critical approaches that are capacious and yet nuanced enough to accommodate cultural, national, and class differences despite seemingly raced and gendered similarities. The acquisitive, indeed, voracious French appetite for empire building and the attraction France held out as a site of equality and color blindness demand that the terms "black French women" and "black women in France" and their intellectual engagement resist papering over the multiple meanings and experiences of Frenchness and French identity.

Black French Women and the Struggle for Equality, 1848–2016 cuts through the myths, ideas, and ideals about France to allow a view into the lived experiences of the social actors—black women—who have attempted to move France and the countries it had annexed "with sword in hand," in the words of historian Jules Michelet, toward its ideals, to make those myths of social equality, liberty, and fellowship real for all.

Introduction

Marianne Is Also Black

FÉLIX GERMAIN AND SILYANE LARCHER

> Des millions de personnes sont mises en cause quand on me traite de guenon. Des millions de gamines savent qu'on peut les traiter de guenons dans les cours de récréation!
> When they call me monkey, they are also calling millions of people monkey. Millions of girls also see that they can be called a monkey.
> Minister of Justice Christiane Taubira, *Libération*, November 5, 2013

In the interwar period, Josephine Baker seduced the French, singing and dancing to the rhythm of jazz and other African American musical genres. While her bodily expression enriched France's dancing repertoire, her stage costume—or lack thereof—is perhaps what kept her audience spellbound. Sometimes topless, Baker often wore a distinctive banana belt that evoked "phalluses" and sparked the sexual imagination and fantasies of European men.[1] In many ways, Baker reinforced French perceptions of Africans as primitive and uncivilized people sharing similarities with "animal kingdoms." But Baker was no exception. As Nicolas Bancel and Pascal Blanchard note, "During this era Africans were encouraged to show their bodies in movement (dances in cabaret and in human zoos, a showing of their motivity at the theater, the eroticization of masculine and feminine bodies in almost all forms of representation), which also put them closer to the animal world."[2] Nearly a century after Baker's first performance with her notorious banana belt, the banana—usually used as a symbol of bestiality and primitivism—still surfaces in French society to codify black lives. Indeed, recently, Christiane Taubira, a black woman from French Guiana who served as minister of justice in François Hollande's administration, was unwillingly thrown into the muddy field of racism and colonial misrepresentation. In 2013 Taubira's effort to pass a law granting gays equal marriage rights infuriated social conservatives, causing Anne-Sophie Leclere, a candidate of the Front National (the Far Right political party), to react "violently." Leclere posted a picture on her Facebook account likening Taubira to a monkey. The humiliation continued in the streets when a twelve-year-old white girl handed Taubira a banana during a public rally.

While the above events reverberated across the Atlantic, causing the *New Yorker* and the *New York Times* to publish "The Justice Minister and the Banana: How Racist Is France?" and "'Anti-Racism' of the Left Reaps Scorn in France," respectively, they did not surprise the minister of justice.[3] In an interview with French newspaper *Libération*, she revealed that many elected officials and activists have either compared her to a monkey or told her "Y a bon Banania" (a racist slur addressed to blacks in France). For Taubira, however, it is another phenomenon, one that unfolded without scrutiny, that is most troublesome. She recalled that during the anti–gay marriage protests the crowd chanted, "Taubira, t'es foutue, les Français sont dans la rue" (Taubira, you're done, the French are in the streets). She wondered why they chanted "les Français sont dans la rue," because French protesters are usually very specific about their claims; they would typically say "les parents sont dans la rue" or "les médecins [doctors] sont dans la rue."[4] In hindsight, she understood that the protesters utilized the event to challenge the legitimacy of her nationality and citizenship. In claiming "the French are in the streets," they reacted to what they believed was an immoral law proposed by a minister of justice from a different country, a "foreigner." Apparently, for these French protesters, Taubira, a black woman from French Guiana, cannot be a French native.

What these protesters ignore, however, is that Taubira comes from a *département d'outre-mer* (overseas French department) that has historically embraced and followed French republican ideals to justify its place within the French nation.[5] The protesters may also ignore that many black individuals in France come from countries that were willingly, and more often forcefully, involved in the construction and imagination of the French republic.[6] This old relationship between France, African, and Caribbean countries has, among many other factors, given France an important place in the construction of the black Atlantic.[7] In the twenty-first century, as noted in *Decolonizing the Republic*, France, particularly the Parisian region, is now Europe's largest "black region."[8] Many white French individuals struggle with or flatly deny this French reality. The French citizens who refer to black French citizens as people *issus de l'immigration* (from an immigrant background)—as if white French citizens were not also *issus de l'immigration*—exemplify this condition of denial plaguing contemporary France. In many ways, this dilemma—whites are natives, but people of African descent are not—fuels the research of many scholars, including ours.[9]

Black French Women and the Struggle for Equality, 1848–2016 is a multifaceted narrative presenting France as a former empire and a postcolonial democracy deeply entangled with Africa and the Americas. Though the anthology contributes to the growing scholarship on black France and Overseas France, its scope and breadth differ from previous studies.[10] The essays shed light on the specificities of black female experiences, a subject that for the most part has eluded French scholars, including experts in women's studies. Indeed, in the early 1990s scholars such as Michelle Perrot, Geneviève Fraisse, Michèle Riot-Sarcey, and Françoise Thébaud added layers of complexity to French social studies and history by utilizing gender as a category of analysis.[11] But while they underscored the shortcomings of male-centered and chauvinistic scholarship, they hardly explored how racism, colonialism, (transnational) migration, and xenophobia structured French society, consequently dismissing the experiences of women of color, particularly black women. Their groundbreaking works gave the impression that all French women were white women from continental France.

The same could be said for *Clio*, a prestigious journal advancing women and gender studies in France. Since the mid-1990s the journal has published on themes such as women in the labor market, religion, war, music, and the construction of the nation. But in each issue "women" is basically an acronym for "white women." When the journal published special issues dedicated to women of the Maghreb and the Amériques métisses, it generally located them outside the boundaries of the French nation.[12] Simply put, the study of gender relations and French women ignored how race, origin, and religion structure French society, consequently silencing the presence and experiences of nonwhite subjectivities. Accordingly, the idea of *femmes françaises noires* (black French women) became a *non-objet de pensée* (nonobject of intellectual imagination).

In the last fifteen years or so, the wind of intersectional analysis blowing from across the Atlantic has brought fresh perspectives on studies of social inequalities in France. Seeking to better understand the various processes of social insertion into the French republic and how globalization connects France with the Global South, certain sociologists and anthropologists analyzed the conditions of migrant women and their children (*les femmes de l'immigration*).[13] A few historians have produced outstanding works on women in Francophone Africa. But here again, as Africanists they do not explore the connections between African women and the construction of the French nation.[14]

Building from the aforementioned studies, this volume invites scholars to reflect on the ways in which black women became an integral part of the French nation while also constructing social fields in Overseas and colonial France. Altogether the essays suggest that French imagination and representation of Africans and their descendants, as well as the dialectics between blackness, gender relation, identity formation, colonialism, sexism, xenophobia, and nationalism, among other things, are subjects of inquiry that inform the making of France. Similar to intellectuals from the former sub-Saharan African colonies and the French Caribbean, the authors of the essays in this volume underscore that French constructions of blackness call for developing a scientific discourse shedding light on the role of racism in French history and, evidently, the implications of being black and female in France and Overseas France. In many ways, the volume stands out from others by analyzing black female experiences through the lenses of African, Caribbean, American, and French scholars situated in North American, French, and French Caribbean universities. That said, *Black French Women and the Struggle for Equality, 1848–2016* does not portray black people in France and its former colonies as a coherent or unified group. As the contributing authors demonstrate, blackness in France and Overseas France is neither a prescriptive category nor a label defining a fixed identity that corresponds to a particular social group.[15] Blackness in the French republic is both transnational and profoundly rooted within the nation. Indeed, as we examine the experiences of people of African descent in France and Overseas France through gendered lenses, we merely call for inserting black female subjectivity, in a plural and heterogeneous sense, into the French national narrative.

As a transatlantic collaboration, this volume also builds on scholarship addressing "the Black International as a liberation narrative; and Black Internationalism as an insurgent consciousness formed over and against retrogressive practices embodied in slavery, colonialism, imperialism, and globalization, from the early modern period to the present."[16] Like Paulette Nardal, the famous Martinican intellectual who helped found the negritude "movement," the contributors seek to engender the historical record. Indeed, in the early 1930s, Nardal had already noted the pattern of silencing black women, claiming: "There was a group of Caribbean women students in Paris whose aspirations began to crystallize around *La Revue du monde noir*. Women of color living alone in the metropolis, less recognized than their male counterparts before the Colonial Exhibition, felt long before they did the need for racial solidarity that was not only material: this is how race consciousness was awakened."[17]

Inspired by Nardal's black internationalism and commitment to mapping the presence, role, contribution, and influence of black women in France and Overseas France, this book aims to answer the following questions, among many others: How do the experiences of black women in France vary according to their class, origin, generation, and nationality? How do they differ from those of their white counterparts? How do the lives of black women in France and Overseas France complicate French narratives of universal equality? How does the intersection of race, class, gender, and culture generate new political identities in France and Overseas France? What can we learn about black France and black women in France and the French Caribbean from the perspective of black female writers? How has French visual culture misrepresented black women? What are the different black feminist expressions in France and Overseas France?

The book is divided into five parts, each of which in one way or another addresses themes related to colonialism, imperialism, nationalism, sexism, racism, feminism, gender relations, and globalization. The first part, "Black Women in Politics and Society," draws back the veil on the political agency and influence of French Caribbean and African women in France and their respective societies. In short, readers can see how black French women work through their community to achieve change or spin the wheel of the system for justice and equality. The second part, "Feminist and Postcolonial Movements for Equality," highlights the heterogeneous dimension of "black French feminism" and the ways in which black women lobby and protest to enjoy the full attributes of French citizenship. In analyzing black women's social movements, part 2 also sheds light on the intricacies of power relations in France in Overseas France. Accordingly, when black women embrace French republican universalism, challenge the viciousness of patriarchy, or assert their political identity they are often misrepresented as "dangerous" or "licentious." It is the price they pay for "not staying in their place." The third part, "Respectability, Resistance, and Transnational Identities," complicates the notion of respectability in black women's lives. In addition to exploring the local and personal politics of black female respectability, the authors invite readers to ponder on the intersection between black female subjectivity, respectability, and the nation. Not only do they call for reflecting on "who is French," but they also demonstrate how the social activism of individuals like Jean McNair invites the French state to reflect upon notions of respectable behavior, especially as it pertains to its racialized citizens.[18] The fourth part, "The Dialectics between Body, Nation, and Representation," also touches upon the idea of nation. While the authors describe how the black female body has often been appropriated to define the "other," they also cast light on the ways in which black subjects struggle to represent the black female body on their own terms, particularly during the present era. Finally, the last part, "Black Women Critique the 'Empire,'" underscores the continuity of black women's struggle against colonialism and imperialism from the interwar era to the twenty-first century, when Senegalese author Fatou Diome invited the French republic to live up to her own standard of liberty, equality, and fraternity.

As a transatlantic collaboration, the volume reaffirms that race, gender, origin, ethnicity, nationality, and sexuality intersect to paint a multidimensional mosaic of black women's lives in France and Overseas France. It dismantles imagined notions of black female identity—for instance, that there is no black feminism in France and Overseas France—and opens new avenues of research.[19] To be sure, *Black French Women and the Struggle for Equality, 1848–2016* is an interdisciplinary study reminding readers of the heterogeneous character of French society. Taking into account French social history in the *longue durée*, the black female experiences and expressions that the volume unveils speak to the global dimension of French identity. The book encourages asking if the "imagined community" of a French republic as "indivisible, laïque, démocratique et sociale" has a political or even a philosophical meaning. In particular, the essays question the social foundation of the republic, suggesting that it must take into consideration that race, gender, religion, culture, and history shape social hierarchies and social inequalities. As readers shall see, by broadening the study of historically marginalized and minimized subjects, the book provides different reference points to imagine France and Overseas France.

Notes

1. Alicja Sowinska, "Dialectics of the Banana Skirt: The Ambiguities of Josephine Baker's Self-Representation," *Bodies: Physical and Abstract* 19 (Fall 2005–Spring 2006).
2. Nicolas Bancel and Pascal Blanchard, "The Invention of the Native," in *Colonial Culture in France since the Revolution*, ed. Pascal Blanchard, Sandrine Lemaire, Nicolas Bencel, and Dominic Thomas (Bloomington: Indiana University Press, 2013), 174.
3. Alexandre Stille, "The Justice Minister and the Banana: How Racist Is France?," *New Yorker*, November 14, 2013; Celestine Bohlen, "'Anti-Racism' of the Left Reaps Scorn in France," *New York Times*, December 2, 2013.

4. Fabrice Rousselot and Sonya Faure, "Des inhibitions disparaissent, des digues tombent," *Libération*, November 5, 2013.
5. For a discussion of French Guiana's relationship to France, see Fred Réno and Bernard Phipps, "The Dichotomy of Universalism and Particularism," in *Post-colonial Trajectories in the Caribbean: The Three Guianas*, ed. Rosemarijn Hoefte, Matthew L. Bishop, and Peter Clegg (New York: Routledge, 2017); and Miranda Spieler, *Empire and Underworld: Captivity in French Guiana* (Cambridge MA: Harvard University Press, 2012). For the other overseas French Caribbean departments, see Silyane Larcher, *L'autre citoyen: L'idéal républicain et les Antilles après l'esclavage* (Paris: Armand Colin, 2014); and Félix Germain, "In Search of Full Citizenship: The French West Indian Case (1848–2009)," *Journal of Contemporary Thought* 32 (Winter 2010): 99–112.
6. See Alice Conklin, *A Mission to Civilize: The Republican Idea of Empire in France and West Africa 1895–1930* (Stanford CA: Stanford University Press, 1998); and Raoul Girardet, *L'idée coloniale en France de 1871 à 1962* (Paris: Hachette, 2005). For the relationship that African and Caribbean intellectuals have nourished with French republicanism over time, see Christopher L. Miller, *Nationalists and Nomads: Essays on Francophone African Literature and Culture* (Chicago: University of Chicago Press, 1998); and Gary Wilder, *The French Imperial Nation-State: Negritude and Colonial Humanism between the Two World Wars* (Chicago: University of Chicago Press, 2005).
7. See Christopher L. Miller, *The French Atlantic Triangle: Literature and Culture of the Slave Trade* (Durham NC: Duke University Press, 2008); Laurent Dubois, "The French Atlantic," in *The Atlantic World: A Critical Appraisal*, ed. Jack Greene and Philip Morgan (Oxford: Oxford University Press, 2008).
8. See Felix Germain, *Decolonizing the Republic: African and Caribbean in Postwar Paris, 1946–1974* (East Lansing: Michigan State University Press, 2016), xiv.
9. Some of the interesting works addressing this subject include N'Diaye Pap, *La condition noire: Essai sur une minorité française* (Paris: Calmann-Lévy, 2008); Trica Keaton, *Muslim Girls and the Other France: Race, Identity Politics, and Social Exclusion* (Bloomington: Indiana University Press, 2006); Trica Danielle Keaton, T. Denean Sharpley-Whiting, and Tyler Stovall, eds., *Black France / France Noire: The History and Politics of Blackness* (Durham NC: Duke University Press, 2012); Rashan Maxwell, *Ethnic Minority Migrants in Britain and France: Integration Trade-Offs* (New York: Cambridge University Press, 2012); and Dominic Thomas, *Black France: Colonialism, Immigration, and Transnationalism* (Bloomington: Indiana University Press, 2007).
10. Many scholars in the United States have written about black female experiences in France. For a few good examples, see T. Denean Sharpley-Whiting, *Negritude*

Women (Minneapolis: University of Minnesota Press, 2002); Sharpley-Whiting, *Beyond Negritude: Essays from Women in the City* (Albany: SUNY Albany Press, 2009); Emily Musil, "In Search of Seven Sisters: A Biography of the Nardal Sisters of Martinique," *Callaloo* 36, no. 2 (2013): 375–90; Félix Germain, "Jezebels and Victims: West Indian Women in Postwar France (1946–1975)," *French Historical Studies* 33, no. 3 (Summer 2010): 475–95; and Claire Oberon Garcia, "Black Women Writers, Modernism, and Paris," *International Journal of Francophone Studies* 14, no. 1 (2011): 27–42. When examining the black diaspora, certain scholars have also made a point not to exclude the black female voice. For instance, see Brent Hayes Edwards, *The Practice of Diaspora: Literature, Translation, and the Rise of Black Internationalism* (Cambridge MA: Harvard University Press, 2003); Elizabeth Ezra, *The Colonial Unconscious: Race and Culture in Interwar France* (Ithaca NY: Cornell University Press, 1992); Jennifer Boittin, *Colonial Metropolis: The Urban Grounds of Anti-imperialism and Feminism in Interwar Paris* (Lincoln: University of Nebraska Press, 2010); and Brett Berliner, *Ambivalent Desire: The Exotic Black Other in Jazz-Age France* (Amherst: University of Massachusetts Press, 2002).

11. Michelle Perrot, *Les femmes ou les silences de l'histoire* (Paris: Flammarion, 1998); Geneviève Fraisse, *Les femmes et leur histoire* (Paris: Gallimard, 1998); Michèle Riot-Sarcey, "L'historiographie française et le 'genre,'" *Revue d'histoire moderne et contemporaine* 47, no. 4 (2000): 805–14; Françoise Thébaud, *Écrire l'histoire des femmes* (Fontenay/Saint-Cloud: ENS Éditions, 1998).

12. Special issue, "Femmes du Maghreb," *Clio: Femmes, genre, histoire* 9 (1999); special issue, "Amériques métisses," *Clio: Femmes, genre, histoire* 27 (2008).

13. Among others, see Jules Falquet et al., eds., "Femmes, genre, migrations et mondialisation: Un état des problématiques," *Cahiers du CEDREF* (Université Denis Diderot, Paris, 2008); Marion Manier, "Cause des femmes *vs* cause des minorités: Tensions autour de la question des 'femmes de l'immigration' dans l'action publique française," *Revue européenne de l'immigration* 29, no. 4 (2013): 89–110; Elise Palomarès, "Contester le racisme en mode mineur: Engagements associatifs de femmes originaires du Mali," *Sociétés contemporaines* 70, no. 2 (2008): 45–69; Christian Poiret, "Articuler les rapports de sexe, de classe et interethniques: Quelques enseignements du débat nord-américain," *Revue européenne des migrations internationales* 21, no. 1 (2005): 195–226. On the complicated connection between gender and history of immigration in French academia, see Linda Guerry, "Femmes et genre dans l'histoire de l'immigration: Naissance et cheminement d'un sujet de recherché," *Genre & histoire* 5 (2009).

14. Catherine Coquery-Vidrovitch, *Les Africaines: Histoire des femmes d'Afrique noire du XIX*ᵉ *au XX*ᵉ *siècle* (Paris: Desjonquères, 1994); Odile Goerg, ed., *Perspectives historiques sur le genre en Afrique* (Paris: L'Harmattan, 2007); Fatou Sow, ed., *La*

recherche féministe francophone: Langues, identités, enjeux (Paris: Karthala, 2009); Marie Rodet, *Les migrantes ignorées du Haut Sénégal, 1900–1946* (Paris: Karthala, 2009); Pascale Barthélémy, *Africaines et diplômées à l'école coloniale, 1918–1957* (Rennes: Presses Universitaires de Renne, 2010). See also Anne Hugon, ed., *Histoire des femmes en situation coloniale, Afrique et Asie, XXᵉ siècle* (Paris: Karthala, 2004).

15. For further information, see Jean-Paul Rocchi and Monica Michlin, eds., *Black Intersectionalities: A Critique for the 21st Century* (Liverpool: Liverpool University Press, 2014).
16. This quote is actually the statement of purpose of *Palimpsest: A Journal on Women, Gender, and the Black International*, which draws on African diasporic studies and womanist/feminist thoughts to produce articles on women of African descent.
17. Paulette Nardal, "Eveil de la conscience de race," in *La revue du monde noir*, 1931.
18. In fact, who is French from both racial and gender standpoints is the topic that Stovall and Boittin sought to complicate in a special issues of *French Historical Studies*. Jennifer Anne Boittin and Tyler Stovall, "Who Is French?," *French Historical Studies* 33, no. 3 (Summer 2010): 349–56. In French, this issue is also addressed in Cécile Vidal, ed., *Français? La nation en débat entre métropole et colonies, XVIᵉ–XIXᵉ siècles* (Paris: École des Hautes Études en Sciences Sociales, 2014).
19. Elsa Dorlin, *Black Feminism: Anthologie du féminisme africain-américain, 1975–2000* (Paris: L'Harmattan, 2008), 12.

PART 1 Black Women in Politics and Society

1

Originaire Women and Political Life in Senegal's Four Communes

HILARY JONES

On June 7, 2010, the gender parity law proposed by President Abdoulaye Wade of the Republic of Senegal became law. The law specified that women must comprise at least half of the party candidates for all local and national elections. In 2012 sixty-five women succeeded in becoming members of Senegal's National Assembly.[1] Subsequently, the law has stimulated debate and provoked controversy over the struggle for gender equality in Senegal, the legacy of French rule, and the role of women in government. Considering Senegal's *originaire* women offers valuable perspective on the making of an African citizenry in Senegal's French colonial towns.[2] It shows the gendered notions of power and politics that urban Senegalese brought to the public arena in the early colonial period and also shines a light on the connections between gender and colonialism, especially in the arena of government and politics. This study, while not exhaustive, offers a fresh perspective on the intersection of urban life, citizenship, and gender in French West Africa.

In the late nineteenth and early twentieth centuries, neither African women nor French women possessed the right to vote, and yet women of Senegal's colonial towns exercised influence within the masculine domain of electoral politics. Taking a closer look at African understandings of female power and the ways in which women interacted with politics in the colonial towns makes the role of daughters, mothers, wives, and sisters visible in our narratives about Africa under French rule. Prior to the formal colonial era, women in urban and rural settings held access to power even though patrilineal systems and patriarchal norms limited women's authority. The advent of colonial conquest subordinated the role of elite women in public life to the authority of male chiefs, male officials, and, in the case of the towns, notable men who held elected office. Senegal's *originaire* women, in this case, withdrew from politics and instead focused attention on networks of civil society that could be mobilized to protect the reputation of their families, secure needed services for their neighborhoods, and weigh in on political debate at critical moments. This essay examines the specific skills and strategies that African women brought to the making of the urban citizenry and the art of politics during the early phase of French colonial rule in Senegal.

Toward a Gender Perspective on Colonial Citizenship in French West Africa

The literature on politics in French West Africa necessarily deals with the concept of citizenship as the central idea that structured the assimilationist rhetoric of French empire and also because Africans, particularly after World War II, based their claims for equal rights on the long-established notion of citizenship as integral to the French "civilizing mission."[3] In his research on Senegal's dockworkers at the height of colonialism, historian Frederick Cooper demonstrated that even trade unionists used the idea of citizenship to make demands on the French state and to claim equality with other French citizens.[4] Mamadou Diouf argues that the origins of African concepts of citizenship date to the mid-nineteenth century, when Senegal's *originaires* transformed the French idea of citizenship by fighting for their right to vote as "citizens" of the towns without renouncing their personal or Islamic status, a condition of colonial citizenship required by the French state.[5] Indeed, Senegal's modern political history cannot be understood without reference to how the idea of colonial citizenship became articulated in the urban administrative district of the Four Communes and thus served as a model for future rights claims in French West Africa.

Although the literature is replete with cases that show the importance of the idea of citizenship for people of French West Africa, none consider the gendered aspects of colonial citizenship nor how women understood and proclaimed the rights of Africans under French rule to be treated as citizens rather than subjects.[6] One reason for this absence has to do with the fact that French women did not achieve voting rights until the Fourth Republic extended the franchise to women in 1944. Even though France confirmed the legal status of Senegal's *originaires* as citizens with the Diagne laws of 1916, only adult men had the right to vote. Furthermore, Blaise Diagne tied his legislative proposal to recognized residents of the Four Communes as full French citizens to the fact that Senegalese men had demonstrated their loyalty by fighting and dying for France in the Great War, like all other Frenchmen.[7] Since the historical record does not mention individual women as key figures in urban political life of early colonial Senegal, historians have generally understood electoral politics as men's business. Until recently, scholars have primarily considered African nationalism as the work of male actors.[8] Among Senegal's most well known figures of the "modern" era, the names François Carpot, Blaise Diagne, Lamine Guèye, Modibo Keita, and Leopold Senghor are familiar. Less familiar are the names Soukeyna Konaré (cousin of *originaire* politician Lamine Guèye), Constance Devès (daughter of Saint-Louis political leader Gaspard Devès and sister of Saint-Louis mayor Justin Devès), Ndate Yalla Fall (cousin of *originaire* politician Galandou Diouf), and Caroline Diop (first Senegalese woman elected to the National Assembly). Both the documentation produced by the colonial administration and scholars' assumptions about the role of politics and the history of nationalism underscore male biases in the production of knowledge about colonial Africa.

Second, any study of the role of women in the political activities of Senegal's colonial towns must consider the intersection between French structures of governance and African understandings of power and politics. Scholars of African feminism contend that we cannot approach the study of African women and their search for equality in the same manner that we understand the concerns of women's movements in the West.[9] Elizabeth Schmidt's study of women's entry into party politics in Guinea during the decade of decolonization shows that African women entered the political arena not to fight for gender equality or to articulate their right to be leaders in party politics but rather to right the wrongs of society and to deal with the social and economic realities facing them, their families, and their communities. Schmidt shows us that for Guinean women in politics, "female consciousness held sway over feminist."[10] The absence of *originaire* women in narratives about urban politics underscores the gaps in our understanding of the gender dynamics of colonial rule. In order to fully appreciate colonial citizenship and the emergence of electoral politics in Senegal under French rule, these silences deserve interrogation to advance research on the subject.

Urban Identity and *Originaire* Politics in Senegal's Towns

Today's Republic of Senegal sits at the westernmost point of sub-Saharan Africa. Situated where the Senegal River meets the Atlantic Ocean, Senegal has served as a natural entry point for North Africans and Saharans who crossed the southern edges of the desert, as well as Europeans who approached the continent from the ocean. French recognition of the Four Communes as municipalities stems in part from the long history of Saint-Louis and Gorée as seats of French mercantile trade interests and the locus for imperial expansion. In the mid-seventeenth century, the French built forts on the coastal islands to facilitate the trade in slaves and other trade goods. In the nineteenth century, Saint-Louis became the most viable port for French "legitimate trade" interests. The town also acted as the French cultural capital in the region and the place where the French military launched wars of conquest in the interior.[11] For a short period from 1895 to 1902, the French named Saint-Louis as the capital of French West Africa before moving the federation's headquarters to Dakar.

The long history of French and African engagement in coastal Senegal produced a population of Africans who worked closely around the French forts and who adopted Catholicism (called *gourmets*) and a self-conscious mixed-race group born to African or Afro-European women (called *signares*) and European merchants or soldiers. The towns of Gorée and Saint-Louis in particular fostered the growth of an urban community with long-standing ties to France. The residents of that community served as trade intermediaries and sought integration into French familial, trade, and political networks.[12] As early as the mid-eighteenth century, town residents elected their own mayor from among the notable inhabitants who represented the urban community, who managed affairs related to the town, and who even convened the Catholics for mass and festivals in the absence of a permanent clergy. In addition, Saint-Louis supported the growth of an influential Muslim community. Migrants from the upper and lower Senegal valley brought Islam to the town. After 1830 free Muslim traders gained entry into the middleman trade in the upriver trade posts.[13] Muslim traders owned property on the island and strategically sent their sons to study in both French schools and Koranic schools on the island. The population of nineteenth-century Saint-Louis thus reflected the heterogeneity and cosmopolitanism of a vibrant nineteenth-century port that straddled both African and French worlds.

Historians disagree about when exactly the word *originaire* came to refer to Senegal's urban population under colonial rule.[14] Regardless of when it appeared, it has become synonymous with the struggle by black African residents of Senegal's towns for full status as French citizens. According to the decree of November 5, 1830, all free adult men born and living in Senegal could enjoy the same rights as those granted to French citizens by the civil code. The Second Republic elaborated on the legal rights of Senegal's inhabitants by establishing the General Council for Senegal similar to the departmental assemblies in metropolitan France.[15] The provision further clarified the status of town residents by specifying that these inhabitants did not have to be naturalized in order to vote but rather had only to prove five years' permanent residency. Eligible voters, moreover, did not have to renounce their personal Islamic or "customary" status in order to qualify. The voting laws thus created an opening that gave *originaires* the right to carry out the duties of French citizens without conforming to the requirements of the French civil code.

Although the Second Republic established electoral institutions in Senegal, Napoleon III suspended the practice of local representative offices in the colony. In 1871 the Third Republic recognized the role of the urban population as voters and elaborated on the republican institutions in Senegal's towns. The municipal decree of 1871 established the communes and specified management by an elected municipal council headed by a mayor and deputy mayor chosen from the top of the winning slate of candidates. In addition to Gorée and Saint-Louis, Dakar and Rufisque completed Senegal's Four Communes.[16] At the request of *métis* and French Saint-Louis residents, the Third Republic also reestablished the General Council, which was similar to departmental assemblies in metropolitan France. In 1879 the Third Republic completed the group of electoral institutions in the colony by reestablishing Senegal's seat in the Chamber of Deputies.

Between 1871 and 1900 the electoral campaigns revolved around candidates with close ties to French military, commercial, or administrative interests and factions who opposed these imperial interests. French and *métis* men dominated electoral politics in this period by relying on patron-client networks to mobilize the African vote in favor of their slate of candidates. After 1900 the political winds began to shift as the African urban community pushed for greater representation in the republican institutions. Additionally, the consolidation of French power in the interior led officials to suppress the black vote in the towns and to question the legitimacy of their claim to be "citizens," not subjects.[17] For colonial authorities, the electoral institutions interfered with their ability to implement arbitrary policies or impose authoritarian practices on the Protectorate population with little or no oversight from Paris or Saint-Louis. According to French officials, influential individuals within the urban community at times acted as a "meddlesome elite" who sought to use the republican institutions as a means of surveillance over abuses of power in the colony.[18] The idea that town residents had special status carried particular meaning for *originaires* who worked in the interior as clerks for the colonial administration or as traders in the peanut basin and Senegal River trade depots, where they were often mistaken for or subjected to the same treatment as Africans who lived under the Protectorate administration. In the early 1900s the

Jeunes Sénégalais, a group composed of French-educated African town residents, began articulating *originaire* interests in their newspapers and organizing to actively support black African candidates for elected office.

The emergence of black politics, as historian G. Wesley Johnson termed the struggle for political equality in Senegal's colonial towns, involved the internecine struggles of "electoral clans" and the racial politics of French colonialism, which practiced a de facto exclusion of the majority of black African male voters from holding office. Historians have paid very little attention to the gendered nature of political life or the ways in which women entered into political debate despite the fact that they did not have the right to vote or hold public office. Where and when did women enter into the politics of the Senegal colony? What notions of the art of politics did they bring with them? The following section addresses these questions by considering notions of female power in urban and rural locations of precolonial Senegambia.

Women and Political Power before French Rule

Originaire women's ideas about power and politics did not merely stem from French systems but were also grounded in African ideas about female power and the art of politics that informed the states and societies of precolonial Senegambia. For instance, the Wolof kingdoms relied on both patrilineal and matrilineal principles to determine royal succession. In the Wolof kingdoms of Waalo and Kajoor, the *linger* (princess or queen) represented the matrilineal line of succession.[19] As the mother or sister of the king, the *linger* served as the leader of the community of women of the country. She controlled key territories in the kingdom, and she presided over judicial issues related to marriage and the punishment of young girls who entered into sexual relations outside of marriage. Although men held the right to rule, the *linger* played a key role in determining succession. As keeper of the *meen*, or representative of the matrilineage, she was responsible for negotiating between the noble lineages to determine the ruler of the kingdom. According to Boubacar Barry, these women gave lavish feasts and offered elaborate gifts in order to convince the nobles to vote for their candidate.[20] Indeed, the last two *lingers* of Waalo, Njömbot and

Ndate Yalla, understood the power of patronage for political ends. Both *lingers* transformed the office by becoming de facto rulers in the place of weakened kings.[21] In the mid-nineteenth century, they used strategic marriage alliances and developed networks of patronage to achieve power and to maintain the sovereignty of Waalo in the face of threats by the Moors on the right bank of the Senegal and French invasion from Saint-Louis.

The Lebou population of Ndakaru (Dakar) organized politics among the twelve villages according to a community assembly, or *peñc*. Traditionally fishermen and farmers, the Lebou recognized a male leader (*seriñ*) but practiced politics through group discussion among elders and people of the village. While men played a dominant role in community meetings, elder women held a special position. The Wolof notion of *saani ci sa kaadu*, meaning "to throw in the last word," has a particular connotation when related to women's speech during group meetings. Aissatou Diop-Hashim explains that *saani kaadu* indicates the space reserved for the elder women of the community to give the last word in making the case for a marriage between families or during the community meeting.[22] Indeed, the idea that women are given the right to launch the last appeal may have originated among the original Wolof speakers of the Lebou villages on the Cap-Vert peninsula. It is, therefore, not surprising that Blaise Diagne (Lebou on his father's side) recognized the importance of campaigning in Wolof by speaking to the Lebou community assemblies and addressing key issues of community well-being that must certainly have resonated with Lebou women of Dakar and Rufisque.[23]

Lastly, the *signares* of Saint-Louis and Gorée also constituted a class of viable political actors in Senegal before the formal era of colonial empire. These propertied women of "social consequence" emerged in the early eighteenth century as the companions and wives of European merchants and soldiers who resided in Senegal temporarily.[24] As scholars have shown, these women gained notoriety from travel accounts that described their beauty and their keen entrepreneurial skills. These women profited from their in-between position to capitalize on the upriver trade markets in gold and slaves and the Atlantic market of imported luxury goods. They also owned the majority of real estate (houses and river boats) on the island towns. By the mid-eighteenth century, *signares* rented their slaves to the French and British forts for public works and up-river trade. While these *signares* operated in the French bureaucratic register of the towns, they did not sit on the governor's advisory council or hold public office. The administration recognized *signares* as town notables, even though they were denied the franchise. The most successful used their position as property owners and their reputation as esteemed members of the urban community to influence administrative policy and the political debates among town residents.

Originaire Women and the Art of Politics

How did *originaire* voters bring their understanding of female power to bear on electoral politics in Senegal's Four Communes? In what ways did *originaire* women rely on both French systems of administration and Senegambian ideas of politics to make their voices heard in the public arena? Historians have typically divided the history of urban politics in the communes into two periods: the period of French and Creole domination (1872–1900) and the period of African "awakening" (1900–1920), culminating with Blaise Diagne's election to the French National Assembly.[25] In both periods, politics operated as a male affair. Women did not campaign for office nor hold elected positions. In addition, documents by the colonial administration rarely ever mention women's roles in the political life of the towns. On the one hand, the absence of women from politics reflects the bias of the time period. For Senegal, the few avenues of power open to (mainly) elite women were closed to male chiefs and elected officials, who became the primary representatives of African interests within the colonial state. In 1920 the Ministry of the Colonies approved of the creation of an assembly called the Colonial Council to replace the General Council. Chiefs of the Protectorate appointed men to represent the interests of their district to the assembly, and town residents elected men among the notables to serve as representatives from the Four Communes.

In spite of the clear separation between female and male space, occasionally women of the colonial towns used their reputation as upstanding wives and mothers to challenge the status quo or to vocalize their support for particular candidates. In mid-March 1887 Frenchwomen and elite women of the mixed-race population of Saint-Louis launched their complaints against the "rancorous nature" of political discourse in the local press by writing a public letter to the governor of the colony, followed by a second letter to Jean Jauréguiberry, the naval minister.[26] The women accused *Le réveil du Sénégal*, the only newspaper not affiliated with the administration, of putting "public peace and good order" at peril by publishing scandalous accounts of the clergy, officials, and notable men of the community. The women who comprised the Mothers of Families included the wives, mothers, and sisters of the French and mixed-race town elite. In particular, they tended to side with the electoral faction in the 1887 electoral campaign, which held closer ties to the administration and the clergy and which stood in contrast to the Devès faction, which publicly challenged abuses of colonial power. The Devès group advocated for anticlericalism at a time when debates about secularism, freedom of the press, and controversial displays by Freemasons dominated the political debate in France and in the capital of the Senegal colony. This letter is one of the few recorded instances of women who came together as an interest group to intervene in a key event that affected their families but that also inserted them in the debate concerning freedom of the press under the Third Republic.

In the early 1900s, as political life in the communes shifted in favor of the interests of black African town residents, politicians did place more emphasis on appealing to the concerns of everyday inhabitants. In these instances, candidates for electoral politics began to appeal to issues of particular interest to women. François Carpot, for example, campaigned for Senegal's representative to the French National Assembly by claiming that he would make sure that each community had running water. Carpot gained the nickname Borom Robinets, or "Chief of the Water Taps," for his efforts. According to folklorist Fatou Niang Siga, partisan women of Saint-Louis developed a new hairstyle called Pilimu Karpo in order to demonstrate their support for the candidate.[27] Similarly, an informant explained to me that the wives and daughters of elite men from all of the neighborhoods in Saint-Louis often held meetings at their houses in support of candidates for mayor and the municipal council, even if they did not have the right to vote in elections. These examples show that *originaire* women did not sit on the sidelines but actively engaged in electoral campaigns despite their exclusion from the formal process.

Shifting our attention to the era of nationalism and decolonization may allow for further elaboration on how women of the towns understood and navigated the political environment as women and as "citizens." For instance, in 1945 Soukeyna Konaré, the cousin of Lamine Guèye, joined forces with Ndate Yalla Fall, cousin of Galandou Diouf, to protest French reforms that extended the franchise to metropolitan women in the Four Communes but not to African women.[28] Konaré and Fall supported their cousins, each of whom led opposing political parties but united to convince France to reverse the decree. According to sociologist Fatou Sarr Sow, these women "opened up the long march in the struggle for gender equality in Senegalese politics."[29] After Senegal gained independence from France on April 4, 1960, politics remained primarily a male affair. In 1963 Caroline Faye Diop became the first female deputy elected to the National Assembly of Senegal from the Socialist Party. In the late 1970s Marie-Angélique Savané emerged as a feminist voice in journalism and women's civil society who also took a leadership role in party politics.[30] These examples show *originaire* women's engagement in the political process despite the exclusions that prevented them from voting and holding elected office. In retrospect, French rule reinforced the patriarchal systems of governance and politics within Senegalese society. Although urban women had access to education and benefited from close proximity to French rule, *originaire* women, like women in the interior, necessarily focused their attention on family, community, and society rather than electoral politics.

Conclusion

Originaire women occupy an ambivalent position in the history of colonial citizenship in French West Africa. On the one hand, women of Senegal's Four Communes constituted part of the urban community, which had a long tradition of electoral politics and an intimate understanding of French republican institutions. On the other hand, politics remained a man's affair throughout the colonial era. Women did not have the same right to vote as adult males who were permanent residents of the towns. Women did not hold electoral office, and male military and administrative officers dealt primarily with male clerics, merchants, clerks, chiefs, soldiers, and assemblymen. In the first phase of urban politics in the Senegal colony, European and *métis* men monopolized electoral institutions. In the second phase, black men such as Galandou Diouf and Blaise Diagne broke the color barrier in public life by mobilizing the urban Senegalese electorate. In this environment, *originaire* women faced exclusion from the public arena. This exclusion, one informant suggested, meant that Senegalese women withdrew from the public sphere to focus on issues related more directly to family and society.

Despite the limitations placed on *originaire* women in the colonial period, they cannot simply be dismissed as nonactors. Voters in the towns most certainly understood and relied on notions of female power in Wolof and Lebou societies. In the late nineteenth and early twentieth centuries, *originaire* voters most likely knew firsthand or heard tell of the influence of women such as Njömbot, Ndate Yalla, and the *signares* of Saint-Louis and Gorée within the governing systems of the neighboring Wolof kingdoms and urban areas. Reports of town women participating in electoral campaigns and rallies and even showing their support for particular candidates by inventing new hairstyles and forms of dress suggest that *originaire* women understood and actively participated in the art of commune politics. Shifting our focus to commune politics in the period of decolonization and nationalism, moreover, may indeed render *originaire* women more visible in electoral politics than historians have previously thought.

French rule tended to reinforce the patriarchal systems that bolstered male political power in Senegalese society over women. In the Senegal case, the withdrawal of women from the public arena may indeed be one factor that accounts for the robust nature of women's civil society groups in the nation today. The debate regarding gender equality in party politics brings to the forefront issues regarding the dominance of men in power in Senegalese society, the legacies of the colonial moment, and neocolonialism as a state response to this disparity. In order to understand the struggle for gender equity for black women in the French-speaking world, we have to appreciate the role that *originaire* women played in this struggle.

Notes

1. Wade's proposal for Senegal's parity law followed a decade after France enacted a parity law to ensure equal representation for women in party politics. "Senegal Adoption of Gender Parity Law," Global Legal Monitor, U.S. Library of Congress, June 7, 2010 (accessed June 29, 2016), http://www.loc.gov/law/foreignnews/article/senegal-adoption-of-gender-parity-law/; Alan Hirsch, "Has Senegal's Gender Parity Law for MPs Helped Women?," *Guardian*, November 15, 2012 (accessed June 29, 2016), https://www.theguardian.com/global-development/2012/nov/15/senegal-gender-parity-law-mps-women; Fatou Sarr Sow, "La parité au Sénégal: Leçons d'hypocrisie," *Le soleil*, August 5, 2014 (accessed July 9, 2016), http://www.ndarinfo.com/La-parite-au-Senegal-Lecons-d-hypocrisie-Par-Fatou-SARR-SOW_a9964.html.
2. The cities of Gorée, Saint-Louis, Dakar, and Rufisque constituted the Four Communes, or the Quatre Communes de Plein Exercices. The municipal decree that established Senegal's communes designated these cities as municipalities governed under French law, unlike the Protectorate, which encompassed the vast peasantry of Senegal's countryside and which was subject to administration by the Political Affairs Bureau. Africans had little or no right to participate in that government.
3. Michael Crowder, *Senegal: A Study in French Assimilation Policy* (London: Methuen, 1967); Raymond Betts, *Assimilation and Association in French Colonial Theory, 1890–1914* (New York: Columbia University Press, 1961); Alice Conklin, *A Mission to Civilize: The Republican Idea of Empire in France and West Africa, 1895–1930* (Stanford CA: Stanford University Press, 1997); Catherine Coquery Vidrovitch, "Nationalité et citoyenneté en Afrique occidentale français: Originaires et citoyens dans le Sénégal colonial," *Journal of African History* 42 (2001): 285–305.
4. In his most recent work, Frederick Cooper has taken up the idea that citizenship structured the French approach to rule, thus differentiating the French colonial state from its British counterpart. For a discussion of the history of this idea, see Frederick Cooper, *Citizenship between Empire and Nation: Remaking France and French Africa, 1945–1960* (Princeton NJ: Princeton University Press, 2014), 11–21.
5. Mamadou Diouf, "The French Colonial Policy of Assimilation and the Civility of the *Originaires* of the Four Communes (Senegal): A Nineteenth Century Globalization Project," *Development and Change* 29 (1998): 671–96. According to Cooper, the precedent set by *originaires* of the Four Communes instilled the idea that Africans could be recognized as citizens without renouncing their customary

or personal status. This principle was applied to French West Africa and French Equatorial Africa under the 1946 Lamine Guèye Law. Cooper, *Citizenship*, 8.

6. In my monograph, I argue that political life in Senegal's colonial towns cannot be fully understood without examination of the intersection of the personal and the political. See Hilary Jones, *The Métis of Senegal: Urban Life and Politics in French West Africa* (Bloomington: Indiana University Press, 2013), introduction.
7. G. Wesley Johnson, *The Emergence of Black Politics in Senegal: The Struggle for Power in the Four Communes* (Stanford CA: Hoover Institution Press, 1971), chap. 9.
8. Since the 1980s there has been robust production of studies on women and African nationalism. Similarly, several historians have examined the gendered nature of power in precolonial Africa. Fewer works deal with women and urban politics in colonial Africa for the reasons explained below. For some examples of work on women and African nationalism, see Susan Geiger, *TANU Women: Gender and Culture in the Making of Tanganyikan Nationalism, 1955–64* (Portsmouth NH: Heinemann, 1997); and Elizabeth Schmidt, *Mobilizing the Masses: Gender, Ethnicity, and Class in the Nationalist Movement of Guinea, 1939–58* (Portsmouth NH: Heinemann, 2005). On the silences and gaps around women and the struggle for African nationalism, see Jean Allman, "The Disappearing of Hannah Kudjoe: Nationalism, Feminism, and the Tyranny of History," *Journal of Women's History* 22, no. 3 (2009): 13–35.
9. Obioma Nnaemeka, "Neo-feminism: Theorizing, Practicing, and Pruning Africa's Way," *Signs: Journal of Women in Culture and Society* 29, no. 2 (Winter 2004): 357–88; Drew Allison, "Female Consciousness and Feminism in Africa," *Theory and Society* 24, no. 1 (February 1995): 1–33; Ali Mari Tripp, "Rethinking Difference: Comparative Perspectives from Africa," *Signs: Journal of Women in Culture and Society* 25, no. 3 (Spring 2000): 649–76; and Nwando Achebe, *Uhebi Ugbabe: The Female King of Colonial Nigeria* (Bloomington: Indiana University Press, 2011), especially "Nkwado: The Preparation."
10. Elizabeth Schmidt, "Emancipate Your Husbands! Women and Nationalism in Guinea," in *Women in African Colonial Histories*, ed. Jean Allman, Susan Geiger, and Nakanyike Musisi (Bloomington: Indiana University Press, 2002), 283–304.
11. David Robinson, *Paths of Accommodation: Muslim Societies and French Colonial Authorities in Senegal and Mauritania, 1880–1920* (Athens: Ohio University Press, 2000); Regine Bonnadel, *Saint-Louis du Sénégal: Mort ou naissance?* (Paris: L'Harmattan, 2000).
12. Jones, *The Métis of Senegal*, chaps. 1–3; and James Searing, *West African Slavery and Atlantic Commerce: The Senegal River Valley (1800–1863)* (Cambridge: Cambridge University Press, 1993).
13. Mamdou Diouf, "Traitants ou négociants? Les commerçants Saint-Louisiens (2e moite du 19eme siècle–début 20eme siècle): Hamet Gora Diop (1846–1910), étude

de cas," in *Commerce et commerçants en Afrique de l'Ouest: Le Sénégal*, ed. Boubacar Barry and Leonhard Harding (Paris: Harmattan, 1992), 107–53.

14. The word *originaire* appears in administrative reports in the years leading up to the electoral campaigns of the early 1900s before Blaise Diagne's 1914 election as the first African to serve as Senegal's representative in the Chamber of Deputies of the French National Assembly. His election signaled *originaire* victory over the monopoly that French and "Creole" politicians had held over the legislative position since its creation in 1848. On the one hand, the term *originaire* can be taken as an inclusive term to mean all permanent town residents. On the other hand, the term *originaire* holds a particular association with the black African struggle to break the French and *métis* monopoly on politics. For the purposes of this essay, I will use it to mean all permanent residents of Senegal's Four Communes.
15. Johnson, *The Emergence*, chap. 2.
16. The 1871 municipal law conferred municipal status to Gorée and Saint-Louis in 1872. In 1880 Paris granted Rufisque municipal status when the town became the central port for cash crop exports from Senegal's peanut basin. Dakar completed the Four Communes when Paris granted municipal status to the city in 1887.
17. In particular, see the case of letter writer Mody Mbaye, an *originaire* who worked as a public letter writer in the rural district of Baol. He wrote complaints to the administration on behalf of his clients in the Protectorate and brought complaints against the administration for denying voting and legal rights to *originaires* who lived in the Protectorate. For official attitudes toward *originaire* voting in the 1890s and 1900s, see "Mon Cher Amiral, Saint-Louis 7 Décembre 1892" and "Envoi d'un projet de décret réglementant les conditions de l'électorat au Sénégal, Saint-Louis 7 Avril 1891," 4PA, Archives Nationales d'Outre-Mer (ANOM), Aix-en-Provence, France. The meeting was held in the building of "citizen Hamet Gueye." See "Ordre du Jour, les membres du Bureau Justin Devès, Pierre Chimère, Jaques Blondin," Saint-Louis, July 29, 1906, 4E6, #86, Archives Nationales du Sénégal, Dakar.
18. Lieutenant Governor of Senegal to the Governor General of French West Africa, April 18, 1903, 4E6, #4, Archives Nationales du Sénégal.
19. Pathe Diagne, *Pouvoir politique traditionnel en Afrique Occidentale* (Paris: Presence Africaine, 1967), 110–11, 130–31; and Boubacar Barry, *The Kingdom of Waalo: Senegal before the Conquest* (New York: Diasporic Africa Press, 2012), originally published as *Le royaume du Waalo: Le Sénégal avant la conquête* (Paris: Karthala, 1985), 45–47.
20. Barry, *The Kingdom of Waalo*, 212–13. One example of this occurred in 1841, when *linger* Njömbot made lavish gifts to the assembly of Waalo notables in order to influence their decision for succession to *brak*, or "ruler," of the kingdom.
21. Barry, *The Kingdom of Waalo*, chaps. 11 and 12.

22. Aissatou Diop-Hashim, "Sanni kaddu: A la redécouverte du discours féministe au Sénégal" (PhD diss., University of Maryland, College Park, 2010).
23. Blaise Diagne also had to campaign in this way in order to combat the rumors that François Carpot, his opponent, spread about Diagne and to sow doubt among the *originaire* population. Still, the Jeunes Sénégalais, an organization of young *originaire* men who threw their support behind Diagne, recognized him as someone who understood the local tradition of politics and the *palabre* or *plaver* (meeting). For more on Diagne's campaign, see Johnson, *The Emergence*, 166–72.
24. For more on the term *signare* and the evolution of "Nharship," see George Brooks, *Eurafricans in Western Africa* (Athens: Ohio University Press, 2003), 101, 124–29, 206–21.
25. Johnson, *Emergence of Black Politics*, chap. 11; F. Zuccarelli, *La vie politique sénégalaise: 1798–1940* (Paris: CHEAM, 1987); and Jones, *The Métis of Senegal*, chap. 7.
26. "À Monsieur le Gouverneur des Dames, mères de familles," Saint-Louis, Sénégal, March 15, 1887, 3G3/4, #272, and "À Ministre de la Marine," March 19, 1887, 3G3/4, #336, both in Archives Nationales du Sénégal.
27. Zuccarelli, *La vie politique*, 80–85; and Fatou Niang Siga, *Reflets de modes et traditions saint-louisiennes* (Dakar: Éditions Khoudia), 28–29.
28. Born to *originaire* parents, Lamine Guèye (1891–1968) headed the Parti Sénégalais de l'Action Socialiste. In 1945 he was elected to represent Senegal in the French National Assembly along with Leopold Senghor. The 1946 Lamine Guèye Law granted French citizenship to all inhabitants of French overseas colonies. Born in Saint-Louis, Galandou Diouf became a clerk in the postal service and a peanut trader. In 1906 he was the first black candidate to be elected to the General Council (Senegal's departmental assembly) from Rufisque. Diouf's candidacy launched a challenge to *métis* politicians to open their electoral lists to black candidates.
29. Sarr, "La parité au Sénégal."
30. Both women became key political figures in postcolonial Senegal. Diop trained as a teacher in the École Normale de Jeunes Filles de Rufisque. Her husband, Demba Diop, played a key role in the Bloc Démocratique Sénégalais (the nationalist political party founded by Leopold Senghor and Mamdou Dia). He served as minister of youth and sport under Senghor. Born in Dakar, Marie-Angélique Savané worked for the United Nations Institute of Social Research and served as chief editor for the journal *Famille et développement*. She married Landing Savane, who founded an oppositional Communist party. In 1974 he founded the party And-Jëf (Act-Together). Marie-Angélique Savané headed the party during the time that her husband was imprisoned for his political views (1974–75).

2

Christiane Taubira, a Black Woman in Politics in French Guiana and in France

STÉPHANIE GUYON

The political landscape in France and French Guiana has always been dominated by men.[1] In France until the 1990s, the typical politicians, particularly in the upper echelon of French politics, were white heterosexual men.[2] In May 2012, following François Hollande's election as president, Christiane Taubira became France's minister of justice. This was the first time that a black person was appointed to lead a ministry since the advent of the Fifth Republic.[3] From her nomination to her resignation in January 2016, Taubira was overscrutinized and subjected to virulent attacks, suggesting that many French politicians and citizens were uncomfortable with a black woman leading one of France's highest offices. Through a biographical approach that takes into consideration power relations in French Guiana and France, I examine Taubira's political itinerary from the French Guianese to the French political space, shedding light on her career and challenges on both sides of the "French Atlantic." In analyzing Taubira's political life in these two postcolonial spaces (the former metropolis is indeed no less postcolonial than the former colony but is rarely imagined as such in French academia), I utilize an intersectional analysis, understood as the coconstruction of relations of domination; that is, "categories like gender, ethnicity and class construct each other, and they do so in myriad ways, dependent on social, historical and symbolic factors."[4]

Taubira is one of the few black women elected into office in both an overseas French department and mainland France. She actually has the distinction of entering politics from outside the traditional French Guianese political networks, even though she shares, to a great extent, the same social and biographical characteristics of most French Guianese politicians. Her political career is of particular interest for scholars interested in race, gender, and ethnicity studies because she belongs to French Guiana's dominant ethnic group while being a racial minority in mainland France. Thus, in the following paragraphs I propose to analyze her trajectory from 1993, when she became French Guianese deputy to the French National Assembly, to 2012, when she was nominated minister of justice.[5] In the first section, I contextualize her rise to politics, paying close attention to the ways in which colonial hierarchies, class, gender, and generation informed the political process in French Guiana. In the second section, I analyze her experiences in French national politics, where her identity as a black woman affected her very differently.

From Anticolonial Student Activism to the Election

The Emergence of a Generation of Militant Creoles

Taubira emerged in the political landscape when French Guiana's political culture was undergoing major changes. In 1946 French Guiana experienced decolonization without independence. Similar to those in Martinique, Guadeloupe, and Réunion, the French Guianese political elites had sought since the beginning of the Third Republic to progressively align the local administrative, judicial, and political institutions with French institutions. A culmination of this process, the law of March 19, 1946, removed French Guiana, Martinique, Guadeloupe, and Réunion from the French colonial empire, transforming them into overseas French departments. But in the 1960s the political consensus about departmentalization ended. French Guianese political life of the 1960s and 1970s was polarized across party lines, ideology, and goals: on the one hand, the Gaullist Right favored departmentalization, while on the other hand, the Left, broadly speaking, pursued autonomy. The Right wanted to maintain departmentalization and expand local political agency (decentralization), while "colonial continuities" fueled the Left's desire for a stronger political autonomy and possibly a change of political status.

The polarization of political life occurred with the emergence of new political elites who competed with the older French Guianese or West Indian business families political elite. Coming from the upper fraction of middle-class creole society, these newly elected French Guianese officials benefited from higher education, a sector that had been restricted to a handful of individuals.[6] In fact, for the French Guianese generation born between 1948 and 1952, Taubira's generation, only 7.63 percent (7.9 percent of women and 7.4 percent of men) held university degrees. This is low in comparison to France (19 percent of France's citizens of this generation held at least an undergraduate degree). However, it shows an increased access to higher education. Indeed, the rate of master's level and doctoral level degrees increased from 1.15 percent (in the generation born between 1913 and 1917) to 3.40 percent (in the generation born between 1923 and 1927), then to 4.48 percent (in the generation born between 1938 and 1942), and to 5.75 percent (in the generation born between 1943 and 1947).[7] At that time, among the native-born French Guianese, only the Creoles benefited from higher education, as the Amérindiens (natives) and the Noirs-marrons (Maroons—descendants of escaped slaves from neighboring Surinam) were completely excluded from secondary and higher education.[8] Because there were no universities in French Guiana, these generations of French Guianese undertook their university studies in France, principally in Paris, Bordeaux, Montpellier, and Aix-Marseille.

Taubira and her contemporaries studied in France in the late 1960s and early 1970s. This generation was strongly marked by their militant experience at the heart of the Union des Étudiants Guyanais (Guianese Students Union, UEG), a student organization founded in the Sorbonne in 1949. By 1964 the UEG, which became the central body of socialization and politicization, advocated for French Guiana's autonomy. Depending on the period during which they did their studies, French Guianese students participated in either the May 1968 events or the Complot de Noël (Christmas Conspiracy), the arbitrary arrests of French Guianese nationalists in December 1974, which actually triggered protests in Cayenne and Paris.[9] The youth who participated in these protests shared markedly different experiences.

The French Guianese students who participated in the Parisian protests, particularly those organized by the UEG, returned to Guiana in the early 1970s, hoping to continue the anticolonial struggle.[10] They founded new organizations, including the Mouvement Guyanais de Décolonisation, or Moguyde (Guyanese Decolonization Movement, created in 1974), Fo Nou Libéré la Guyane (National Front for the Liberation of Guyana, created in 1975), and Unité Guyanaise (Guyanese Unity, created in 1978). Strongly influenced by the Maoist and anticolonial movements, these organizations defied the Parti Socialiste Guyanais (Guyanese Socialist Party, PSG), the most important leftist political party, and poured their energy into trade unions and popular education.[11] Their politics, however, kept them on the margin of the political sphere.

Many French Guianese students who participated in the Christmas Conspiracy entered into the institutionalized political parties. Their effort to free French Guianese prisoners fueled collaboration with leaders of the PSG in French Guiana and the Socialist Party in France.[12] Additionally, these UEG militants returned to French Guiana at a moment when this party directed the collective principles of French Guiana and when the party's leaders adopted an autonomist position that was compatible with the ideology of the UEG. In many ways, the participation of UEG members in the French Guianese political scene changed the balance of power.

The Electoral Confirmation of Activist Male Creoles

Many male activists from the UEG began their political careers under the patronage of the established Creole politicians. Though very young, they played an important role in political parties, particularly but not exclusively in the PSG, as some individuals found a home on the right side of the political spectrum. This is in many ways the story of Antoine Karam (president of the Regional Council from 1992 to 2010), who after returning to French Guiana in 1975 entered immediately into the office of the National Committee of the Guianese Workers Union (Union des Travailleurs Guyanais, UTG). In February 1977 the mayor of Cayenne named Karam deputy mayor. He was only twenty-seven years old.[13] But the careers of the former female activists from the UEG diverge from those of their male counterparts, as some of the women were involved in the UTG but were excluded from responsibilities. Moreover, none of them entered quickly into politics.[14] Only Eugénie Rézaire was elected regional councilor on the list of the PSG in 1998, almost twenty years after her male colleagues from the UEG.

A student from the generation of the Christmas Conspiracy, Taubira falls into the category of the aforementioned militant generations. Born in 1952 in Cayenne, Taubira comes from a working-class Creole family: her father was a grocer, and her mother was a nurse who, after separating from her partner, raised eleven children single-handedly. In 1971 Taubira studied economics at the Université Paris 2 Panthéon Assas and sociology and African American ethnology at the Jussieu Campus. As a student, she participated in mobilizations of the UEG against the Christmas Conspiracy, as well as numerous student mobilizations for international solidarity. She writes:

> My major opportunity was—because I hadn't lived May 1968 and everything that resulted from it—to experience Allende's Chile. During this period, I often frequented locations where there was talk of the revolutions of Latin America. I knew all the revolutionary convictions of the Izquierda, the revolutionary Left. . . . I remember the arrests of the separatists in Guyana during Christmas 1974. It was under the authority of the National Security Court, it was the time of Special Courts. . . . I can assure you that we mobilized ourselves with heart and fervor. . . . In order to support the separatist movement, we organized protests, large meetings in which, incidentally, I intervened.[15]

But her marital trajectory rooted her equally in the earlier militant generation of the UEG. In fact, her second husband, Roland Delannon, nine years her senior, campaigned for the UEG during the events of May 1968 and contributed to the creation of Moguyde upon his return to French Guiana in 1974. When she returned to French Guiana in 1979, Christiane Taubira also became a member of Moguyde. Hoping to educate the people, Moguyde's activities included protests; street theater; workshops; conferences; and redaction and diffusion of the magazine *Mawina* (the Maroni River in the language of the Noirs-marrons), the comic *Kromanti* (Kromanti is a Marronne language from Jamaica), and even classic texts on Marxism and anticolonialism.[16] But Taubira maintained a distant relationship with the various political parties, including the PSG. Twenty years later, when she remembered this period in an interview published in the form of a book, she explained why she felt different from these politicians: "[They] became technocrats, first of the unions, and later of the political parties. . . . These are people who are so poor thinking, who are of such great intolerance, and who always have such a bland sense of life, so conformist to square thinking. I think that they cordially detest me."[17]

Taubira's Entry into Politics: Toward an Alternative to the French Guianese Socialist Party?

Unlike her predecessor Élie Castor, who had conquered the local mandates of general councillor and mayor before being elected president of the General Council and deputy of French Guiana, Taubira had never been elected to any office before winning her seat as deputy in 1993. Additionally, she built her political capital and became a legitimate political actor through her work outside of the established French Guianese political parties.

After the election of François Mitterrand and the implementation of decentralization, the separatist parties experienced a sharp decline in French Guiana. Taubira was able to take on important professional roles in the public and private sectors.[18] Indeed, young French Guianese graduates easily gained access to management positions upon their return to French Guiana. After having been a professor of economics and then director of a training center, in 1982 Taubira demonstrated an interest in economic development and regional cooperation. The same year, she cofounded the Coopération Agricole Antilles-Guyane (West Indies–Guiana Agricultural Cooperation), which she led until 1985. She subsequently became director of technical services in maritime fishing. Finally, in 1990 she took the head position of a regional agency that promoted cooperation between the Caribbean, the Americas, and Southeast Asia. Her anticolonial activism found itself thus redirected into the professional world, agricultural development, and regional cooperation, with the prospect of having a more autonomous French Guiana with mutually dependent economic and political organizations. In the beginning of the 1990s, Taubira held a prestigious professional position that offered her a certain amount of media visibility in French Guiana. In addition to occasional appearances in the media, she also broadcast a daily economic chronicle for eighteen months on Radio France Outre-Mer.

Her start in politics took place in 1993, outside of the traditional channels of mobilization and partisan circuits, in the context of a crisis in the PSG. The party succumbed to internal strife and judicial troubles. Radio Jam, a popular radio station, first promoted Taubira's candidacy. The radio denounced the corruption of the PSG's elected officials and called for political renewal. When she announced her candidacy in December 1992, Taubira also denounced the cronyism, voting logistics, and pressure that PSG leaders put on electors. Her support committee was comprised of several well-respected personalities. The title of her campaign document, "Charte pour un souffle nouveau" (Charter for a new beginning), characterized the class renewal and the political practices that she wanted to incarnate. She highlighted her moral qualities: "our love for freedom of opinion and expression in spite of the risk of reprisals, our moral and political courage in the face of preconceived ideas, the establishment, and the cliques." When she asserted, "We offer you as a guarantee not promises for the future but references from the past: our wholehearted engagement in all professional activities, and our activist curiosity for all the subjects and problems that affect our Guyanese society," she justified her candidacy by her professional expertise and experience.[19]

After she won her first legislative seat, Taubira's political career flourished outside the PSG structure. Her husband and the father of her four children was her campaign director; she mainly benefited from the support of activists, family, and friends. With her husband, she then created the Walwari movement, allowing her to strengthen her political career in certain places. In 1994 she was elected European deputy. In 1998 she declined to run as chief candidate in the regional elections after her husband submitted without her knowledge a different list of candidates from the Walwari movement. She would, however, lead the Walwari list in the regional elections from 2004 to 2010, her ex-husband having withdrawn from political life after their divorce.

Taubira belongs to the French Guianese postcolonial elites. She has an educational and vocational trajectory similar to that of her male counterparts. Yet she remained a political outsider, because in French Guiana women are often excluded from the most important political circles, offices, and responsibilities. She became a member of parliament outside the traditional partisan paths. It is precisely her position as an outsider—a woman in politics—that allowed her to embody a renewal in politics in the 1990s, thereby successfully challenging the political parties.[20]

Equipped with a National Stature: Female and Black in the National Political Space

Unlike most deputies from the overseas departments, Taubira grabbed national attention by focusing on big and sensitive issues like the memory of slavery. In the first decade of the twenty-first century, she also gained notoriety from participating in debates about the representation of immigrant populations. In other words, she was a visible actor in debates about diversity, an issue that haunted the French.

From Overseas to Diversity

French Guianese deputies usually focus on local issues. Deputization is about raising awareness about the overseas departments' needs and obtaining financing or extra provisions for the department. Unlike her counterparts, Taubira intervened regularly in national and international issues, such as the bill on antipersonnel mines she presented in 1997. She was also very active on the issue of interest to the overseas French departments, which also had national ramifications. She also introduced the May 21, 2001, law "aiming to recognize the slave trade and slavery as a crime against humanity," which concerned all of France. According to the law's first article, which was crafted by Taubira, "The French Republic recognizes that the transatlantic slave trade, as well as in part the slave trade in the Indian Ocean, and slavery . . . constitute a crime against humanity."[21] This law is emblematic of Taubira's political positioning; with evidence on her side, she argued for recognizing the suffering caused by slavery, thereby putting an end to the invisibility of victims of the slave trade. She made slavery a national issue, calling for communal memory (communal education, establishment of a national commemoration) and clearly situating herself in favor of national unity. She claims, "Commemorating slavery—and not just its abolition—is a manner of recognizing the black part of the French citizenship, emphasizing the angle of 'cultural diversity.' It is, in this way, an integrative project."[22] Taubira and the other promoters of the law rejected all approaches involving material reparations; for them, the memorial and symbolic recognition of slavery was not only for the descendants of slaves. If the law recognized victims, it did not designate a guilty party, nor did it present excuses. It intended to confront the past in order to strengthen the national community.

After joining the National Assembly, Taubira entered rapidly into the national political arena. In 1994 she was fourth on the Radical Energy list, led by Bernard Tapie during the European elections. In 2002 she was the presidential candidate of the Radical Leftist Party (Parti Radical de Gauche, PRG). The fact that she garnered 2.32 percent of the vote indicates her capacity to rally voters beyond the overseas French departments and the PRG. Yet, like women in general, elected officials from the overseas departments were constantly reduced to their defining feature: they were perceived as unsuitable to represent the nation.[23] In fact, with the exception of Gaston Monnerville, elected officials from the overseas departments have rarely been able to earn national recognition. During this presidential campaign, Taubira took advantage of her departmental identity while at the same time remaining grounded in the French political sphere. The declaration of intent for her program France Plurielle, République Fraternelle (Plural France, Fraternal Republic) reads as follows: "It is strong and united with regard to the diversity of its population, the vitality of the identities assumed, the liberated territorial dynamism. It is founded on the secularism that undoes the tensions between identity and universality, on the humanism that dictates the fragilities to be protected, the talents to fertilize, ones that the republic will inspire in public institutions that represent the French population."[24]

Similar to Gaston Monnerville and Aimé Césaire, Taubira called for a process of republican political integration that was respectful of difference. Following the example of the law of May 2001, the emphasis on diversity went hand in hand with the affirmation of the universal values of the republic and the promotion of national unity. Taubira incarnated a plural France, one that she presented as socially and culturally heterogeneous. She did not talk about racial differences or national origins. She even asserted, "I symbolize, in a certain manner, this diversity in the social composition of France, that is, in its population. France is plural by the existence of strong cultural identities, strong regional identities."[25] She rejected the presentation of her candidature by the press as a "minority" candidate, claiming, "I am not here to represent minorities. I am what I am and I fully accept it, and I don't feel like I belong to a minority."[26]

Taubira was very conscious of the improbable and transgressive character of her candidacy without actually making it explicit as such in the interview book that she published during her campaign. She affirms, "I am at a place where it is inconceivable that I be, I am breaking down the prejudices within those that watch us and the inhibitions within ourselves. . . . I am in the process of really putting France face to face with its history, with its past."[27] Her campaign also focused on the question of suburbs and the process of exclusion. She avoided discussing the connection between race, ethnicity, and exclusion. That said, not only does Taubira frequently cite intellectuals from the negritude movement in her writings and interviews, she also evokes the color of her skin and her Creole identity. She proudly asserted, "My color strikes the eyes, and it is clearly part of the interaction from the first contact. I wear my cultural identity without the slightest effort."[28] However, she did not make "black identity" the foundation of her political engagement. She abstained from waving the race and ethnicity flag, claiming, "I stop thinking that people are statistics, one group here, a category there, in function of this, here is what we can do. Me, I'm not part of that logic." The evocation of the colonial past or cultural affirmation is always associated with universal values: "I look straight into their eyes and I say voilà, there are values that don't have an age, that don't have a place, there are these universal values that I carry within my flesh."[29]

Although she defended herself, the reception of her 2002 presidential political campaign focused on "diversity." The term "diversity" constitutes a manner of "designating without naming people of African, Southeast Asian, and, to some extent, Caribbean origin."[30] In the 2000s diversity as an issue of representation made its appearance in the public space. In the middle of the decade, it even supplanted the issue of gender equality.[31] The riots of 2005 also contributed to raise awareness about diversity issues and, in fact, the "racial question" in France. Taubira's presence at the sides of the families of Ziad and Bouna, whose deaths provoked the riots, reinforced the symbolic work that she began in parliament as a representative of diversity.[32]

Becoming a Stateswoman

By the turn of the twenty-first century, the diversity issue loomed large over French political parties. The social climate gave women of color a special purpose: their presence at events or in organizations killed two birds with one stone—it checked the race and gender box.[33] For instance, during the presidential campaign of 2007, Rachida Dati and Najat Vallaud-Belkacem were designated spokespersons for Nicolas Sarkozy and Ségolène Royal, respectively. Sarkozy later named Dati, Rama Yade, and Fadela Amara to the government, showcasing his party's commitment to diversity.[34] Hollande also wished to integrate representatives of diversity into his government. Jean-Marc Ayrault, the prime minister appointed by President Hollande, knew Taubira because of his role as mayor of Nantes, a port city during the triangular slave trade.[35] He wanted her to be part of the government. Since no woman headed the most important ministries, Taubira was a perfect candidate for minister of justice. Other female representatives of diversity, Najat Vallaud-Balkacem and Fleur Pellerin, also joined the government, and all three assumed roles that are not traditionally reserved for representatives of "diversity."[36] Victoria Lurel, George Pau-Langevin, Harlem Désir, Myriam El Khomri, and Kader Arif, all natives of overseas departments and/or racialized individuals, were also part of the Ayrault and Valls governments.

Taubira's stature as stateswoman was established during the parliamentary debates preceding the adoption of the law of May 17, 2013, which legalized marriage for same-sex couples. The Left praised the minister of justice's speech during the opening of the bill's review process, which inscribed homosexual marriage into the republic, thereby continuing the secularization of marriage. Taubira even made it the embodiment of the republican motto "freedom, equality, fraternity," declaring:

> We say that marriage open to couples of the same sex is a good illustration of the motto of the republic. It illustrates the freedom to choose for one's self, the freedom to decide to live together. We proclaim by this text the equality of all couples, of all families. Finally, we also say that there is in this act an approach to fraternity, because no difference can serve as a pretext for discrimination from the state. . . . Marriage, which has been an institution of exclusion, will finally become, by the inclusion of same-sex couples, a universal institution.[37]

During the parliamentary debates, Taubira demonstrated her great mastery of the parliamentary arena and her oratory competency, all while maintaining a singular tone, particularly through her literary references to Léon Gontran-Damas, a French Guianese poet of the negritude era.[38] From January to April 2013 she was the most ardent defender in the government of a bill that was challenged by the Right, eclipsing the other responsible minister, Dominique Bertinotti, the minister of family affairs. The following year, Taubira also defended a project of penal reform that led to the creation of a new probationary sentence. (She wanted to make penal constraint a separate sentence without reference to prison time.)[39]

Since her entry into the government, the disagreements between Taubira and Manuel Valls, the interior minister, have been numerous. The minister of justice proved that she could take great liberties with tone, several times criticizing governmental positions. The solidity of Taubira's position within the government was ambiguous; in a period of budgetary restriction, she secured important funds for her ministry but lost crucial political arbitration when facing Valls. Indeed, her bill to reform aspects of the penal code failed. Taubira also had a weak personal network among senior public servants in France.[40] She did not have an adequate team and remained dependent on the Elysée to choose her councilors.[41] Additionally, her cabinet, characterized by great instability, was frequently commented upon by the press, which blamed the dysfunction on her personality.[42]

In spite of these difficulties, she did not resign from the government until January 2016, when a bill denaturalizing individuals who committed terrorist acts was introduced.[43] She immediately published a book reflecting on the attacks of November 2015, denouncing the solutions envisioned by Hollande and Valls, which she argues contradicted the principles of equality. Praising diversity and refusing to stigmatize Muslims and dual citizens, she claims: "Because in order to strip them of their nationality without making them stateless people, it is necessary that they have dual citizenship. This loss of nationality would include an inequality. The same acts perpetrated by a French person without a substitute nationality would not produce the same effects. . . . One time it's the Jews, another it's the Arabs, then the blacks, then the Muslims, sooner or later it's women, then homosexuals, then binationals."[44]

In sum, Taubira was on the margin of parliament. She did what she needed to do to prove her allegiance to the group; but the flimsy grip that her political party held over her allowed her to maintain a distinctive political identity.[45]

In the 2000s the law for gender equality in politics does not apply to the government. Even though they are not required to do so, the president and prime minister take gender parity and the inclusion of ethnic minorities into account as they choose their ministers. Being a black woman was thus an opportunity for Taubira to hold a ministerial position. Still, it was a very fragile resource, as the bills that she defended (homosexual marriage and the penal reform of 2014), both of which provoked strong opposition to her freedom of speech, generated much criticism. Additionally, she was also subjected to violent racist and sexist attacks.

Racist and Sexist Attacks

While she belonged to the majority group in French Guiana, where her blackness was not a liability, in France Taubira faced antiblack racism. Certain French individuals depicted her as inherently primitive and lazy. From the moment of her nomination to her resignation, Taubira endured a series of attacks by the press and by politicians from the Far Right; they criticized her supposedly lazy behavior. Her first ministerial trip, on May 18, to the final game of the National Penal Basketball Challenge, during the course of which a prisoner managed to escape, initiated the salvo of accusations of laxity and naive optimism. Then on May 22 Taubira reaffirmed her intention to suppress criminal court proceedings for minors and aroused violent critiques from the Right. Laxity is classically ascribed to political personnel on the Left by those on the Right, but the pointed character of this accusation in the case of Taubira resulted in doubt based on the intersection of her sex, race, and overseas origins. Thus, many of her detractors equated her with a mother or grandmother—this was the case of editorialist Eric Zemour and again of humorist Nicolas Canteloup—in order to criticize her supposed indulgence toward delinquent youths. As Frédérique Matonti demonstrates, different imitations by Canteloup dating from January, August, and December 2013 present her as indolent, lazy, and incompetent, in perfect agreement with the stereotypes of black Caribbean women that have developed since the slave trade.[46]

Pointing to her "revolutionary past," the leaders of the Right and Far Right constantly questioned Taubira's allegiance to the nation. When Taubira attended the commemoration of the abolition of slavery ceremony without singing "La Marseillaise" (the French national anthem), she endured attacks from Marine Le Pen, the president of the Front National, and Christian Estrosi and Jean-François Copé, two national leaders from the Right. The other ministers or white personalities present did not sing either, but no one doubted their loyalty to France. Numerous rumors also spread on social media, where Taubira was likened to a rebel.

Taubira also fell victim to caricatures and racial insults that emerged during the nineteenth century.[47] On October 17, 2013, during a televised report, a candidate from the Front National showed a collage of photos on his Facebook page comparing Taubira to a monkey. This would be the first episode in a long series of caricatures and slogans—the Far Right was relentless. On November 12, 2013, the newspaper *Minute* ran the article "Sly Like a Monkey, Taubira Finds Her Banana Again," which embodied the classic racist attacks against blacks.[48] Taubira did not sue her offenders. However, the government prosecuted the newspaper for "injures à caractère raciste" (the equivalent of a racial discrimination lawsuit). An antiracist organization and Walwari, Taubira's Guianese political party, also sued. These different affairs led to convictions, but the governmental majority waited until the end of 2013 to express widely and publicly its support for the minister of justice.

First in French Guiana and later in the national political space, Taubira embodied a renewal of politics, a condition that allowed her to gain national recognition. She was a political outsider from multiple angles: not only is she black, but she is also a woman who gravitated to the margin of the party and its traditional political networks. In the last decade, the politics of minority representation and the issue of diversity lessened and perhaps transformed these "handicaps" into "assets." Nevertheless, the racist attacks demonstrate how a black woman's access to the highest governmental functions disrupts the nation. While racialized women can use their gender and race as assets in the political space, they are continually threatened and stigmatized—the script can flip at any minute, so to speak.[49] White men are still the norm in positions of political leadership in France, and partisan networks and upper civil service networks still decide political careers.

Notes

1. This article follows up on certain elements of Stéphanie Guyon's article "Des marges ultra-marines de la République au parlement: Trajectoires de députées guyanaises," *Parlement* 19 (2013): 91–106.
2. Catherine Achin, Elsa Dorlin, and Juliette Rennes, "Capital corporel identitaire et institution présidentielle: Réflexions sur le processus d'incarnation des rôles politiques," *Raisons politiques* 31 (2008): 5–17.

3. Under the Third Republic, a black man, Henri Lémery of Martinique, was briefly minister of justice from October 15 to November 7, 1934.
4. Baujke Prins, "Narrative Accounts of Origins: A Blind Spot in the Intersectional Approach?," *European Journal of Women's Studies* 13 (2006): 277–90.
5. After defeating Rodolphe Alexandre (Guyanese Socialist Party), Christiane Taubira was deputy of the First District of Guyana from 1993 until 2012.
6. The word "creole" designates the local descendants of the entire important population living in the colonial context, be they descendants of white colonizers or of black slaves. In Guyana, in the absence of a white creole population, they call "Creoles" those descendants from black slaves and from different migrant groups of the nineteenth century. The Guyanese Creole population in fact absorbed the native Creoles from Sainte Lucie and the French Antilles and colonial migrants (principally Chinese and Lebanese) toward the end of the nineteenth century and during the first half of the twentieth century.
7. National Institute of Statistics and Economic Studies (INSEE), results of the census of the population of the overseas departments, March 9, 1982, Guyana, May 1983.
8. Until the 1970s, young American Indians were schooled separately in religious institutions and Indian residential homes and could not gain access to regular high schools or to universities.
9. Thirteen Guyanese independence activists were imprisoned and brought before the Security Court of the State, a special court created in 1963 by Gen. Charles de Gaulle. The incriminated activists were freed in January 1975 after the charges against them were deemed unfounded.
10. In particular, on May 2, 1968, the Jeune Guyane stormed an organization connected to the senator of Guyana, Robert Vignon, and on May 4 the student organization also participated in the takeover of BUMIDOM, an organization dedicated to helping citizens of the overseas departments migrate to France. From an interview with author Alain Michel, ex-leader of the UEG and then leader for Guyanese independence, Cayenne, December 2005.
11. The PSG is a Guyanese party founded in 1956 by a group that separated from the SFIO. At first favorable to a simple reform of department status, it adopted a separatist position in 1979.
12. Interview by the author with Antoine Karam, Cayenne, 2005.
13. Karam interview.
14. Interview by the author with Eugénie Rézaire, Cayenne, 2016.
15. Elizabeth Drévillon and Christiane Taubira, *Une campagne de folie, comment j'en suis arrivée là* (Paris: Editions First, 2002), 93–95.
16. Christiane Taubira, *Mes météores, combats politiques au long cours* (Paris: Flammarion, 2012), 207.

17. Drévillon and Taubira, *Une campagne de folie*, 103.
18. On the reconversion of dissenters in the professional sphere, see Julie Pagis, "Incidences biographiques du militantisme en Mai 68," *Sociétés contemporains* 84 (2011): 25–51.
19. "Charte pour un souffle nouveau, dignity/creativity/efficaciousness, Walwari, legislative elections from the 21st–28th March 1993," 13.
20. In mainland France at the beginning of the 2000s, women were encouraged to enter politics, as they were supposed to promote democracy and change politics. See Catherine Achin and alii, *Sexes, genre et politique* (Paris: Économica, 2007).
21. See *Journal officiel de la république française*, May 23, 2001, 8175.
22. Renaud Hourcade, "L'esclavage dans la mémoire national française: Cadres et enjeux d'une politique mémorielle en mutation," *Droits et cultures* 66 (2013): 71–86.
23. See Programme électoral de Mme Christiane Taubira, candidate du Parti radical de gauche à l'élection présidentielle de 2002, intitulé "France plurielle, République fraternelle," March 2002, http://discours.vie-publique.fr/notices/023001395.html.
24. This failure at universality was ascribed to women to justify their exclusion from representation. Laure Bereni, *La Parité: de la cause à la loo* (Paris: Économica, 2012).
25. Drévillon and Taubira, *Une campagne de folie*, 192.
26. Drévillon and Taubira, *Une campagne de folie*, 194.
27. Drévillon and Taubira, *Une campagne de folie*, 216.
28. Drévillon and Taubira, *Une campagne de folie*, 214.
29. Drévillon and Taubira, *Une campagne de folie*, 218.
30. Patrick Simon and Angéline Escafré-Dublet, "Représenter la diversité en politique: Une reformulation de la dialectique de la différence et de l'égalité par la doxa républicaine," *Raisons politiques* 3 (2009): 127.
31. Martina Avanza, "Qui rep'resentent les élus de la diversité: Croyances partisanes et points de vue des 'divers,'" *Revue française de sciences politiques* 60 (2010): 745–67.
32. These riots became the object of a racial reading both by intellectuals and politicians from the Right who highlighted the cultural particularities of families from the suburbs as an explanation of their recourse to violence and by those from the Left who focused on the discrimination of which the rioters were victims. Éric Fassin and Didier Fassin, *De la question social à la question raciale?* (Paris: La Découverte, 2006).
33. Achin and alii, *Sexes*.
34. Frédérique Matonti, *Le genre présidentiel* (Paris: Découverte, 2017), esp. chap. 4, "De Rachida Dati à Christiane Taubira: Diversité et racisation."
35. Nantes was one of the principal French ports involved in the slave trade from the seventeenth to the nineteenth century and was one of the first in France to put in place, in the 1990s, important policies regarding the remembrance of slavery.
36. Matonti, *Le genre présidentiel*.

37. Speech by C. Taubira, account of the meeting of the National Assembly on January 29, 2013, http://www.assembleenationale.fr/14/cri/provisoire/p20130118.asp.
38. She quoted the poem "Nous les gueux" by Léon Gontran Damas, to which she had already made reference during her speech at the opening of the parliamentary debate.
39. Translator's note: Penal constraint is a form of probation, separate from any prison sentence, that requires the individual to abide by certain restrictions and report to a probation officer.
40. Jean-Michel Eymeri-Douzans, Xavier Bioy, and Stéphane Mouton, *Le règne des entourages: Cabinets et conseillers de l'exécutif* (Paris: Presses de Sciences Po, 2015).
41. C. Vigouroux, C. Moguée, G. Le Châtelier, and A. Christnacht are close to the Socialist Party or belong to Hollande's personal network. The same is true for Taubira's deputy directors, J. F. Beynel, F. Pion, and A. Bérriat.
42. Franck Johannès, "Les départs se succèdent au cabinet de Christiane Taubira," *Le monde*, March 20, 2013.
43. The other ministers embodying the left wing of the government quit in 2014.
44. Christiane Taubira, *Murmures à la jeunesse* (Paris: Philippe Rey, 2016).
45. As an unaffiliated deputy, Christiane Taubira joined the parliamentary group République et Liberté during her first mandate, then the Socialist group during her second mandate, then finally the group RCV, which brought together the PRG, the Greens, and the MDC, during her last two mandates. As a deputy from the Left, she voted with the government from the Right of E. Balladur in 1993.
46. Matonti, *Le genre présidentiel.*
47. William B. Cohen, *The French Encounter with Africans: White Response to Blacks, 1530–1880* (Bloomington: Indiana University Press, 1980).
48. W. E. B. Du Bois, *The Souls of Black Folk* (1903; New York: Bantam, 1989), 63.
49. In a similar way, Catherine Achin and Sandrine Lévêque, studying the implementation of the gender equality law in politics, showed that being a woman was a fragile and temporary resource in the exercise of a local mandate. Achin and Lévêque, "L'une chante l'autre pas: La parité aux élections municipales de 2001 et 2008," in *La campagne à Paris*, ed. Eric Agrikolianski, Jacques Heurtaux, and Brigitte Le Grigno (Paris: Éditions du Croquant, 2011), 243–62.

3

A Passion for Justice

The Role of Women in the Aliker Case

MONIQUE MILIA-MARIE-LUCE

Between the two world wars, the plantation slavery three-tier system still structured Martinican society. The small *béké* caste still dominated the island's economy and sought to maintain its political hegemony.[1] A black middle class mostly comprised of mulattos (the descendants of the *gens de couleur*) stood above the black masses and the small Indian population that had previously served as indentured laborers. Blacks and Indians, at least 61 percent of the population, were confined to sugarcane fields, as sugar and rum were still the island's most important exports.[2] To be sure, the *békés* owned most plantations. But in the 1930s the tide seemed to be turning. The sugar industry was in crisis. Large-scale strikes organized by trade unions forced the *békés* to reckon with the black laboring class. Equally important, members of the black middle class who espoused socialist and communist ideals made significant inroads into the political scene. It is in this context that the affair of André Aliker consumed Martinican society.

On January 12, 1934, André Aliker, a mulatto storekeeper from Fort-de-France and the managing director, administrator, and treasurer of *Justice*, a weekly communist newspaper, was found dead on Fond Bourlet beach in the village of Case-Pilote.[3] The circumstances surrounding his death, which was reclassified as murder, aroused strong emotions on the island. In 1933

Aliker was in fact the first to publish a series of articles on the collusion between figures from the worlds of the sugar industry, politics, and the law in Martinique. The articles pointed the finger at Eugène Aubéry, a rich planter and politician, and his wife, Marie-Joséphine-Berthe Hayot, who belonged to one of the richest and most influential *béké* families of the island.[4] Aliker was the first individual to publish such accusatory articles. Perhaps, for this reason, from July 1933 until his death, André Aliker routinely received anonymous (and sometimes not so anonymous) threats.

Aliker's murder was a tragedy that greatly affected the other residents of the island. Each year, via television and radio shows, Martinicans commemorate his death. While his death deeply scared Martinique of the 1930s, it is first and foremost a family tragedy that is enshrined in Martinique's collective memory by his younger brothers. Indeed, in 1936 Marcel, known as Souloute, avenged his brother by shooting the alleged murderer; throughout his long life (he died at the age of 106), Pierre, a doctor and career politician, wore white as a sign of mourning. But Aliker's brothers and the male members of the family were not the only ones affected by Aliker's death. Rarely mentioned in all the documents relating to the case are Louise-Anne Aliker, the mother who lost her son; his sister, Renée; and above all, Émilie Tenitri (Émilie Aliker), the woman who lost her husband and the father of her children.

In this chapter, drawing from interviews and private archives, I suggest that these women are an integral part of the story surrounding André Aliker's life and death. Indeed, André Aliker's wife and other female relatives used all the legal means at their disposal to ensure that the law was fairly applied to the case. After the murder, Aliker's widow became personally involved in the criminal proceedings. For her, it was a way to survive a tragedy that left a deep imprint on the family memory. But most importantly, Mrs. Aliker's fight for justice demonstrates how women of color in Martinique—both black and mulatto women—stood up against the *béké* caste, which not only controlled Martinique's economy but also constantly tried to regain the reins of politics that they had gradually lost during the Third Republic. These acts of resistance preceded the efforts of black politicians and intellectuals like Aimé Césaire, who, following

World War II, promoted departmentalization to protect the interests of people of African descent in Martinique. They also fall within the black feminist tradition, which from the United States to the Caribbean has silently but relentlessly fought for justice and equality.[5]

A Widow Who Was Closely Involved in the Proceedings

In Guy Deslauriers's 2009 film *Aliker*, actress Joan Titus gives a voice to Aliker's wife for the first time in the history of French and French Caribbean cinema. This may seem surprising, but very few artists, filmmakers, and novelists have shown interest in the rather sensational Aliker story. Deslauriers admits, "There are no documentaries or plays about André Aliker," a phenomenon that undoubtedly motivated him to make this timely and important film.[6] That said, the lack of information about Aliker's widow is also closely linked to the current state of knowledge about the history of women in Martinique.

Marie Antonine Émilie Tenitri, usually called Émilie, was born on May 5, 1905, in the commune of Ducos.[7] She married André Aliker on July 24, 1928, and had two children with him.[8] She, like her husband, lived under constant threat.[9] The threats against the Aliker family emerged after *Justice* published articles accusing wealthy *békés* of fraud. The Alikers feared for their lives. Luckily, a network of family and friends in which women played an important role united around them. For example, André Aliker's sister Renée slept at their home in Fort-de-France so that Émilie would not be alone with the children, as people would regularly beat on their door at nightfall. Ultimately, the disappearance of her husband in January 1934 dramatically altered Émilie Aliker and her family's lives.

On January 12, 1934, at around 6:30 p.m., a lifeless André Aliker bound with ropes was fished out of the sea at Fond Bourlet beach.[10] His death, just days before his fortieth birthday (he was born on February 10, 1894, in the town of Lamentin), stunned his family and friends, as well as a large section of the Martinican population. Philibert Duféal, a militant communist and trade unionist who was nine years old at the time of the events, recalls how news of Aliker's death filled the hearts of most Martinicans with sadness. According to Duféal, during the funeral, which occurred the following day, a gloomy atmosphere loomed over the island: "The funeral procession went along rue Brithmer (now avenue Jean-Jaurès), the boulevard de la Levée, and finally rue Schoelcher to André Aliker's home. Thousands of people lined the route—a mourning, silent crowd. One could read the sadness and anger on the faces of these workers, employees, and young people. Aliker's wife experienced weakness in her legs and had difficulty walking."[11] For the young widow, this was also the beginning of a long journey to discover the cause of her husband's death and seek justice for herself and her children.

The discovery of Aliker's body raised questions about the cause of his death. There were plenty of hypotheses about his strange death—people talked about the settlement of scores relating to arms trafficking or even a possible heinous crime. The theory of suicide also persisted for several months. An anonymous pamphlet, *In Search of the Truth about the Aliker Case: History of a Legend, the Underside of a Tragedy*, helped nourish suspicions of suicide. These rumors forced an investigation into the cause of Aliker's death. In fact, the investigation became particularly important to his wife because he had purchased a life insurance policy for 200,000 francs with the Nationale company. Aliker's "enemies" wanted to prevent her from receiving her well-deserved life insurance benefits. Moreover, she felt compelled to clear her husband's name. Émilie braced herself for a tough fight, because her husband's enemies kept on spreading false rumors. They claimed Aliker killed himself and disguised his suicide as murder so that his wife could receive life insurance benefits; according to the pamphlet, "Aliker's failing business and his apparent moral confusion preceding his death confirmed that he committed suicide."[12]

This allegation placed a burden on Émilie, who lived in a precarious financial situation. To receive her life insurance benefits she had to demonstrate that her husband did not commit suicide. She battled both the accusers and the insurance company, which quickly asked the legal authorities about the state of the investigation surrounding Aliker's death.

Although the suicide theory was disseminated in public, the term "murder" quickly appeared in the police records. While the cause of death had not yet been confirmed by the autopsy, Adolphe Duchemin, the first judge of inquiry in charge of the criminal investigation, was open to the idea that

Aliker was murdered. Later, the findings of medical experts submitted to the judge on January 19, 1934, rejected the possibility of suicide. In fact, the autopsy report stated "death by drowning" and "a hypothesis of suicide to be ruled out because the body was tied up."[13] Months later, in April 1934, the insurance premium was finally paid to Aliker's widow. But she did not receive it without a fight. *Justice* noted this unjust treatment, highlighting the difficulties Aliker's widow had with completing the administrative procedures following the sudden death of her husband. Moreover, since the suicide hypothesis had been ruled out, *Justice* questioned the progress of the investigation. The murder had been confirmed, yet there were no culprit(s). Émilie and Aliker's family worked hard to ensure the investigation would result in the conviction of the person they held responsible for his assassination: the wealthy *béké* Eugène Aubéry.

A Crime without a Conviction?

The findings of Judge Duchemin suggested that Aliker was assassinated because of his journalistic activities. In his first report, dated January 15, 1934, the judge wrote, "On account of the personality of André Aliker, managing director of the newspaper *Justice*, who recently conducted a number of press campaigns and was even convicted of this offense, it does not seem impossible that a causal relationship can be considered."[14] The testimonies, anonymous letters, and incidents preceding Aliker's death sped up the investigation. In fact, in January the judge ordered the arrest of four men and two women, "all six held and charged with murder and complicity in the murder."[15] However, the classification of the offense as "complicity in the murder" suggests there were one or more primary perpetrators to be identified, but no one else was charged. The investigation got off to a good start but quickly stalled.

Émilie played an active role in the criminal proceedings: she initiated a civil action, seeking legal redress in her name and that of her minor children, on March 19, 1934. As the historian Hervé Piant notes, "The person who initiates a civil action is not a victim; she is a victim who is making a claim."[16] Émilie stood fearlessly against the rich *békés* and their extensive judicial, political, and business network.

Émilie hoped the individuals who harmed her husband in the months preceding his murder would appear before the court. She contacted the judge of inquiry and asked him to lead an "investigation into the actions of Mr. Aubéry, Lavigne, and Maugee and their relationships with those charged with the murder."[17] Because she had access to the case records, Émilie was able to relay information to the rest of the family, especially Aliker's brothers-in-law residing in France. When she initiated the civil action, the judge of inquiry, Adolphe Duchemin, was provisionally replaced by Albert Pouzoulet on March 25, 1934.[18] Duchemin was obliged to go to Paris to report on his general course of action in relation to the inquiries and in particular his stand on the Aliker case. According to the public prosecutor, "Mr. Duchemin, the judge of inquiry, revealed his bias by refusing to consider any other hypotheses. He continued to consider one and only one alternative: a political crime committed by individuals, ordered and paid for by Aubéry or his entourage."[19] Thus, changing the judge of inquiry indicated an attempt to quickly close the investigation. The rich *békés* under scrutiny were apparently as untouchable as most Martinicans imagined.

On May 25, 1934, the case against the six suspects was dismissed. This dismissal was immediately opposed by the public prosecutor and the civil plaintiff. Eventually, four of the six individuals who had initially been suspected and charged were released, and only Mellon Herbert and Cephinis, known as Darcy-Moffat, were accused of complicity in the murder. They were referred by the grand jury of Martinique to appear before the court of assizes of Martinique on June 11, 1934. The judicial inquiry that opened on January 12, 1934, was thus closed without indicating the person who might have been directly responsible for Aliker's murder.

The expatriation of the judge also helped to create the impression that this was a troublesome case. As legally permitted on the grounds of legitimate suspicion, the two defendants requested not to stand trial in Martinique. The attorney general who approved the request also recommended that the case be referred to another jurisdiction on the grounds of public disorder. He felt that doing so "would prevent racial, class, and nationality/colonial problems from becoming even more acrimonious."[20] The court of cessation in a decision dated December 21, 1934, decided that Cephinis and Mellon should be brought before the court of assizes in the Gironde.[21]

The trial opened in Bordeaux on January 21, 1936, two years after the murder of Aliker. But it was extremely costly to Émilie Aliker. As journalists noted, the trial was prohibitively expensive because of the distance between Martinique and France. One journalist remarked, "For each Martinican witness she wished to produce, the plaintiff had to pay 5,000 francs. The Alikers were poor. They were unable to raise 10,000 francs, let alone the 100,000 that would have been necessary."[22] For the young widow attending the trial, there was probably also the heartbreak of having to leave her children in Martinique. What must also have added to Émilie's sorrow was the fact that she and her in-laws were held accountable for Aliker's murder because they did not come to testify in court. (Eugène Aubéry and his son-in-law Lavigne were also summoned to appear before the court of assizes but did not show.) The jury of the court of assizes of Gironde, which acknowledged the premeditated homicide and ambush, cleared Darcy-Moffat and Mellon of their complicity in the murder. In conclusion, "the widow of the unfortunate Aliker was denied the symbolic franc of damages."[23] With the case thrown out of court, the plaintiff was ordered to pay all the fees and expenses of the civil proceedings resulting from her intervention.[24] Although the archival papers relating to the judicial investigation reveal that Émilie had a fighting spirit (she even went as far as writing to the minister for the colonies), she battled and eventually lost to a judicial system tainted by class, racial, and gender biases. Still, despite the verdict, the family of Aliker did not abandon their quest for truth and justice.

Epilogue: Surviving the Tragedy

The Aliker family took several initiatives in the days and months following the trial in Bordeaux. The most drastic one was an act of revenge by Aliker's younger brother, Marcel (Souloute), that truly captured the public's attention. On January 31, 1936, Marcel Aliker shot Eugène Aubéry, although he did not kill him. Following the request by the jury in Bordeaux to reopen the criminal investigation to find Aliker's murderer(s), his other younger brother, Pierre Aliker, was very active in Paris. Pierre successfully involved the local Antillean community in Paris and human rights organizations in the struggle to find his brother's murderer(s). The Comité Aliker, which was founded in 1935, and the Ligue pour la Défense des Droits de l'Homme et du Citoyen (League for the Defense of Human and Citizens' Rights), a major French organization promoting justice, equality, and human rights for all, both lent their support to Pierre. Pierre Aliker was relentless. He mobilized the press and questioned parliamentarians and members of the government. His main objective was bringing Eugène Aubéry to court.

Émilie now took more of a back seat. (She had expected to testify in the trial of Marcel Aliker, but in the end she was not called.) She did not, for financial reasons, contemplate bringing another civil action. However, Aliker's mother was prepared to lead the fight. Louise-Anne Aliker (1872–1952), also known as Fenfemme (according to the register of civil status), sought justice for her son's murder. On May 9, 1936, she wrote a four-page letter to the minister of the colonies, stating that she was prepared to file a civil suit that would target Eugène Aubéry: "As it is now established by a court ruling that my son was murdered with premeditation and ambush, which should in the eyes of all have the authority of a *res judicata*, I ask you to proceed to the prosecution of the murderer or murderers and their accomplices. One name appears to stand out among others; which is why I am depositing in your hands a formal complaint of murder against Mr. Eugène Aubéry, a planter from Martinique, whom I accuse of being the instigator of the crime."[25]

This letter is extremely interesting. It reveals a family using all the means at their disposal. Indeed, according to George Aliker, "Louise-Anne, his paternal grandmother, belongs to the first freeborn generation. But she didn't know how to read or write."[26] Although Aliker's mother was illiterate, she and her family found a way to capture her anger and disillusionment with the law in writing. Perhaps, after all, Louise-Anne was the most affected by the murder. She experienced the tragedy of losing three of her sons within the space of four years: Evrard in 1932, André in 1934, and Ernest in 1936 (there were seven children in the family: Emmanuel, André, Ernest, Marcel, Evrard, Pierre, and Andrée). In May 1936 she was awaiting the trial of her son Marcel (he was acquitted on July 21, 1936). Alexandre Aliker remembers that whenever his grandmother saw a man of the church, she cursed him or spat, saying, "Sa Bon Dié ni an ko mwen kon sa? Dépi an ich pé endé mwen, i ka pran" (Why is the good Lord mad at me? As soon as one of my kids is able to help me, he takes them away).[27]

Louise-Anne Aliker suffered greatly, but she kept the memory of her son André alive. Each year on All Saints' Day she took her grandchildren to clean their father's grave. Keeping their father's memory alive was just as painful for Émilie Aliker, who very rarely spoke about the case with her children. Her early widowhood was a turning point in her life. A housewife until 1934, Émilie became the head of the family, responsible for the material well-being of her children. She had no other income, and for a few months, assisted by her uncle Fernand Tenitri, she took over her late husband's business. Eventually, she had to close the business. From the late 1940s to the early 1950s she operated a boardinghouse and ran the Hôtel de la Paix in Fort-de-France. She reorganized her entire life and was able to draw on a family support network. With financial assistance from her aunt Camille Vandam, Émilie bought a home, and her mother came to live with her to help take care of the children. Émilie Tenitri never remarried. She died on September 27, 1997.

Pierre Aliker, who played a prominent role in the Martinican political landscape, often stated that his brother's murder was "the greatest assault to justice and the biggest scandal in Martinique of the twentieth century."[28] His voice echoes the sentiments of many Martinicans who also feel that the Aliker case is a tragic episode in the history of their island. But while many Martinicans remember how Aliker was killed for his tough-minded and transparent journalism, they ignore the struggle for justice led by the Aliker women. The story of Émilie Aliker in particular symbolizes how women have been neglected in Martinican history.[29] When reflecting on her accomplishments, which seemingly amount to a failed civil lawsuit, scholars can appreciate how this wife and mother from the privileged black population of Martinique stood up against the *béké* hegemony in the island. Her act of resistance was bold and courageous. In many ways, it figures in the long history of race relations in Martinique, a history in which black women from various social classes have covertly and overtly fought against the local structure of white supremacy.

Notes

I would like to express my thanks to the following people for sharing their family memories for this ongoing research into the Aliker case: Alexandre Aliker, son of André and Émilie; and Georges Aliker, son of Marcel and Christine Aliker, the granddaughter of Evrard, an older brother of André, who grew up with Renée, the only girl among the siblings.

1. *Béké* is the Antillean Creole term used to describe a descendant of the early European, usually French, settlers in the French Antilles: it "refers to a member of race/ethnicity occupying a dominant socioeconomic position" (Mervyn C. Alleyne, *The Construction and Representation of Race and Ethnicity in the Caribbean and the World* [Kingston: University of the West Indies Press, 2002], 189). Locals also referred to the few French travelers and administrators as *békés*. See Jacques Dumont, *L'amère patrie: Histoire des Antilles françaises au 20e siècle* (Paris: Fayard 2010), 57–58.
2. Dumont, *L'amère patrie*, 57.
3. The newspaper, founded in 1920 by Jules Monnerot, was a propaganda tool of the Jean Jaurès Communist Group. See "La vie du journal" (The life of the newspaper), *Justice*, February 1, 1934, JO 9097, Bibliothèque Nationale de France (BNF). Communism in Martinique had not yet made a political breakthrough. For example, the results of the cantonal elections on October 21, 1928, show that André Aliker only obtained 22 votes in the canton of Fort-de-France, where he stood as a candidate, as against 1,518 votes for the elected candidate. See *Journal Officiel de la Martinique*, no. 45, October 27, 1928, 659. The eight elected councilors obtained more than a thousand votes. See http://gallica.bnf.fr/ark:/12148/cb34418558f/, accessed December 27, 2016.
4. *Journal Officiel de la Martinique*, no. 52, December 13, 1924, 625, BNF Gallica, http://gallica.bnf.fr/ark:/12148/cb34418558f/, accessed December 27, 2016.
5. For example, see Patricia Bell-Scott, Barbara Smith, and Gloria Hull, eds., *All the Women Are White, All the Blacks Are Men, but Some of Us Are Brave: Black Women's Studies* (Old Westbury NY: Feminist Press, 1982); Patricia Mohammed, *Gendered Realities: Essays in Caribbean Feminist Thought* (Kingston: University of the West Indies Press, 2002); Ula Taylor, *The Veiled Garvey: The Life and Times of Amy Jacques Garvey* (Chapel Hill: University of North Carolina Press, 2002).
6. "Parti de gauche, Midi-Pyrénées," http://www.gauchemip.org/spip.php?article9571, accessed December 27, 2016. It should be noted that in 1969 the writer Vincent

Placoly wrote a play titled *La fin douloureuse et tragique de André Aliker: schéma pour une représentation de la société coloniale* (The tragic and painful end of André Aliker: Outline for a representation of colonial society).

7. She was the natural and only daughter of Marie-Joséphine Tenitri, originally from the municipality of Trinité. According to Alexandre Aliker, his grandmother was sent to an aunt in Ducos to give birth so as to preserve appearances.
8. Acte no. 145 de l'année 1928, 23W54–55, Archives municipales de Fort-de-France.
9. The threat followed the publication by *Justice* on July 11, 1933, of a special edition with the headline "Alert! The Lareinty Panama. The Chéquards of Tax Evasion. Magistrates Caught Red-Handed." See Armand Nicolas, *Histoire de la Martinique de 1848 à 1939* (Paris: L'Harmattan, 1996), 2:223.
10. Rapport de gendarmerie (police report), 1M3622, Archives de la Collectivité Territoriale de Martinique (ACTM).
11. http://madjoumbev2.free.fr/aliker.html.
12. "A la recherche de la vérité dans l'affaire Aliker: Histoire d'une légende, les dessous d'un drame," undated, 38J47, ACTM.
13. "Expertise medico-légale" (Forensic expertise), copy of the doctors' report, January 16, 1934, 38J10, ACTM.
14. Report by the judge of inquiry to the public prosecutor, January 15, 1934, 1M3622, ACTM.
15. Extracts from the minutes of the office of the court of appeal in Martinique, 1M3622, ACTM.
16. Hervé Piant, "Victime, partie civile ou accusateur? Quelques réflexions sur la notion de victime particulièrement dans la justice d'Ancien Régime," in *Les victimes des oubliées de l'histoire?*, ed. Benoît Garnot (Rennes: Presses Universitaires de Rennes, 2000), http://www.openedition.org/6540, accessed December 27, 2016.
17. Émilie Aliker to Adolphe Duchemin, March 19, 1934, 1M3622, ACTM.
18. *Journal Officiel de la Martinique*, no. 15, April 14, 1934, 217, BNF Gallica, http://catalogue.bnf.fr/ark:/12148/cb34418558f, accessed December 27, 2016. Adolphe Duchemin's temporary departure from the colony was actually made permanent by a provision available to the minister of the colonies.
19. Public prosecutor to the attorney general, March 6, 1934, 1M3622, ACTM.
20. Attorney general to the secretary general of the government of Martinique, July 4, 1934, 1M11467/A, ACTM.
21. Attorney general to the secretary general, July 4, 1934.
22. Jean-Maurice Herrmann, "Le procès Aliker s'ouvre aujourd'hui," *Le populaire*, January 21, 1936, BNF Gallica, http://catalogue.bnf.fr/ark:/12148/cb34393339w.
23. Jean-Maurice Herrmann, "Un verdict honteux pour la justice française," *Le populaire*, January 23, 1936, BNF Gallica, http://catalogue.bnf.fr/ark:/12148/cb34393339w.

24. Trial of the accused Cephinis and Mellon, the acquittal order and ruling of the court dismissing the plaintiff's action, 38J101, ACTM.
25. Louise-Anne Aliker to the minister of the colonies, May 9, 1936, 1M922/E, ACTM.
26. Association Martiniquaise de Recherche sur l'Histoire des Familles (AMARHISFA), bulletin no. 28, 11, http://www.amarhisfa.fr/wp-content/uploads/2014/09/bulletin-28.pdf.
27. Interview with Alexandre Aliker, Fort-de-France, May 27, 2016.
28. Georges Mauvois, *Château Aubery* (Fort-de-France: K Éditions, 2008), 13.
29. Muriel Descas-Ravoteur and Micheline Marlin-Godier, *Femmes de la Martinique: Quelle histoire?* (Fort-de-France: Conseil Général de la Martinique / Archives Départementales, 2009), 5.

PART 2 Feminist and Postcolonial Movements for Equality

4

French Caribbean Feminism in the Postdepartmentalization Era

FÉLIX GERMAIN

This may come as a surprise, but after World War II France shared many similarities with Martinique and Guadeloupe.[1] Food was scarce, poverty was widespread, and access to core items of modernity such as toilets eluded many citizens in urban and rural areas. Yet despite these common challenges, as reflected by the ratification of the female suffrage law in 1944 and new labor laws guaranteeing citizens a minimum wage in 1951, better days for both men and women seemed to lie ahead.[2] By the sixties, after a decade of dependency on American dollars to achieve modernization projects, France had finally turned the dark corner of despair and poverty. The Gallic nation boasted a strong industrialized sector and a growing service economy.[3] French women also benefited from this wind of change. Young women from the middle and upper classes in particular enrolled in universities, hoping to participate in the labor market and reap the full benefits of a revitalized French society.[4] Simultaneously, French feminists of the postwar period worked diligently to change French perceptions of women's role and for the rights to control their destinies and bodies. After May 1968 they began to win hard-fought battles, particularly in regard to contraception and abortion.[5]

While the struggle of women in France to achieve liberty and equality has been well documented, perhaps because it emerged from a different social context, the struggle of French Caribbean women to achieve liberty and equality after World War II has not earned sufficient scholarly attention. This essay remedies this situation. Indeed, the French Caribbean, truly a crossroad for different cultures, political ideologies, and social identities, has a vibrant feminist tradition.[6] Women of the postwar period have relentlessly tried to improve the female condition and the overall quality of life in Guadeloupe and Martinique. Below I discuss their initiatives to achieve liberty and equality and to make sure that each individual has, in the words of Amartya Sen, "The substantive freedoms he or she enjoys to lead the kind of life he or she has reason to value."[7]

In 1952 Frantz Fanon, the famous Martinican intellectual who studied the influence of French colonization on colonized subjects, made the following pseudoscientific assertion. In analyzing French Caribbean women's identity formation, Fanon dismissed quantitative or qualitative research protocols and reduced all women to self-hating beings, claiming, "It is always essential to avoid falling back into the pit of niggerhood, and every woman in the Antilles, whether in a casual flirtation or in a serious affair, is determined to select the least black of the men."[8] Fanon not only exaggerated the connections between the colonial legacy, colorism, and gender relations but also failed to recognize the diversity of female identities and experiences in Martinique. Indeed, *béké* women, the wealthy white descendants of plantation owners, shared experiences that were markedly different from those of black women from the lower classes, the farmers, household workers, market women, and agricultural workers who toiled under the sun. Likewise, the experiences of black women from the lower classes were drastically different from those of their middle-class, educated, and generally lighter-skinned counterparts (the class/group of women who allegedly inspired Frantz Fanon's pen).

That said, in 1946 departmentalization arrived in a Trojan horse, promising to bridge the gap between the races and classes. The majority of women, who were still confined to sugarcane plantations and the kitchens of the bourgeoisie, expected higher wages or new positions in the growing public and private sectors. But unlike in France, where the economy grew rapidly and jobs multiplied over the years, the private sector in Guadeloupe and Martinique remained small, the public sector grew moderately, and due to higher labor costs the agricultural sector nearly collapsed.[9] It is in this climate of underdevelopment and persistent poverty that a new wave of feminism swept these new French departments.

The first public displays of feminism did not come from women of the lower classes.[10] Privileged women of the black middle class, who often maintained cordial relations with elite *béké* women, implemented initiatives to improve the female condition, thereby building the foundation of a modern feminist movement in Martinique and Guadeloupe. One of the most famous of these "unruly" women is Paulette Nardal, one of the founding mothers of the negritude movement.[11]

In December 1944 Nardal created the Rassemblement Féminin, a women's association that provided a safe space for women seeking to initiate social change and participate in the island's political system. Nardal and her companions wanted women to vote for officials who cared about women's needs; they craved a more egalitarian society. As reflected in the pages of *La femme dans la cité*, the feminist journal she launched in January 1945, Nardal and the women of the Rassemblement Féminin were multifaceted. They sought to develop democratic institutions; promote legislation that conformed to their spiritual values; elect officials capable of implementing sound economic and public health policies; and reform the civil code to strengthen families, protect children, and foster respect for women. Nardal and the Rassemblement Féminin also pledged to fight against tuberculosis, alcoholism, immoral behaviors, the deterioration of the agricultural sector, and the high cost of living and for social programs and laws promoting the well-being of single working women, housewives, mothers, and families, particularly working-class families.[12]

Throughout its existence *La femme dans la cité* maintained its original agenda. Always faithful to French republican values, Nardal and her colleagues seemed to embrace Catholic humanist ideals. In other words, they viewed and promoted equality between men and women from a Christian perspective.[13] Similar to Christian feminists, they believed women should be moral leaders and play important roles in their society; they were comfortable with the idea of women both as active participants in the labor market and as housewives and mothers managing households.[14] However, evidence from *La femme dans la cité* also suggests that Nardal and the women from the Rassemblement Féminin were more than mere Catholic humanists or Christian feminists. In an era when people put French culture on a pedestal, *La femme dans la cité* promoted Afro-Caribbean folklore, music, and literature.[15] The journal was a mouthpiece for women who believed in using local culture and folklore to advance women's issues. In other words, these women can also be categorized as "post-Christian feminists" because they challenged the universalist approach of Western epistemology, suggesting that French Caribbean women should turn inward to solve their own problems.

Ironically, the Rassemblement Féminin and *La femme dans la cité* figured on the right side of the political spectrum. They adored Charles de Gaulle. Like most Martinicans and Guadeloupeans they admired his prominent role in the French resistance movement of World War II.[16] But this might be one of their most glaring similarities with women from the lower classes, as the French Caribbean class and caste system often put them at odd with their least privileged counterparts. This was particularly true in regard to the women's professional aspirations. For instance, many poor women from rural areas wished to escape from the rigid demands of the agricultural sector, yet Nardal and the Rassemblement Féminin wanted them to stay on plantations. Also, many urban women from humble social backgrounds aspired to obtain some sort of administrative positions, but Nardal and the Rassemblement Féminin asked municipalities to offer them training in household management, a pseudonym for domestic work.[17] In hindsight, the conservative planters' class could not agree more with the ways in which the Rassemblement Féminin was positioning poor black women in the labor market.

There was a noticeable social and cultural gap between women from the Rassemblement Féminin and their counterparts from the lower classes. But this gap paled in comparison to the political differences that black feminists from the privileged classes shared. In fact, their political perspectives were so different that it generated toxic social relations, encouraging women to create different organizations. Indeed, in 1945 Jane Léro, a card-carrying Communist from Martinique, founded the Union des Femmes, a Martinican version of the French organization founded in 1881 to provide medical assistance and educate women about hygiene methods.[18] In Guadeloupe, Gerty Archimède, who became deputy to the National Assembly on the Communist ticket, also created a chapter of the Union des Femmes.[19] Since their creation, these organizations, which would later become the Union des Femmes de la Martinique (UFM) and the Union des Femmes de la Guadeloupe (UFG), have fought alongside women and workers to improve their quality of life; simply put, Léro, Archimède, and the subsequent leaders of the organizations have always believed that happier workers made healthier families, and healthier families made happier women.

Despite ideological differences, Nardal's, Léro's, and Archimède's quest to improve the condition of women shared many similarities. In the late forties and early fifties, they educated women about the new social security law and highlighted the importance of civic responsibilities. The feminists' effort to change the political landscape did not target women exclusively, as they continuously tried to convince men that women were fully capable of exercising their right to vote.[20] But for the most part, the Union des Femmes (in Guadeloupe and Martinique) and the Rassemblement Féminin's initiatives focused on the well-being of women and their families. This was an important and much-needed task, because women were generally submerged with the challenges that poverty, illiteracy, and limited access to contraception brought upon them. Whether single or married, most women in rural and urban areas shared the burden of caring for many children. Yet, to their dismay, due to limited access to health-care facilities and poor nutrition, infant mortality (from birth to three years old) was alarmingly high.[21]

In sum, the initiatives of early postwar feminists aimed to alleviate the burden of poor mothers. Responding to the dire social condition that most women in Guadeloupe and Martinique confronted, their feminism was pronatal and civic oriented; they advocated for children's and women's health while actively promoting female civic engagement. There were also parallels between French Caribbean feminism and French demographic policies and nationalism. In other words, feminists also believed in women's empowerment because women played a central role in keeping families healthy, and like French demographers and politicians, they viewed healthy families as an essential element to achieving sustainable national growth.[22] Thus, moderate nationalistic views were also couched in French Caribbean feminism.

The late fifties marked a turning point in the history of French Caribbean feminism. In this era, nationalistic sentiments were surging in Guadeloupe and Martinique as a new generation of students and intellectuals criticized the stagnant socioeconomic growth that had been affecting their society since departmentalization. The increasing presence of *métropolitains* (white professionals from France) in the islands also angered this politically engaged section of the population, whose members too often tasted the boredom and frustration of unemployment. Influenced by African nationalist movements and the Algerian War, they began to question departmentalization, accusing France of maintaining neocolonial relations with the overseas French Caribbean departments. Reflecting this phenomenon, between 1959 and 1968, numerous nationalist organizations sprouted in Martinique, Guadeloupe, and Paris, the home of a growing French Caribbean diaspora.[23]

Their distrust in the French republic encouraged Guadeloupean and Martinican feminists to reconfigure their center of gravity. They effectively distanced themselves from their French counterparts to address issues that specifically affected Martinican and Guadeloupean women. In a symbolic gesture, the chapters of the Union des Femmes in Martinique and Guadeloupe became the Union des Femmes de Martinique (1960) and the Union des Femmes Guadeloupéennes (1958).[24]

Throughout the sixties the UFM and the UFG continued advocating for workers' right. They participated in numerous strikes and protests to improve the quality of life of Domien people from the overseas French Caribbean departments.[25] Most importantly, they kept on working to provide services for poor women, stressing the importance of prenatal care and postpartum care. As health-care professionals of the era noted, too many women were giving inappropriate food to their infants (in Martinique, for instance, women often gave their young children chocolate *matété*, a sort of thick consommé comprised of cassava flour, milk, and chocolate).[26] In other words, feminists of the sixties focused on core social issues, particularly health care and access to affordable housing. They still encouraged female civic engagement, but they prioritized informing mothers about keeping their children healthy by connecting them to health-care practitioners offering precious advice. The members of the UFM and UFG reached out to poor women in rural and urban areas, deploying a number of strategies to touch their lives. For example, they organized the "most beautiful baby contest," a game that encouraged mothers to follow certain nutritional guidelines in order to have the healthiest child.[27] At the end, mothers who participated in the contest won an invaluable prize: a healthy child.

By the seventies, new battles were on the horizon. While nationalist currents encouraged Guadeloupean and Martinican feminists to distance themselves from their French counterparts, they were still aware of French social movements. In France, the May 1968 events spearheaded a women's movement (Mouvement de Libération des Femmes, or MLF) that called for women's access to contraception and abortion services and for abrogating the *puissance paternelle*, a law granting fathers the power of decision over children (it was abolished in 1970).[28] The MLF's ideas resonated loudly among French Caribbean feminists who felt that women bore the brunt of responsibilities in their usually large families. But these ideas contradicted the principles of the Catholic Church, which has traditionally played a very important role in French Caribbean societies. Thus, the seventies was a decade fraught with tension between feminists and the leaders of the Catholic Church who opposed abortion and access to contraception.[29]

During the following decades, Guadeloupean and Martinican feminists expanded their organizations, opening various centers and offices lobbying for women's right and reaching out to women needing help. The UFM and UFG became the dominant feminist organizations in their respective islands. They organized and participated in numerous events and movements to improve the condition of workers and the overall quality of life in the islands. They protested to increase access to public transportation; they supported agricultural workers striking for fair wages; they repeatedly denounced the high cost of living in the overseas French departments.[30] Protesting for social equality in Martinique and Guadeloupe and against the persistent socioeconomic disparities with France is important to French Caribbean feminists. For example, in 2009 the UFG figured prominently in the general strike against the high cost of living that paralyzed Guadeloupe for over a month.[31] That year, many labor unions had joined hands, demanding an increase of 200 euros per month for workers earning the minimum wage. Showing their support, the UFG issued a statement that truly demonstrated how French Caribbean feminists are determined to fight against the power structure that allegedly oppresses Domiens. The UFG affirmed: "We pledge to support LKP [the movement that organized the strike and demanded higher wages]. We are determined to spread knowledge about Guadeloupe's dire economic situation; we invite all Guadeloupean women to participate in the struggle and help change the status quo; we reaffirm our support for dispossessed Guadeloupeans and encourage local politicians to negotiate new accords with Paris."[32]

As indicated by the above quote, the UFG and UFM have supported movements that questioned the integrity of French republican ideals—the LKP movement, for example, claimed that racist and colonial thoughts encouraged *métropolitains* to treat Domiens as second-class citizens. By participating in grassroots social movements, French Caribbean feminists seek to help dispossessed people achieve the freedoms and the valuable life defined by Sen. But despite their French citizenship, French Caribbean feminists, who often position themselves on the left of the political spectrum, are apparently embracing liberation paradigms from the Global South to address issues of gender inequalities and economic opportunities in their homeland. It is a strange phenomenon, inviting scholars to acknowledge that these women are living proof that race, gender, class, and origins still determine one's social position and political identity in the French republic. Indeed, French Caribbean feminists are EU citizens, yet their initiatives suggest that they share a common fate with individuals from the Global South.

Despite the obvious parallels between Global South development paradigms and French Caribbean feminism, the women's actions remained firmly rooted in their local environments. In particular, since the turn of the twenty-first century, French Caribbean feminists have intensified their efforts to demystify local notions of masculinity. They want to contest the image of *hommes ntillais* (French Caribbean men) as born leaders who are free to lead the kinds of moral, sexual, and family lives they desire at the expense of women. This new dimension of French Caribbean feminism is most noticeable in their relentless fight against what I would call the plague of French Caribbean societies: domestic violence.

In previous work, while discussing how Guadeloupean and Martinican nationalists used women to advance their cause, I demonstrated how domestic violence has traditionally gone unnoticed and uncensored in Guadeloupe and Martinique. Even Frantz Fanon, one of the most famous French Caribbean intellectuals, had been known to brutalize his partner.[33] Yet his acts of violence have been shoved under the rug, reflecting French Caribbean cultural norms. After all, many Domiens consider domestic violence to be an ordinary event, almost a ritual.[34] For that reason, domestic violence has been increasing throughout the overseas departments. To be sure, it would take a team of scholars from numerous disciplines to explain, in a serious and rigorous manner, how this problem has evolved and persisted over time.[35]

The UFM and UFG tried relentlessly to change the French Caribbean collective consciousness about domestic violence. They reached out to couples in isolated rural areas, conducted town hall meetings, and raised money to publish short pieces in the daily newspaper. For example, in 2008, the UFG wrote: "The UFG is aware that a wind of violence has been blowing over our department. For this reason, we invite all Guadeloupeans to reject and combat violence, which is too often the product of social marginalization, unemployment, and the influence of dubious foreign role models. . . . We call for unity against violence, particularly against violence committed toward Guadeloupean women. The UFG pledges to take a series of initiatives to improve this situation."[36] Other smaller women's organizations that have recently surfaced in the islands have been inspired to join hands with the UFM and UFG in the fight against this recurring problem. As this symposium's title indicates—"Violence faite aux femmes: Bilan et perspective" (Violence against women: Assessment and direction)—they organized numerous conferences and symposiums to assess the depth of the problem and offer a serious plan of action.[37]

The UFM and UFG quickly delivered on their promises of helping battered women, opening sanctuaries for women who experienced such traumas. Notwithstanding their success, they struggled tremendously to convince government officials to subsidize, at least partly, these life-saving endeavors.[38] Eventually, in 2014, important government officials like Laurent Prévost, Martinique's *préfet*, acknowledged the severity of the problem in French Caribbean societies. In fact, he attended the opening of Solange's sanctuary (named after the UFM's first president), claiming that the center, which is partly subsidized, would play a vital role in the island, since more than 1,100 women had complained of domestic violence in the previous year.[39] Still, Rita Bonheur, the UFM's president, recalls that women of the organization had to storm the *préfecture* to get the *préfet*'s attention.[40] His awareness of the problem was a result of the women's intervention.

As we move deeper into the twenty-first century, French Caribbean feminists campaign vigorously to end violence against women. But they are not neglecting the issues that preoccupied early postwar feminists like Paulette Nardal. Helping women parent, for example, has remained a top priority. Reflecting on motherhood, contemporary feminists suggest that the compression of time and space, technological innovations, and transnational cultural flows have a profound effect on the new generation of women—and not necessarily in a good way. French Caribbean feminists do not believe in a linear progression of women's rights and gender equality. For instance, regarding motherhood and families, Guadeloupean and Martinican feminists suggest that society has taken a step backward. They assert, "Children have changed; they have lost their self-esteem; they have little respect for their bodies and their community; families don't communicate enough; and children are exposed to the dangers of globalization and individualism."[41] In other words, despite the progress that women have made in society, feminists fear that younger women, particularly those from the lower classes, live in much more precarious conditions than women of the previous generation. But not only do they associate precariousness with socioeconomic factors such as unemployment, unequal pay, and dependency on eroding welfare programs, but they also view moral decay and the negative impacts of globalization on traditional French Caribbean values as part of the problem.

For this reason, as reflected by their communiqués and bulletins, the UFM, UFG, and other smaller women's organizations work assiduously to change "women's image in music, iconography, comedy, folklore, television, and video games; female hypersexualization, sexism, and the degradation of women in the streets; women's self-esteem; violence against young women via new technologies; societal perception of household responsibilities; and the representation of women in French Caribbean history."[42] Not a month goes by in Martinique and Guadeloupe without an exhibit on women, a conference exploring facets of the female condition, a small or large demonstration, or a press release voicing women's opinion on sociopolitical and cultural issues. Contemporary French Caribbean feminists are extremely proactive in their effort to remedy the pernicious effects of patriarchy and other social ailments affecting women, children, and men. To be sure, they seek to change local perceptions of women and men while encouraging public officials—the wheels of the French republican system—to make sure that all citizens enjoy the same rights, opportunities, privileges, and respect.

In the past decade, French Caribbean feminists have also turned their attention to the plight of foreign women. As French departments, Martinique and Guadeloupe attract many transnational Caribbean workers. Dominicans from Dominica, Dominicans from the Dominican Republic, Haitians, and St. Lucians are constantly crossing borders, settling in the departments for short or long stays. French Caribbean feminists embrace an intersectional analysis, to shed light on the experiences of women from these island nations; in short, Guadeloupean and Martinican feminists contend that gender, class, and nationality present female migrants with unique challenges. One of the worst manifestations of this migration is sex trafficking. Many women, especially women from the Dominican Republic, have been lured to the wealthier French Caribbean islands and then subjected to various forms of abuse.[43] Aware of the growing presence of

Dominican sex workers in Fort-de-France and Point à Pitre, the UFM and UFG advocate intensifying efforts to dismantle networks of traffickers and penalize "clients."[44] Additionally, they have taken to the streets, protesting against acts of violence—the murders of sex workers, for instance.[45] However, in spite of their tough rhetoric, the organizations have been reluctant interventionists. They highlight the plight of exploited sex workers, yet at the same time, perhaps because of the discomfort that sex work generates in French Caribbean culture, Martinican and Guadeloupean feminists refrain from intervening in these women's private lives. Indeed, the *fanm'kolokett*, a pejorative Creole (kreyol) term referring to promiscuous women and prostitutes, stands in stark contrast to French Caribbean women's notion of womanhood and femininity—the *fanm poto mitan*, the strong black woman who is the pillar of the family, or the *belle Creole*, an elegantly confident woman in control of her destiny.[46]

The decline of traditional family values and the increasing presence of trafficked women in Guadeloupe and Martinique, two of the unfortunate results of globalization, are posing new challenges to feminists. But globalization in the French Caribbean has also brought what many would consider progressive changes—the legalization of same-sex marriage, for example. In many ways, the relationship that French Caribbean feminists have nourished with the proponents of same-sex marriage reveals much about the particularities of French Caribbean feminism. Like French feminists, Guadeloupean and Martinican feminists supported the movement to legalize same-sex marriage. The UFM, for instance, expresses its allegiance to the cause on its website. The organization uses a statement issued by the Centre d'Information sur les Droits des Femmes et des Familles, a French feminist organization, to demonstrate that it endorses same-sex marriage and understands the struggle of LGBT people.[47] But neither the UFM nor the UFG ever organized events for the cause, much less promoted tolerance of *zanmi* and *makoumè*, the pejorative kreyol words for "lesbians" and "homosexuals," respectively.[48] Presumably, feminist organizations took this position because even though the words *zanmi* and *makoumè* have pejorative connotations, they have always been an integral part of French Caribbean culture. No one wants to be identified as *zanmi* or especially as *makoumè*, but everyone has either a vague or even a clear idea of who is *zanmi* or *makoumè*, and that's okay, as long as the individual conforms to local notions of femininity and masculinity.[49] In other words, the particularities of the French Caribbean same-sex ecosystem has led feminists to maintain a rapport with gays and lesbians that is different from that of their French counterparts. While France has produced openly lesbian feminists like Monique Wittig, who since the early eighties has argued that women, in particular lesbians, should fight and emancipate themselves from the constraining effects of heteronormativity, Martinique and Guadeloupe have not.[50]

But this absence may mirror a generational divide, as a young generation of *zoukeuses* and *zoukeurs* (*zouk* is a form of popular music from Guadeloupe and Martinique) are making full use of new media to challenge conventional notions of sexuality and gender relations. For example, Jean Lycinaïs, a young French Caribbean woman, legitimizes lesbian relationships in her song and video clip, which has been viewed by more than 1.5 million viewers on YouTube. In the video, she convinces her female lover to stop conforming to societal expectation, leave her male partner, and come back into her arms, because she is the only one capable of giving her true love and affection. Similar to many young French Caribbean subjects, Lycinaïs uses new media as a weapon to fight against the marginalization of female identity and sexuality. Her actions and creative arts typify the new unorganized, sporadic, yet calculated and effective mode of social protest utilized by young users of new media to improve their society.[51]

Whether through their "soft but steady" support of same-sex marriage, noninterventionist advocacy for the rights of female sex workers, promotion of traditional French Caribbean family values, battle to end domestic violence, or practice of liberation paradigms from the Global South to address issues of gender inequality and economic opportunity in their homeland, French Caribbean feminists are deploying a feminism that is connected to France yet rooted in their local experiences. French Caribbean feminists advocate for gender equality while praising gender differences. They suggest that the *belles kreyols* and *poto mitans* share attributes and, arguably, social roles that are different from those of French Caribbean men. They also call for reflecting on the idea of womanhood. All French Caribbean subjects are invited to think about new ways of imagining femininity and masculinity. In particular, feminists invite French Caribbean men to understand and relinquish the privileges of patriarchy. Simultaneously, younger women, women born at the dawn of the twenty-first century, who are not always affiliated to feminist organizations are explicitly inviting society to reflect, accept, and understand that citizens share different sexual orientations. They confront homophobia, a phenomenon that eludes feminist organizations, even if they condemn it. Still, despite their modest effort to change French Caribbean perceptions of sexuality, French Caribbean feminists have relentlessly fought to improve their society; for them, the *belle kreyols* and *poto mitans* are entitled to the same rights, opportunities, and respect as French Caribbean men.

Notes

1. In 1946 Martinique's and Guadeloupe's political status changed from colonies to overseas French departments, effectively granting Martinican and Guadeloupean people full French citizenship.
2. Dana Simmons, "Wages and the Politics of Life in Postwar France," *Journal of Modern History* 81, no. 3 (2009): 579–606; Janine Mossuz-Lavau, "Les électrices françaises de 1945 à 1993," *Vingtième siècle: Revue d'histoire* 42 (1994): 67–75.
3. See Gérard Bossuat, "L'aide américaine à la France après la seconde guerre mondiale," *Vingtième siècle: Revue d'histoire* 9 (1986): 17–35; and Chris Howell, *Regulating Labor: The State and Industrial Relations Reform in Postwar France* (Princeton NJ: Princeton University Press, 1992).
4. Susan Weiner, "Two Modernities: From 'Elle' to 'Mademoiselle'; Women's Magazines in Postwar France," *Contemporary European History* 8, no. 3 (1999): 395–409.
5. For a brief discussion of feminist movements and intellectuals in postwar France, see Christine Delphy, "Les origines du mouvement de libération des femmes en France," *Nouvelles questions féministes* 18, no. 16 (1991): 137–48; Catherine Rodgers, "Elle et Elle: Antoinette Fouque et Simone de Beauvoir," *MLN* 115, no. 4 (2000): 741–60.
6. Because of the lack of data on women from French Guiana, this chapter explores the experiences of feminists from Martinique and Guadeloupe.
7. Amartya Sen, *Development as Freedom* (Oxford: Oxford University Press, 1999), 87.
8. Frantz Fanon, *Black Skin White Masks*, trans. Charles Lam Markmann (New York: Grove Press, 1967), 47.

9. See Félix-Hilaire Fortuné, *La France et l'Outre-Mer antillais* (Paris: Harmattan, 2001); and Laurent Jalabert, "Les mouvements sociaux en Martinique dans les années 1960 et la réaction des pouvoirs publics," *Études caribéennes*, December 17, 2010, published online.
10. In the nineteenth century, women from the lower classes had already asserted their presence as political agents. Lumina Sophie, a Martinican woman who participated in protests for equality and was then jailed, earned the titles "instigator" and "man hater." See Gilbert Pago, *Lumina Sophie dite surprise: 1848–1879 insurgée et bagnarde* (Martinique: Ibis Rouge, 2009).
11. T. Denean Sharpley-Whiting eloquently describes Nardal's contribution to negritude in *Negritude Women* (Minneapolis: University of Minnesota Press, 2002).
12. *La femme dans la cité*, no. 1, January 15, 1945.
13. Emily Musil, "In Search of Seven Sisters: A Biography of the Nardal Sisters of Martinique," *Callaloo* 36, no. 2 (2013): 375–90.
14. For a discussion of post-Christian feminism, see Lisa Isherwood and Kathleen McPhillips, eds., *Post-Christian Feminisms: A Critical Approach* (Burlington VT: Aldershot, 2008).
15. A few numbers of *La femme dans la cité* are available on the Bibliothèque Nationale de France's website. Nardal stopped publishing the journal in 1951, but the library features issues published until 1950.
16. William Miles, *Elections and Ethnicity in French Martinique: A Paradox in Paradise* (New York: Praeger, 1986).
17. *La femme dans la cité*, no. 1, January 15, 1945.
18. Union des Femmes de la Martinique, *Mémoires* (Fort-de-France, Martinique: UFM, 2000). For information on the Union des Femmes de France, see *Union des Femmes de France, Conférence faite à Chartres* (Chartres: Imprimerie de Durand, 1989), available in the Bibliothèque Nationale de France, Paris.
19. Archimède sparred with her Gaullist counterparts in Guadeloupe, including Albertine Baclet, the first female mayor in Guadeloupe. Their rivalry intensified in the late sixties as nationalist currents and the French political malaise spilled over Guadeloupe. See Martin Laventure, "Les femmes prennent doucement mais sûrement le pouvoir," *France-Antilles Guadeloupe*, February 15, 2008. For a more comprehensive study of women in politics from 1828 to the early 1990s, see Myriam Cottias and Annie Fitte-Duval, "Femme, famille et politique dans les Antilles françaises de 1828 à nos jours," *Caribbean Studies* 28, no. 1 (1995): 76–100.
20. According to Rita Bonheur, the current president of the UFM, in its early days UFM members spent much time raising awareness about women's civic responsibilities, including inciting women to vote and convincing men that women were politically

savvy individuals capable of choosing their own candidate without their husband's patronage. Interview by the author with Rita Bonheur, April 21, 2016.

21. Rapport d'activité du Dr. Perronette, médecin du P.M.I., document 9J68, Archive Départementale de la Martinique.
22. For a discussion of womanhood, motherhood, and nationalism in postwar France, see Kristin Ross, *Fast Cars, Clean Bodies: Decolonization and the Reordering of French Culture* (Cambridge MA: MIT Press, 1995).
23. Félix Germain, *Decolonizing the Republic: African and Caribbean Migrants in Postwar Paris, 1946–1974* (East Lansing: Michigan State University Press, 2016).
24. Gerty Archimède, *Fleur et perle de Guadeloupe* (Pointe-à-Pitre: Jasor, 1996); also, the Banque Numérique du Patrimoine Martiniquais features a dossier on Solange Fitte-Duval, a former president of the UFM, that details when the association changed its name. See http://www.patrimoines-martinique.org/?id=198.
25. The term "Domien" is often used in France to refer to people from Réunion and the French Caribbean. It is also used in the French Caribbean, though people on the left side of the political spectrum prefer using Antillean.
26. Rapport d'activité du Dr. Perronette.
27. Interview with Rita Bonheur.
28. See Françoise Picq, *Libération des femmes: Les années-mouvement* (Paris: Seuil, 1993). For the ideological and theoretical underpinnings of French feminism, consult Dani Cavallaro, *French Feminist Theory: An Introduction* (New York: Continuum, 2003).
29. Interview with Rita Bonheur.
30. *Femmes martiniquaise*, a bulletin published by the UFM, details how women protested for decent housing and better access to affordable public transportation. *Femmes martiniquaise*, Fort-de-France, Martinique, August–September 1985.
31. Yarimar Bonilla, *Non-sovereign Futures: French Caribbean Politics in the Wake of Disenchantment* (Chicago: University of Chicago Press, 2015).
32. The statement of support appeared throughout the virtual world, a space increasingly used for social protest. For example, see the Blog d'Azzédine Tabi, "Appel de l'Union des Femmes Guadeloupéennes," http://azzedinetaibi.over-blog.com/page/53, accessed May 29, 2016.
33. Germain, *Decolonizing the Republic*, 90.
34. In chapter 9 of this volume, Stéphanie Mulot and Nadine Lefaucheur use the example of a woman who escapes from a physically abusive relationship. My interview with the current director of the Union des Femmes de la Martinique was also very insightful. She asserted that many women experience domestic violence yet remain silent about it. She discovered that women were and still are being battered by

reading between the lines; in other words, she and her colleagues know the coded language of Martinican women. Interview with Rita Bonheur.

35. One of the few serious works dealing with domestic violence in the French Caribbean is Nadine Lefaucheur, ed., *Pouvoir dans la Caraibe: Genre et violence interpersonelle en Martinique* (Paris: L'Harmattan, 2012).
36. "Un appel contre la violence," *France-Antilles Guadeloupe*, April 28, 2008.
37. "Droits des femmes: La route est encore longue," *France-Antilles Guadeloupe*, July 3, 2015. Some of the smaller organizations include the Association Agape Guadeloupe, Culture et Égalité (Martinique). Also, because there are many women's organizations in Guadeloupe that share diverse interests, women have created a federation titled FORCES (Fédération Féminine d'Organisation et de Revalorisation Culturelle Économique et Sociale).
38. In 2005 a Martinican man immolated his ex-companion in the middle of the capital, forcing many Antilleans to come to terms with, or at least acknowledge, the presence of deadly violence against women in their society. In 2013 domestic violence in France and the overseas French departments resulted in the deaths of 146 women. This information is posted on the UFM's website. See Union des Femmes de Martinique, "Violence dans le couple," http://www.unionfemmesmartinique.com/?cat-9-dans-le-couple, accessed June 1, 2016.
39. In both Martinique and Guadeloupe, the *préfet*, a government official in charge of the islands' security forces, has almost exclusively been a white man. No woman has ever been a *préfet*. The *prefet*'s interview can be seen on Martinique Première's website (TV station). See Martinique Première, "'La maison de Solange' accueille les femmes victimes de violence," http://la1ere.francetvinfo.fr/martinique/2014/11/25/la-maison-de-solange-accueille-les-femmes-victimes-de-violence-210004.html, accessed May 31, 2016.
40. Interview with Rita Bonheur.
41. "La parentalité au cœur des discussions," *France-Antilles Guadeloupe*, March 11, 2015.
42. The quote is taken from a flyer published by the Union des Femmes de Martinique detailing their agenda for 2016. The flyer is titled "Konfyans nou sé fos nou: Actrices dans nos vies!" (Our self-esteem is our strength: Agents of our destiny!). Similar themes can be found on flyers and announcements of meetings sponsored by other organizations.
43. "L'autre visage de la communauté dominicaine," *France-Antilles Guadeloupe*, August 13, 2013.
44. Union des Femmes de la Martinique, "Prostitution: Les clients crient avant d'avoir mal," http://www.unionfemmesmartinique.com/?article-1235-prostitution-les-clients-crient-avant-d-avoir-mal, accessed June 6, 2016.

45. "Meurtre d'une prostituée: L'accusé vide son sac," *France-Antilles Guadeloupe*, June 6, 2011; "Commémoration de la mort de Sandra," *France-Antilles*, June 13, 2015.
46. For a description of the *poto mitan* woman, see Bonnie Thomas, "Identity at the Crossroads: An Exploration of French Caribbean Gender Identity," *Caribbean Studies* 32 (2004): 45–62. Brenda Berrian uses contemporary *zouk* songs and old beguine music to describe the idea of the *belle kreyol* in French Caribbean society. See Brenda Berrian, *Awakening Spaces: French Caribbean Popular Songs, Music, and Culture* (Chicago: University of Chicago Press, 2000), 76.
47. Union des Femmes de Martinique, "Adhésion féministe à la cause LGBT," http://www.unionfemmesmartinique.com/?article-1161-adhesion-feministes-a-la-cause-lgbt, accessed June 13, 2016.
48. In her excellent dissertation, Vanessa Agard-Jones discusses gender and sexuality in Martinique and Guadeloupe: "Sovereign Intimacies: Scaling Sexual Politics in Martinique" (PhD diss., New York University, 2013).
49. There are many parallels between same-sex relationships in the African American communities of the South and the French Caribbean. As Patrick E. Johnson demonstrates, they are part of the community's cultural fabrics. See *Sweet Tea: Black Gay Men of the South* (Chapel Hill: University of North Carolina Press, 2008).
50. Namascar Shaktini, "Monique Wittig's New Language," *Pacific Coast Philology* 24, no. 1/2 (1989): 83–93.
51. See Jean Lycinaïs, *Mwen enmé'w*, https://www.youtube.com/watch?v=l2fE2KZnvcU.

5

The End of Silence

On the Revival of Afrofeminism in Contemporary France

SILYANE LARCHER

> I no longer want to accept being accepted provided that I deny a part of myself, that I do not contradict white people's understanding of race, that I do not assert my legitimacy as a concerned and an aware person. I am fed up with tolerating that my experiences, my experience of racism, are ignored, diminished, compared with what is not comparable, silenced.
>
> Amélie Koulanda, "Être ou ne pas être soi-même dans une société blanche," *Péri-phéries* blog, August 14, 2015

On June 29, 2015, a teach-in organized by the University of Paris 8 titled "Défaire l'empire" (Undoing the empire) was held at the premises of the Centre National de la Recherche Scientifique (National Center for Scientific Research, CNRS) in Paris. Researchers and activists were invited to discuss the theoretical issues raised by the treatment of ties between race and the colonial past in academia and, more broadly, in intellectual and political debate in both France and Belgium. Within this framework, a roundtable was organized around the theme of feminisms and postcolonial critiques. The discussions were rich, passionate, even heated at times. In this context, a lively controversy between two feminist activists, Sharone Omankoy and Maya Surduts, shook up the sequence of exchanges.

The conflict opposed Omankoy, the twenty-nine-year-old founder of the Afrofeminist Mwasi Collective (Collectif Mwasi; *mwasi* is the Lingala word for "women"), and Maya Surduts, a seventy-eight-year-old second wave feminist, Trotskyist, spokeswoman for the National Collective for the Rights of Women (Collectif National Droits des Femmes, CNDF), and member of the Coordination of Associations for the Right to Abortion and Contraception (Coordination des Associations pour le Droit à l'Avortement et à la Contraception, CADAC).[1] At the end of the talk that Omankoy presented with Annette Davis, also twenty-nine and a member of Mwasi, in which both women explained their feminism, Omankoy decried having been interrupted by someone in the room. In midpresentation, in fact, and at the precise moment that she pronounced the words "white feminism," a disparaging voice escaped from the audience.[2] Consequently, the representative of Mwasi asked that this person express herself freely and proposed that she be given the floor. Maya Surduts then responded at length, triggering a bitter conflict.

"What I deplore," explained Surduts, "is that I have the impression that there is a misapprehension, which is in part our responsibility, of what the movement is, of the history of the women's movement in France. I can assure you that there is a history, that there is a past—"

"And ours? And ours, our history?" Omankoy countered.

"But wait! Listen," replied Surduts. "I'm not talking about yours; but actually, that's what I wanted to say to you: we have worked toward the cause for years with the black women's movement—uh—for years we have worked together. Among other things, we protested against apartheid in South Africa. I don't know how many initiatives we took on this subject; we participated in—uh—I remember, there was a feminist collective against sexism and racism at the women's house in Paris, and Christine Delphy and I participated actively.[3] . . . During the Marche des Beurs in '83, '84, the Socialist Party co-opted our participation.[4] But there were struggles, and important struggles of contestation, actually of a certain conception of society—we weren't only—the women's movement isn't only the movement of women against patriarchy. It is also a part of the class struggle, it is also a part of a certain conception of society. . . . And the movement was divided in this respect. I'm not saying that we were on the right side—but we were indeed often aligned with those struggles. . . . Well, it's a whole series of things that it is difficult to summarize in three words. . . . All of a sudden, I nonetheless had the feeling that we, white women, were reactionaries—"

"That's not what we said," Omankoy replied, contradicting her.

"No, no, no—but I felt like that—uh, white women's feminism, uh—I don't know what that is! Personally, we participated. Every time and always when we could, in the struggle against both race and class domination—but we didn't theorize it as a matter of race—we theorized it as a relationship of domination, of exclusion, of discrimination. It's rather in that language, in that dynamic that we situated ourselves. Thank you."

At the conclusion of this long commentary, two women took the floor. The first, also a member of the National Collective for Women's Rights, stood up to remind listeners of the place of the organization Black Women's Coordination (Coordination des Femmes Noires) in the history of the women's liberation movement. She lamented the continued absence of a written record of this history, although a conference had been organized on this theme in 2010.[5] The second woman who spoke underscored the profound divisions between feminists that had come to light in 2004 surrounding the law on the display of religious symbols in schools.[6] More recently, women in headscarves, wanting to join the ranks of the other feminists, had been excluded from a demonstration by CADAC in November 2014. On hearing this last remark, Maya Surduts hastened to respond vigorously. A tumult rose up immediately in the room.[7] Then Sharone Omankoy cried out: "Excuse me; seriously, excuse me. Is it possible on the other hand that you listen to us? Why did you come here? Why did you come here, in fact? That's my issue. As it is, for the last few minutes you've been giving us history lessons as if our Afrofeminism had fundamentally no kind of meaning, holds no kind of interest. Honestly, hold on! Our lives are political! So to give us, so to lecture us on the Black Women's Coordination—I went to university too. I was at the School for Advanced Studies in the Social Sciences [École des Hautes Études en Sciences Sociales, EHESS], okay! I learned some things about feminism, but the Black Women's Coordination wasn't one of them. So my history, me, my identity, when do I write it? When do I write it? On what foundation? You all have yours; and us?" Then she added before the uncomfortable gaze of her interlocutor, "No, but it's indecent. You don't even have the nerve to look me in the eyes!"

Exasperated, jumping up from her chair, Maya Surduts muttered, "I have no place here—"

"Exactly! I think you can leave. Exactly! You have no place."

The activist from the National Collective for the Rights of Women stood up too, indignant, and asserted: "You're implying that we don't have a place—"

"Well, yes, you have no place!" retorted Sharone Omankoy.

The two members of the historic association stood up, grabbing their purses. Maya Surduts turned back around, justifying herself: "I'm leaving—we didn't lecture you—we simply tried—"

Unable to contain herself any longer, Sharone Omankoy raised her voice. "You cut us off during our presentation!! So a moment ago, the respect, um—the disrespect is coming from you! So you may leave, madam!" she declared, firmly putting her hand on the table.

The two women ended up leaving the room while thanking the audience, several of whose members applauded the Afrofeminists' remarks. "Thank you, thank you. Thanks a lot for all those battles. We'll fight our own," Omankoy commented sarcastically.

"I've already experienced a lot of virulence. But panels like these, I've never known that," Surduts responded.

"And contempt like yours, we see that all the time. And we don't want it anymore!"

"What contempt? What contempt?" Maya Surduts, incredulous, called out from a distance.

"We give a presentation, you cut us off right in the middle of the presentation! *That's* your vision of your feminism? . . . While we were speaking, you were talking over us!? Are you kidding?" Omankoy shot back tersely.

One would be mistaken to see in this clash only a vigorous confrontation between two women, one young, the other older, or even one black, the other white. My analysis here falls within a deconstructivist and processual perspective of interpretation of ethnoracial categories. On this basis, these categories would not be considered as descriptive or "objective" labels but must be approached in their capacity as encompassing positions in power relationships, socially determined of course, but that are never, for all that, fixed or substantialized.[8]

This quarrel crystallizes both the breadth and particularity of the crisis that has been rocking feminist milieus in France for a considerable time. The conflict that opposes these two women from distinct generations, each with her distinct social experiences and even distinct position in the women's movement and in the social system, bears witness simultaneously to the evolutions at work in French society and the transformations that currently affect mobilizations of women descendants of postcolonial immigrants. If we once spoke of movements of "women in immigration," today it should be noted that the daughters and granddaughters of immigrant workers from the former French colonies, engaged in a "postcolonial" or "decolonial" feminism, modify in return the contours of "the space of the women's cause" and call into question the feminist agenda itself.[9] If feminism in France was never homogeneous, as the representative of CADAC recalls, it must now respond to the accusation of speaking for all women.[10] Who are the women whom the principal feminist associations claim to represent? In whose name do they act? And especially, *who speaks* in the name of women in general?

As I demonstrate in this essay—which builds on recent and ongoing qualitative research—the June 2015 dispute between two generations of French feminism opposes not merely two rival conceptions of women's liberation.[11] It especially underscores the extent to which Afrofeminist activists question the limits of a feminism blind to the material effects of racism on the oppression of women and, more broadly, the limits of the French republican color-blind ideology. At the same time, the dispute calls into question the content of the notion of emancipation. From what must women free themselves, and is there a legitimate objective of emancipation? The conflict reconstructed above translates in an exemplary manner what Jacques Rancière defines as a case of disagreement (*mésentente*) "where contention over what speaking means constitutes the very rationality of the speech situation." In fact, as we shall see, "disagreement clearly is not to do with words alone. It generally bears on the very situation in which speaking parties find themselves. . . . The structures proper to disagreement are those in which discussion of an argument comes down to a dispute over the object of the discussion and over the capacity of those who are making an object of it."[12]

The lively exchange that opposed Omankoy and Surduts was in its entirety underpinned by an initial symbolic violence that weighed on the emotions of each woman. The confrontation took place at the administrative seat of the CNRS, symbol of an elitist French academic arena whose codes the Mwasi activists, less comfortable in meetings with researchers than Surduts, did not master. From the moment she took the floor, Annette Davis recalled at once powerfully and modestly that "coming here for a teach-in and speaking out in an academic framework is for [Davis and Omankoy] a little bit frightening."[13] By playing the game imposed by the encounter between two worlds, the two young women thus accepted undergoing a trial that obliged them to "call upon tools that are not [their] tools of choice in [their] struggle," to use "a language that is not natural [to them], that does not make [them] comfortable, and that [they] do not like." Further underlining the distance between their social conditions and the university world, Davis reminded listeners that "the academic universe is accessible neither to all men nor to all women." Moreover, the episode forced them "to cause violence to themselves by using the master's tools to dismantle the master's house," Annette Davis eloquently declared, alluding to the African American feminist Audre Lorde. Because of this violence, very quickly exacerbated by the fact that the two women were noisily interrupted while they had the floor, the two activists, both from a working-class background and daughters of postcolonial immigrants, seized the opportunity to denounce publicly the failure to recognize the struggles of black women at feminist rallies and in academic research.[14] For them, it was a question of speaking in their own names while passing from the rank of "objects of research to [that of] political subjects, by defining [their] own political agenda," and, moreover, of giving voice, in the name of their social experience as black women who have been exposed to both racism and misogyny, to their critique of "whitriarchy," that is, the interpenetration of racism and patriarchy expressed through a sexualized racism and a racialized sexism. Because of their position at the intersection of multiple oppressions combined or crossed with race, gender, and class, as well as the fact that "the space of social movements" addresses the struggles against racism and against sexism as mutually exclusive, the two Afrofeminists stated forcefully that they did not recognize themselves in either movement.[15] They flatly rejected the Occidentalocentric feminism, purportedly aracial, that "is a dead-end on the racial question and excludes de facto black women and, more broadly, nonwhite women." In their eyes, by obliterating the experiences of the most vulnerable women, those from the working classes, the majority from sub-Saharan Africa, North Africa, the Caribbean, and, more broadly, countries of the Global South, the feminists from the dominant associations did not question their own role within this "whitriarchal system," unwittingly reenacting the normativist, racist, and culturalist oppression perpetrated by "white men."

It bears repeating that the point of departure of the altercation between the two women coincided exactly with the moment when a disapproving voice reacted to the expression "white feminism," disrupting the two activists' presentation. As demonstrated by Surduts's pained reaction to the young Afrofeminists' attacks, some second wave feminists do not understand that their own blindness regarding the specific oppressions to which a significant proportion of women are subjected—women who, like them, are fighting for their emancipation and equal rights—constitutes in itself a symbolic act of violence. They do not understand that for some women, even for those in great precarity, gender and class do not suffice to define their unequal socioeconomic conditions nor even their place in society. By the denial of a racism of which they understand neither the causes nor the consequences, as well as by their blindness, these feminists consign the descendants of postcolonial immigrants to an otherness defined according to a norm of feminine and gender experience, ultimately resulting in an implicit barrier between "whites" and "nonwhites." Without being clearly aware of it, by debating the liberation and rights of women by the yardstick of a tacit norm of identification with one's fellow human or, more rigorously, of an injunction to sameness—the very one that defines a purportedly neutral masculine—Surduts and her friends constructed themselves in return as "white."[16] If the space of antiracist rallies is today experiencing profound divisions between activists because of the very interpretation of racism and the means judged indispensable for combatting it, it seems that feminist milieus do not escape this rift for precisely the same reasons: an inability to properly account for race and its very concrete manifestations in French society.[17]

This confrontation essentially constitutes a battle over the history of feminist struggles as the scene of emergence for political subjects. The denunciation of a crossing-out of history, of the erasure of past struggles, appears in the Afrofeminists' eyes as much as proof of their assignation to otherness, and therefore to "race," as it does a demand for points of reference in a fully pluralistic and inclusive history of feminist activism, in other words, for the end of Eurocentric feminism.[18] Far from being negligible, this omission of one group of women from the writing of the history of feminisms in France weighs heavily on the conflicts and, consequently, on the demands of today. Indeed, when searching by key word in the *Guide to the Sources of the History of Feminism in France from the Revolution to Our Time*, out of 368 results, none corresponds to the adjective "black" in its feminine plural form (*noires*).[19] Only one appears for the word "colonies," referring to a file on the Socialist official Guy Mollet in relation to the ties between the SFIO and Socialist women.[20] The term "immigrants" in the feminine plural (*immigrées*) results in five entries, two of which correspond to files on associations for the struggle for the rights of immigrant workers and their equality with French women. A veritable unthinkable concept, this absence is emblematic of the type of language in which the history of women in France is generally thought, judging by a prism above all continental (*hexagonal*) and national. The reference to the "immigrant"—the foreigner whose social condition creates solicitude, even solidarity, and who remains at the same time perceived as "other" due to her legal status—tends to confirm the ethnonationalist bias of French feminist discourse. Consequently, by making their "invisibilization" the effect of a racial relationship—that is, one based on historic power relations and born of the colonial past—the Afrofeminists impose in return a symbolic violence on their detractors.

Omankoy and Davis called on second wave feminists to change the semantics of their activism and to question its construction no longer solely in regard to male power and class struggle but also in its direct relation to minority women. Like Islamic feminists or activists demanding a "culturally mixed feminism" (*féminisme métis*) regarding the Muslim headscarf, the Afrofeminists called upon the "historical feminists" to define themselves by holding up a mirror to them, compelling them to engage in critical reflexivity and to recognize a decentered narrative of their struggles.[21] Confronted with the challenge of overcoming the French colonial past by incorporating the transformation that it introduced into French society into the language of their struggles, these "historical feminists," in the majority, are experiencing what could be called an "unfortunate trial of conscience." Certainly, one may consider the recent affirmation of Afrofeminism in the space of political mobilizations and in the public arena as the second phase of a postcolonial moment of French feminism, henceforth reconfigured but still racked by tensions.[22] This postcolonial moment must be understood as the public critic of colonial legacies and uneven power relations between the West and the Global South.[23]

Responding to the narrow horizon of expression accorded to the cause of Afrodescendant women, the birth of the Mwasi Collective situated itself from the first in relation to the double issues of the statement of a self-narrative—one that does not endlessly relegate racialized women to the margin of a normative and exclusive feminism—and of autonomous political mobilization. In this sense, we must understand the association's creation as an enterprise both constrained and organized by the coming of age of racialized French women hailing from working-class neighborhoods.[24] Born in France to immigrant parents from the Democratic Republic of Congo (DRC), Sharone Omankoy founded with several friends the Mwasi Collective in November 2014 on the International Day for the

Elimination of Violence against Women. The collective initially united twenty-some women of Caribbean and sub-Saharan descent wanting to denounce the wartime rapes committed against women in the DRC. Run only by women of African descent and uniting exclusively "women and people declared women, black and racially-mixed," between twenty and thirty-five years of age on average, the collective was born of a common desire to assemble in order to organize, exchange ideas, and speak out about issues pertaining to members' own destiny.[25] Its creation also constitutes a means for these women, within a framework of care ethics, to grant each other a space of sisterhood," that is, of empathy and support in which they can speak their own truth (*se dire*) and feel understood on the basis of shared social experiences, in particular those of racism, of socialization in predominantly working-class neighborhoods, and of an upbringing in postcolonial immigrant families.[26] Mwasi espouses an intersectional approach to the violence and oppressions that black women undergo.[27] It occupies "numerous battlegrounds: against discrimination linked to class, gender, sexuality, health, religion; against the institutionalization of heteropatriarchy dominations within the white hegemonic capitalist system in all its complexity."[28]

The Mwasi Collective defines itself as "anticapitalist, anti-imperialist, proheadscarf, for the rights of sexually exploited persons, antiracist." It organizes meetings aiming to debate Afrofeminist experiences and problematics, such as the café meetings (*café-rencontres*) "Sist@, talk to me about your afrofeminism" and "Sist@, let's talk between afro-queers" and even the picnic meeting "Afrofem, let's talk hair." These actions aim to debate the aesthetic representations of black women, the gender identity of black people, and their ordinary stigmatization in French society. If Mwasi mobilizes against "acts of sexual violence in the Democratic Republic of Congo and all the acts of violence against women," the collective has also demonstrated against the law known as the Work Law, against the Eurosatory armaments trade show, during the COP 21 in support of climate justice, and even against police violence.[29] Several members of the collective participated in the demonstrations organized in Paris by the Black Lives Matter France movement, which called for justice for Adama Traoré, a twenty-four-year-old Frenchman of Senegalese descent killed while in police custody on July 19, 2016, in the Val d'Oise department.[30] The association also demonstrates "for the rights of women and gender minorities," for sex workers, and for trans and intersex people. It takes action in favor of refugees' rights at parades or demonstrations, as well as through the organization of clothing drives and donations. In the form of celebration days, it organizes clothing swaps aiming to support mutual assistance and recycling and to promote environmentally responsible consumer practices. Finally, the Mwasi activists work in areas ignored by the major feminist associations, modeling in this way a feminism of the margins.

The collective's activism is based on a hybrid perspective, at once postcolonial, transnational, even global, articulating without hierarchy antiracism and feminism.[31] The collective counted several participants in the Decolonial Summer Camp (Camp d'Été Décolonial), an event organized in August 2016 by activists espousing a political antiracism on the model of North American community organizing and seeking to bring, in the form of workshops and conferences, "to any person personally undergoing State racism" theoretical tools of analysis and deconstruction of his or her lived experience.[32] Similarly, Mwasi marched in Berlin alongside Black Lives Matter and participated in the International Forum of Black Feminisms, organized in September 2016 by the Association for Women's Rights in Development (AWID) in Bahia, Brazil.

The essential theoretical resources of the Mwasi activists come from the United States. While asserting their singularity in relation to black feminists in the United States, the collective explicitly builds on the work of Audre Lorde, bell hooks, Kimberlé Crenshaw, the Combahee River Collective, and of course Angela Davis. If these references are crucial, their content of political landmarks reveals as much a dearth of theoretical references specific to the French context as a blatant need, a real necessity, of history. In this regard, the extent of Mwasi's political agenda joins in many respects the struggles and demands of feminists whom one may consider their precursors at the end of the 1970s and the beginning of the 1980s in France. If these earlier initiatives did not self-identify by the Afrofeminist label, a feminism at once black, radical, concerned with confronting jointly the issues of race, anticolonialism, patriarchies (Occidental and non-Occidental), and sexism already figured in the French feminist landscape, in particular on the extreme Left. Thus, the publication in 1978 of the work by sociologist Awa Thiam, *La parole aux Négresses*, with a preface by French journalist, writer, and feminist activist Benoîte Groult, presents itself as the first radical and "black African" feminist manifesto in the French language.[33] Defining itself as "revolutionary," proclaiming itself in the tradition of Aimé Césaire, it undertook the due-process trial of excision, polygamy, assimilationism, and the practice of skin whitening while embracing an internationalist feminism, even a universal sisterhood: "As women, we feel solidarity with that young Italian girl, raped at the age of sixteen by her brother and who wants to have an abortion, although doctors refuse to help her; with all of the imprisoned Angela Davises and Eva Forests wherever they may be from; with Vietnamese women who valiantly fought to ensure victory against the American 'paper tigers'; with Black African women engaged in the struggle for the liberation of Zimbabwe," writes Awa Thiam. She continues: "By the affirmation of her solidarity with other women involved in the fight, it is a sisterhood that the black woman posits. . . . By this, we position ourselves as the sisters of anyone oppressed because she is a woman. Whether accepted or not, this sisterhood is there. Freely given."[34] The same year, a brochure edited by the Black Women's Coordination, of which Thiam was a member, along with the playwright Gerty Dambury, read in part:

> The Black Women's Coordination is [a group of] women who want an end to the social and political ghetto to which they are relegated under the heading of immigration. . . . Starting with the confrontation of our lived experience as women and as blacks, we have become aware that the history of struggles in our countries and in immigration is a history in which we are denied, falsified. . . . No sector of society subjected to oppression, be it composed of racial minorities or of women, can foist off the management and the development of its struggle for liberation on other forces, even if they are allies. . . . That is why our struggle as women is above all autonomous, for in the same way that we are intent

on fighting the capitalist system that oppresses us, we refuse to submit to the contradictions of activists who, all the while claiming to fight for a socialism without qualification, nonetheless perpetuate in regards to women, a relationship of dominance that they denounce in other areas. The Black Women's Coordination has no intention of stagnating in immigration or in a nationalist ideology.[35]

Several of the contributions in this volume, by decentering their gaze, allow the elucidation of forms of struggles and social and political situations indispensable to formulating the historical foundations of an antiracist feminism in France or an anticolonialist feminism in a Francophone context. Yet a more precise history of the complex relationships and tensions between members of the women's liberation movement and women from ethnoracial minorities in France still remains to be documented and written. Apart from the somewhat glossy image of the solidarity of struggles evoked earlier by the activists from the CNDF (Collectif National Droits des Femmes), the reproaches addressed today to a "white feminism" had already been voiced against an "Occidental feminism" in the late 1970s and early 1980s. In a rich interview, the political scientist Françoise Vergès adds precious testimony about the political atmosphere and the complexity of the debates of that time. Of Réunion Islander descent, Vergès participated conjointly in the actions of the women's liberation movement and those of anticolonialist workers' associations. After having frequented the Elisabeth Dimitriev feminist circle (named after the symbol of the so-called class-struggle brand of feminism) beginning in 1979, she also campaigned as part of one of the best-known branches of the women's movement, the Psychoanalysis and Politics (Psychépo) group, run by Antoinette Fouque. Vergès has made an indisputable assessment of the movement: "I would tell myself that I couldn't be exclusively in a feminist group. *I found that they didn't sufficiently discuss racism, immigrants, colonialism*," she declared. Evoking jokes about her, she related in an interview:

I remember a reflection made to me: "Oh, there goes Françoise with her Thirdworldism again!" The women's liberation movement was rather Franco-centric. There were examples of solidarity with and interest in

> the struggles for women from the Caribbean and elsewhere, but the process of decolonizing the feminist movement was never undergone. . . . In Psychépo, I remember the presence of Corsican women and a few Algerians, but I have no memory of a deep reflection on racism, the legacy of colonialism, or the way the left-wing movements had been contaminated by the color line. . . . Therefore we cannot say that there wasn't anything. And with Trotskyist feminist groups, the interest in the struggles of non-European women was more noticeable. But I think that within the women's movement, very few had lived outside of France. There was only a very small awareness of other situations, of the weight of racism. These other situations remained abstract.[36]

In the early 1990s, feminists whose commitment stemmed from the intersection of social and familial problems caused by the feminization of sub-Saharan African immigration, the rejection of traditional patriarchies (embodied notably by the practice of excision) and European ones, and antiracism expressed the same frustration and the same desire for autonomy from the mainstream feminist organizations.[37] Lydie Dooh-Bunya, president of the Movement for the Defense of Black Women's Rights (Mouvement pour la Défense des Droits des Femmes Noires, MODEFEN), created in 1981, has recounted in an interview the extent to which women of sub-Saharan African descent did not find their place in either African immigrant workers' associations (primarily male) or feminist associations, which were often deaf to the "problems specific to women of black culture."[38] But she especially underscored the lack of solidarity between French feminists and feminists of African descent as soon as matters turned to confronting topics directly tied to the social conditions of the latter group within French society:

> Accordingly, our French feminist comrades showed that they had the ability and knowledge to be in solidarity; their solidarity seemed essential to us, and in certain respects irreproachable, on the issue of excision. Having said this, we might have to ask them other questions concerning black women; racism in the workplace, housing, or at school, when our children are not accepted or are killed, for it happened that a child would

be killed because he is African or North African. One may regret that all women do not show more solidarity faced with these violations of rights, or at least that they don't show it more in various actions. That is why it was essential that we, black women, not be wagons hitched to the demands of others, but that we, too, say out loud what oppresses us and what we expect from others.[39]

The conflicts of today therefore grow out of a long history of misunderstanding, of power dynamics, but also of detailed convergences and divergences of struggles between "black feminists" and "French feminists." However, the historical and social position of the rising generation of activists who identify with Afrofeminism renders moot the barrier between "French feminists" and the "others" that has long shaped an ethnonational portrait of feminism in France, be it plurivocal, conflictual, or heterogeneous. And for good reason: if the Mwasi activists defend the rights of refugees and immigrants and demonstrate against sexist and/or racist policies that afflict women and gender minorities in a number of states of the Global South, as well as those who were born or grew up in France and are primarily French citizens, they no longer, in contrast to their elders, make "daily life in migration" a central subject of their political agenda—with an exception when it comes to the living conditions of migrants suffering from HIV or sex workers, both male and female.[40] Nevertheless, the Mwasi Collective, the most visible Afrofeminist association in France, must not be considered as representative of the current black activists' diversity.[41] If we must count among the latter category the November 6 Group and the association Lesbians of Color, created in 2009, numerous are those women and queer activists from the young generation who comprise what can be defined as a "nebulous Afrofeminism."[42] They all are, in a disparate manner, driven by a common determination to confront as a single force the racism and sexism of the society of their birth, which largely shaped the horizon of the opportunities and obstacles that punctuate their young lives. Indeed, the generational renewal of a black feminism in France must be analyzed in the light of a particular sociohistorical configuration that calls for further examination. However, we may assume that this recent visibility derives from the rise of the "civic blogosphere" as a space of the democratization of speech and criticism in which these new voices develop a political Afro-blogging.[43] The interest that some media newspapers and magazines recently gave to Afrofeminism, seduced as they are by its apparent novelty but at the risk sometimes of depoliticizing its reach, cannot be dissociated from the complex social fabric woven between prolific bloggers reading and responding to each other, exchanging texts, at times publishing press articles, meeting each other in forums on social networks and at antiracist demonstrations and Afrofeminist events in the urban framework of the capital or its suburban areas. Products of the democratization of an education system that benefits the daughters of sub-Saharan immigrants more than the sons, these young women, often of a precarious condition but holding diplomas and connected to the world by family ties, cultural references, or travels—by a sort of critical monitoring—strive to give voice to the political subject of a resolutely plural feminism in a society profoundly struck by social and racial inequalities.[44]

Notes

1. "Second wave feminism" refers to feminist movements that emerged from 1968 in France. See Françoise Picq, *Libération des femmes: Quarante ans de mouvement* (Paris: Seuil, 1993); Christine Bard, ed., *Les féministes de la deuxième vague* (Rennes: Presses Universitaires de Rennes, 2012).
2. https://www.canal-u.tv/video/site_pouchet_cnrs/embed.1/defaire_l_empire_2eme_partie_table_ronde_feminismes_et_critiques_postcoloniales_1.18431?width=100%25&amp%Bheight=100.
3. Christine Delphy, a leading figure of French feminism and a sociologist at CNRS, founded with Simone de Beauvoir, Claude Hennequin, and Emmanuèle de Lesseps the academic journal *Nouvelles questions féministes* in 1981. She wrote *L'ennemi principal. 1. Economie politique du patriarcat* (Paris: Syllepse, 1999).
4. Historically called the March for Equality and against Racism and later renamed March of the Beurs (the immigrants from Maghreb) by French media, the Marche des Beurs was the first antiracist march in France. It occurred from October 15, 1983, to December 1983. For further details, see Abdellali Hajjat, *La marche pour l'égalité et contre le racisme* (Paris: Amsterdam, 2013).

5. For the fortieth anniversary of the MLF (Women's Liberation Movement), on September 25, 2010, the CNDF organized a conference titled "Faire et écrire l'histoire: Féminisme et luttes de classes de 1970 à nos jours" (Make and write history: Feminism and class struggle from 1970 to the present) held at the Paris local council building.
6. The veil issue has long provoked battle among French feminist movements and still profoundly divides them. See Natalie Benelli et al., "De l'affaire du voile à l'imbrication du sexisme et du racisme," *Nouvelles questions féministes* 25 (2006): 4–11; Patricia Roux et al., "Féminisme et racisme: Une recherche exploratoire sur les fondements des divergences relatives au port du foulard," *Nouvelles questions féministes* 25 (2006): 84–106; Nicolas Dot-Pouillard, "Les recompositions politiques du mouvement féministe français au regard du *hijab*," *SociologieS* 10 (2007). See also Joan W. Scott, *The Politics of the Veil* (Princeton NJ: Princeton University Press, 2010).
7. The CNDF contested the veil and the 2004 law. See Dot-Pouillard, "Les recompositions politiques."
8. For further developments, see Silyane Larcher, "Troubles dans la 'race': De quelques fractures et points aveugles de l'antiracisme français contemporain," *L'homme et la société* 194 (2015): 215. For a similar approach, see Michel Giraud, "Question noire et mémoire de l'esclavage," *Cahiers d'études africaines* 198/199/200 (2010): 677–86; and with a specialization on discrimination, Christian Poiret, "Pour une approche processuelle des discriminations: Entendre la parole minoritaire," *Regards sociologiques* 39 (2010): 5–20. For an epistemological perspective, see Stuart Hall, "Old and New Identities, Old and New Ethnicities," in *Culture, Globalization and the World System*, ed. Anthony D. King (Minneapolis: University of Minnesota Press, 1997), 41–68; and Elsa Dorlin, introduction to *Sexe, race, classe: Pour une épistémologie de la domination* (Paris: Presses Universitaires de France, 2009), 5–18.
9. For "women in immigration," see Nadia Chââbane, "Diversité des mouvements de 'femmes dans l'immigration,'" *Les cahiers du CEDREF* 16 (2008): 231–50. For "postcolonial" or "decolonial" feminism, see Natalie et al., "Les approches postcoloniales: Apports pour un féminisme antiraciste," *Nouvelles questions féministes* 25 (2006): 4–12. And on "the space of the women's cause," see Laure Bereni, "Penser la transversalité des mobilisations féministes: L'espace de la cause des femmes," in *Les féministes de la deuxième vague*, ed. Christine Bard (Rennes: Presses Universitaires de Rennes, 2012), 27–41.
10. On homogeneity in feminism, see Eliane Gubin et al., *Le siècle des féminismes* (Paris: Éditions de l'Atelier, 2004); Monique Remy, *Histoire des mouvements de femmes: De l'utopie à l'intégration* (Paris: Harmattan, 2000); and Christine Delphy,

Un universalisme si particulier: Féminisme et exception française, 1980–2010 (Paris: Éditions Syllepse, 2010).

11. Started on February 2016, my research bears on ethnographical observation of Afrofeminist events and mobilizations, as well as on biographical interviews conducted in Paris and its suburbs. Because it provides an excerpt of a broader inquiry on French black women and queer feminists in contemporary France, this essay gives less room to the second wave feminists' voices. I would like to thank my colleagues Mahamet Timera and Jules Falquet, both sociologists at Paris Diderot University, for their suggestions and comments at the beginning of my investigation.
12. Jacques Rancière, *Disagreement: Politics and Philosophy*, trans. Julie Rose (Minneapolis: University of Minnesota Press, 1999), xi–xii.
13. See Annette Davis's and Sharone Omankoy's joint intervention at the workshop "Undoing the Empire" (Défaire l'empire), https://www.canal-u.tv/video/site_pouchet_cnrs/embed.1/defaire_l_empire_2eme_partie_table_ronde_feminismes_et_critiques_postcoloniales_1.18431?width=100%25&amp%Bheight=100.
14. Davis is a part-time *auto-entrepreneur* (self-entrepreneur) in private education, and Omankoy is a social worker for an association offering help to HIV/AIDS patients. I interviewed each of them on June 15 and July 25, 2016.
15. "The space of social movements" is a translation of Lilian Mathieu, "L'espace des mouvements sociaux," *Politix* 77 (2007): 131–51.
16. For a compelling analysis of the conceptual stakes of this distinction, see Paul Ricoeur, *Oneself as Another* (Chicago: University of Chicago Press, 1992).
17. Larcher, "Troubles dans la 'race.'"
18. For a reflection on the epistemological stakes of an inclusive feminism, see Naomi Zack, *Inclusive Feminism: A Third Wave of Women's Commonality* (Lanham MD: Rowman & Littlefield, 2005).
19. Guide des sources de l'histoire du féminisme, http://archivesdufeminisme.fr.
20. The Section Française de l'Internationale Ouvrière (French Section of the Workers' International) is the predecessor of the current French Socialist Party.
21. Zahra Ali, *Féminismes islamiques* (Paris: La Découverte, 2012); Cecilia Baeza, "L'expérience inédite et dérangeante du Collectif des Féministes pour l'Egalité," *Nouvelles questions féministes* 25 (2006): 152; Dot-Pouillard, "Les recompositions politiques."
22. The way in which public discourse on Islam in French society fractured feminist mobilizations can be considered as the first postcolonial moment of French feminism. See Abdellali Hajjat and Marwan Mohammed, *Islamophobie: Comment les élites françaises fabriquent le "problème musulman"* (Paris: La Découverte, 2013), 244–50.

23. For a discussion of "colonial legacies," see, among others, Jean-François Bayart and Romain Bertrand, "De quel 'legs colonial' parle-t-on?," *Esprit*, December 2006, 1–27.
24. Only one person among the ones I interviewed had parents belonging to the upper socioeconomic classes (doctor and high-school professor).
25. http://mwasicollectif.com.
26. See Michele Wallace, "A Black Feminist's Search for Sisterhood," in *All the Women Are White, All the Blacks Are Men, but Some of Us Are Brave*, ed. Gloria T. Hull, Patricia Bell Scott, and Barbara Smith (Old Westbury NY: Feminist Press, 1982), 5–12.
27. See Kimberlé Crenshaw, *Demarginalizing the Intersection of Race and Sex: A Black Feminist Critique of Antidiscrimination Doctrine, Feminist Theory, and Antiracist Politics* (Chicago: University of Chicago Legal Forum, 1989).
28. http://mwasicollectif.com.
29. The Work Law (Loi Travail) imposed by the French government introduced more flexibility in French law legislation, in particular in wage-paid work conditions.
30. Sylvia Zappi, "Rassemblement à Paris de 'Black Lives Matter France' après la mort d'Adama Traoré," *Le monde*, July 23, 2016, http://www.lemonde.fr/police-justice/article/2016/07/23/rassemblement-a-paris-de-black-lives-matter-france-apres-la-mort-d-adama-traore_4973930_1653578.html.
31. For a critical approach of the reception of intersectionality in French academia, see Jules Falquet and Azadeh Kian, "Introduction: Intersectionnalité et colonialité," *Les cahiers du CEDREF* 20 (2015), available online, http://journals.openedition.org/cedref/731; Fatima Ait Ben Lmadani and Nasima Moujoud, "Peut-on faire de l'intersectionnalité sans les ex-colonisé.e.s?," *Mouvements* 72 (2012): 11–21. See also Sirma Bilge, "Le blanchiment de l'intersectionnalité," *Recherches féministes* 28 (2015): 9–32.
32. https://ce-decolonial.org. For more details, see also https://www.mediapart.fr/journal/france/010916/le-camp-dete-decolonial-une-rupture-avec-lantiracisme-moral?onglet=full.
33. Awa Thiam, *La parole aux Négresses* (Paris: Denoël/Gonthier, 1978). The English-language edition is titled *Speak Out, Black Sisters: Feminism and Oppression in Black Africa*, trans. D. Blair (London: Pluto Press, 1986). The Mwasi Collective's website cites this book as a theoretical and historical resource. For further information, see Gertrude Mianda, "Reading Awa Thiam's *La Parole aux Négresses* through the Lens of Feminisms and English Language Hegemony," *Atlantis* 36, no. 2 (2014): 8–19.
34. Thiam, *La parole*, 182–83.
35. Coordination des Femmes Noires, July 1978. The booklet is also available on the Mwasi Collective's website. For an example of one of Gerty Dambury's plays, see *Rabordaille* (Éditions Théâtre Ouverture, 1989).

36. Myriam Paris, "Entretien avec Françoise Vergès: Mettre en théorie et en pratique le principe du déplacement," *Comment s'en sortir?* 1 (2015): 12–13, 20–21.
37. Useful elements can be found in Catherine Quiminal, ed., "Mobilisation associative et dynamiques d'intégration des femmes d'Afrique subsaharienne en France," cited in "Faire et défaire les identités avec le religieux: Migrations, ethnicité, 'race' et religion," by Mahamet Timera (thèse d'habilitation à diriger des recherches [habilitation thesis to direct research], Université Paris 7–Denis Diderot, 2007), vol. 2 (appendixes).
38. Philippe Dewitte, "La condition des femmes noires en France: Un entretien avec Lydie Dooh-Bunya, présidente du Mouvement pour la défense des droits de la femme noire (Modefen)," *Hommes & migrations* 1,131 (1990): 81–89.
39. Dewitte, "La condition," 82.
40. Catherine Quiminal, "Comment peut-on être africaines en France," *Journal des anthropologues* 72/73 (1998): 49–61.
41. As of 2017, it is impossible for me to determine the correct number of members of the association. Some of them, like Sharone Omankoy, have left it, while new members have joined.
42. For information on Lesbians of Color, see Jules Falquet, "Lesbiennes migrantes, entre hétéro-circulation et recompositions néolibérales du nationalisme," in *Recueil Alexandries, Collections Esquisses* (2011), http://www.reseau-terra.eu/article1092.html.
43. Dominique Cardon, "Le style délibératif de la 'blogosphère citoyenne,'" *Hermès, la revue* 47, no. 1 (2007): 51–58; Antoinette Pole, "Black Blogosphere," *International Journal of Technology, Knowledge, and Society: Annual Review* 2, no. 6 (2007): 9–16.
44. Even though French women of African descent are more discriminated against than French women of European descent, their rates of unemployment are lower than those of their male counterparts. See Yaël Brinbaum and Jean-Luc Primon, "Transition professionnelle et emploi des descendants d'immigrés en France," *Revue européenne des sciences sociales* 51, no. 1 (2013): 28.

6

Gerty Archimède and the Struggle for Decolonial Citizenship in the French Antilles, 1946–51

ANNETTE K. JOSEPH-GABRIEL

The history of France's vexed relationship with its former colonies once again came to the fore of international debate with the January 2016 resignation of the minister of justice, Christiane Taubira, over a proposed law to strip French nationality from dual citizens convicted of terrorism. As a black woman from French Guiana, Taubira's assertion that "parfois résister c'est rester, parfois résister c'est partir" (sometimes to resist is to stay, sometimes to resist is to leave) places her in a long line of black women who publicly articulated their resistance to exclusionary models of citizenship in France and the Francophone world.[1] From within the corridors of established political institutions such as the French National Assembly and Senate, or through published texts that boasted a transatlantic readership, black women have historically challenged, shaped, and defined notions of belonging at various moments in the debate on French national identity.

Yet with a few exceptions, historical narratives retain a masculine genealogy of the discursive framing of citizenship in the Francophone world. For example, retrospective analyses of the 1946 law of departmentalization, which granted overseas department status to France's *vieilles colonies* (old colonies), situate the Martinican poet and politician Aimé Césaire as the primary architect of this political transformation.[2] While the intellectual contributions of Antillean women such as Suzanne Césaire and the Nardal sisters have gained recognition in recent years and have been the subject of a growing body of scholarship, the grassroots organizing and political advocacy work done by Antillean and Guyanese women, including Gerty Archimède, Eugénie Éboué-Tell, and Jane Léro, remain muted episodes in French Antillean political history.[3] This elision results in at best a partial understanding of notions of belonging in the French-speaking world and limits the terrain of possibilities for imagining more inclusive forms of political affiliation and participation. Centering black women's voices in this ongoing debate allows, then, a radical rethinking of citizenship from a singular allegiance to a nation-state, to a set of practices that emphasize the humanity, presence, and claims to equality of formerly marginalized groups.

The years after World War II were a pivotal period in the intertwined histories of France and the Antilles and therefore a particularly instructive moment for such a study of contested citizenships. The constitution that established the French Fourth Republic in 1946 also redefined the relationship between metropole and colonies. Notably, it founded the French Union. This uneven federation was composed of metropolitan France, which still wielded governing power; Martinique, Guadeloupe, French Guiana, and Réunion as overseas French departments; and the newer colonies in Africa as overseas territories. In short, the constitution did away with the colonial status and made overseas populations French citizens, at least on paper. The promise of citizenship, however, did not always translate into concrete changes in the lived realities of the colonized. Inconsistent application of voting rights left out large segments of the African population. In the Antilles, France dragged its feet on extending social security and other forms of welfare benefits that were already available in the Hexagon. In effect, many former colonial subjects soon realized that they remained recognizable outsiders in the French polity. Their citizenship, juxtaposed with that of their metropolitan counterparts, was, to borrow Homi Bhabha's formulation, "almost the same, but not quite."[4] Even as France had to negotiate the terms of its colonial relations, it was also involved in redefining the role of women as citizens in the metropole. Notably, in 1944 French women won the right to vote. In this historic moment, black women in overseas France were precisely the demographic situated at the intersection of these two changes: France's extension of voting rights to French women and citizenship rights to former colonial subjects.

As Clara Palmiste shows, these transformations in political status had important implications for women in Guadeloupe and Martinique. Women quickly outnumbered men as registered voters for municipal and legislative elections. Consequently, political parties soon recognized the importance of women's vote: "In most of the tracts in Guadeloupe and Martinique, the parties 'courted' the feminine vote, aware of their weight on the future of the colonies."[5] Antillean women were an increasingly formidable force, able to elect officials to governing bodies in the metropole who would advance women's political interests. Gerty Archimède was one such official.

Gerty Marie Bernadette Archimède was born in Morne-à-l'Eau, Guadeloupe, on April 26, 1909.[6] Her mother was a telephone operator, and her father served as mayor of Morne-à-l'Eau between 1912 and 1947. Archimède worked in a colonial bank in Guadeloupe—an experience on which she would later draw as a deputy in condemning the perpetuation of colonial fiscal policies in the Antilles—before leaving to study law in Paris. She was called to the bar in Point-à-Pitre in 1939. A member of the Communist Party, she was elected on the party's ticket in 1946 to the National Assembly, where she represented Guadeloupe until 1951. During her time as a deputy, Archimède was a fierce advocate for the disenfranchised in the Antilles. Alongside other Antillean deputies, including Aimé Césaire and Rosan Girard, she argued for laws and reforms that would be favorable to agricultural workers, women, and children in the Antilles, often facing staunch opposition from her metropolitan colleagues.

While Archimède's political advocacy focused primarily on improving social and economic conditions in Guadeloupe, her legal work spanned a larger portion of the African diaspora. She was particularly committed to political freedom both at home and abroad. She began her legal career defending Guadeloupeans accused of dissidence under the pro-Nazi collaborationist Vichy regime.[7] She was also a member of the legal team that defended the sixteen Martinican agricultural workers accused of killing their *béké* (a term that is used in the Antilles to refer to the white Creole planter class) employer in the infamous case that came to be known as *L'affaire des seize de Basse-Pointe*.[8] In July 1950 Archimède learned of the plight of political detainees of the French colonial administration in the Ivory Coast. In a simple note, she proposed her legal services to Félix Houphouët-Boigny, then deputy in the National Assembly and secretary of the anticolonialist party, the Rassemblement Démocratique Africain (African Democratic Rally). The note read: "I am a better lawyer than deputy. I would like to go and defend my African brothers."[9] This pithy but powerful message clearly articulates Archimède's commitment to Pan-Africanism and her sense of solidarity, fostered over years of working side by side with deputies from French Guiana, Madagascar, and West Africa, with the shared aim of enacting legislation through the National Assembly that would ensure legal protections for France's overseas territories.

Archimède left Paris a few days later with a list of the names of 150 detainees. She arrived in Abidjan to find 3,000 men, women, and children imprisoned by the French colonial administration for charges as vague as "having uttered speech of such a nature as to trouble the morale of populations."[10] A neighboring school had been closed and converted into a detention center to house overflow from the prison. Many of the prisoners had been wounded by gunfire when their villages were raided by the police, and some succumbed to their injuries while in detention. In this atmosphere of repressive colonial violence, Archimède prepared her defense for a series of legal battles that would keep her in Abidjan for four months. She obtained several acquittals and spent some time teaching groups of women to make guava jam to support themselves financially while their husbands were in prison.[11] Three days after her return to Paris, Archimède wrote a letter that was read in the National Assembly, decrying colonial oppression in the Ivory Coast. She cited at length damning examples of the colonial administration's failure to uphold the rhetoric of liberty, equality, and fraternity and called on the National Assembly to act decisively to redress these injustices.[12]

Over a decade later, Archimède provided legal counsel to civil rights activist Angela Davis on her arrest in Guadeloupe for possession and intended distribution of Communist propaganda. In her autobiography,

Davis best articulates the respect that Archimède commanded from her colleagues and the passion with which she defended her cases:

> Maître Archimede was a big woman with very dark skin, penetrating eyes, and unassailable confidence. I will never forget the first meeting we had with her. I felt as if I were in the presence of a very great woman. As for our predicament, there was never any doubt in my mind that she would rescue us. But I was so impressed by her personality, by the respect that she clearly commanded as a Communist, even from the colonialists, that for a while our problem became a secondary concern for me. If I had surrendered to my desires, I would have remained on the island to learn from this woman. Over the next days, she worked tenaciously at negotiating with the customs officials, the police, the judges.[13]

Archimède's tenacity, as Davis describes it, as well as her skillful negotiation of the latter's release from the island, reveal her to be a savvy lawyer and politician who could be at once resolute and conciliatory when necessary. Archimède's legal work and her collaboration with some of the leading figures of anticolonial movements in the twentieth century place her at the forefront of the struggle for freedom and equality in the Francophone world. In each of the aforementioned cases, she challenged the arbitrariness and illegitimacy of colonial rule. Her brand of anticolonial resistance from within used the legal system to counter an oppressive state. For example, in the National Assembly, she often argued against the practice of including a clause in each new law passed in France that limited its application in the overseas departments by making the law subject to decrees by the head of state and implementation by the Ministry of the Colonies. She called these clauses "an anticonstitutional formulation" and continuously reminded her colleagues that "the law is categorical: henceforth, the overseas departments have the same juridical and legislative status as those of the metropole."[14] Archimède firmly believed in the power of legal recourse for disenfranchised Antilleans and therefore advocated for departmentalization as the political structure that would allow Guadeloupeans, formerly at the mercy of arbitrary colonial decrees, to participate democratically in the legislative process through their elected representatives.

Gerty Archimède's legacy is one of resistance to intersecting oppressions based on race, gender, and class. Devoted to the Communist Party even after the fall of the USSR, a fierce advocate for equal treatment of Antilleans under French law, and a voice for black women's equal access to health care and employment, Archimède was, in the words of several Guadeloupean commentators, the voice of the people.[15] Examining her legacy of anticolonial resistance presents a new narrative on departmentalization in the Antilles. No longer a political transformation single-handedly conceived of and implemented by Aimé Césaire and a select few male colleagues in the French National Assembly, this narrative demands the inclusion of the voices of black women such as Archimède who were instrumental in its inception. In my reading of Archimède's contributions over five years of debates in the National Assembly, I show that her vision of departmentalization was about more than an extension of French rights and protections to the overseas departments. It was, fundamentally, a means to claim a decolonized citizenship that would disrupt and ultimately replace the colonial structures that continued to determine and shape the economic, social, and political realities of France's newest departments. Placing Archimède's voice at the center of the heated debates on what it meant to be French in the aftermath of a divisive world war reveals the promise that departmentalization held for black French women in particular, who had been multiply marginalized as colonized subjects along the lines of race, gender, and class. Their citizenship was not to be additive, incorporating Antillean women as second-class citizens into the existing power structures established by the colonial state. It was to be radical, dismantling those systems of power in favor of the recognition of the humanity of the formerly colonized as the underlying tenet of a new way of being French in the Antilles.

Coloniality and the Practice of Citizenship

Archimède's recourse to citizenship was a means to contest what Peruvian sociologist Aníbal Quijano has described as the "coloniality of power." Quijano's work examines the historical processes by which colonial power came to be consolidated and therefore allows us to understand how colonialism functions and, by extension, what decolonization might look like. He argues that European conquest must be understood as the result of two historical processes: Euro-centered capitalist methods of labor control and the codification of racial difference between colonizer and colonized.[16] Quijano's reading of colonial power, grounded in the history of Latin America, is nevertheless applicable in certain ways to the French Empire in the Caribbean because there too we find that colonization dehumanizes the colonized through an institutionalized racial hierarchy. This hierarchy is in turn marshaled as evidence that supposedly legitimizes European conquest and economic exploitation such that "both race and the division of labor remained structurally linked and mutually reinforcing."[17] Recognizing the coloniality of power moves us away from the linear and seemingly straightforward association of political independence with decolonization. Independence that maintains the fundamental elements of the coloniality of power is not decolonization. It leads instead to "a rearticulation of the coloniality of power over new institutional bases."[18]

Aaron Kamugisha cautions, in his study of the coloniality of citizenship in the Anglophone Caribbean, against the view that "independence effected a *radical* break with previously existing forms of citizenship."[19] Independence can be decolonization only if it is accompanied by a "process of dismantling the structures of power and discourses of otherness instituted by the colonial state."[20] Within this framework, departmentalization can also hold the possibility of decolonial citizenship if it is premised on a set of political relationships and democratic practices through which French Antilleans can contest the labor exploitation, racial discrimination, and economic inequality that have historically been perpetrated, or at the very least sanctioned by the state.

Departmentalization, then, is not antithetical to decolonization but is instead a potentially powerful tool of political inclusion. Césaire argued as much in his speech to the National Assembly as the *rapporteur* for the 1946 law that would reclassify some of France's colonial territories in the Caribbean as overseas departments (Loi tendant au classement comme départements français de la Guadeloupe, de la Martinique, de la Réunion et de la Guyane française, law no. 46-451, March 20, 1946). Césaire began by situating the demand for "departmentalization" as the next step in a century-long history of political transformation in the French Antilles that began with the abolition of slavery in 1848: "But we respond that it is the same Montesquieu who wrote scathing pages against the enslavement of blacks, and the matter at hand today is, through a law of assimilation, better, equalization, to liberate more than a million men of color from one of the modern forms of subjection."[21] For Césaire, the proposed law would liberate French Antilleans from the arbitrary decrees of colonial administrators by empowering the populations of the overseas departments as voters and citizens. Ultimately, full citizenship would, for Césaire, result in a redistribution of political power across a wider base of Antillean society, where it had previously been concentrated in the hands of colonial administrators and the white planter class.

Césaire went on to outline his vision for decolonial citizenship in the French Antilles as a dynamic process that would be adaptable over time: "We must add, by the way, that the assimilation which is before you today, far from being a rigid assimilation, a 'geometric' assimilation, an unnatural assimilation, is a flexible, intelligent, and realistic assimilation."[22] As Gary Wilder has argued, Césaire's demand to integrate overseas populations into the French state was also a proposal for "a type of integration that would reconstitute France itself, by quietly exploding the existing national state from within."[23] Ultimately, as Nick Nesbitt shows, Césaire's vision of departmentalization was "a pure initiative of political decolonization" because it "answers not the question 'how do we assimilate or become more "French,"' but instead 'what political form best allows the development and flourishing of our singular capacities of expression?'"[24]

Archimède shared the decolonial model put forward by Césaire and others and worked consistently to keep this vision at the forefront of debates in the National Assembly. Leading the charge on bills and reforms that sought to halt the devaluation of the franc in the Antilles and to extend social security benefits and labor protections to the overseas departments, Archimède argued that anything short of these goals would be a reiteration of a colonial paradigm.[25] Her contributions to National Assembly debates targeted two main elements of the process of decolonizing French citizenship for all: extending French laws to the overseas departments and challenging the persistence of women's second-class citizenship despite their acquisition of the vote.

Decolonizing Citizenship in the Transition from Colony to Overseas Department

Archimède's focus on equality and legal protections for Antilleans in general and Guadeloupean women in particular was a response to the limitations imposed on departmentalization by her metropolitan colleagues in the National Assembly. Departmentalization in the Antilles is often summarized as the extension of French laws from the metropole to the *départements d'outre-mer* (DOMs). Yet the 1946 law was, in reality, more limited than this description suggests. The transformation from colonies to departments did not guarantee a blanket and default application of French laws to the DOMs but instead required that the applicability of a law to the overseas departments be stipulated at the time of passing the law. For Archimède, this constant bracketing of the Antilles in a separate clause written into each law was but a continuation of the colonial regime of inequality and a perpetuation of the second-class citizenship of Antilleans. Her argument to this effect in the National Assembly is worth quoting at length here because it allows us to foreground her voice and her important contribution to the ongoing debate on decolonial citizenship in the early years of departmentalization, a contribution that has all but disappeared from contemporary narratives. Archimède exhorted her colleagues to recognize that metropolitan France continued to fall short of the decolonial promises held forth by the 1946 law: "Well, each time we present a new provision, the Government, especially if it is a provision that will be advantageous to the overseas departments, never fails to introduce a clause into the text, something along the lines of: 'a later law will extend the provisions of the present law to the overseas departments'—this is in the event that we oblige the Government to remain within the limits of the Constitution—or else simply: 'a later decree.'"[26]

Archimède argues here against French lawmakers' practice of marking Antilleans as separate citizens who could continue to be governed by unilateral decisions made by the Ministry of the Colonies, rather than by laws voted in by their elected representatives. For Archimède, such a policy of exclusion was but a repackaging of colonialism in the obfuscatory language of vaguely defined laws, decrees, and quotas. As Archimède and other Antillean deputies fought for and only acquired state protections in a piecemeal manner, she argued that each denial of such rights to Antilleans was not an isolated case. Rather, she described France's unwillingness to recognize Antilleans as fully French and therefore eligible for the same rights accorded all French citizens as a willful repetition of colonial practices, "an omission which recurs too often to be involuntary."[27]

In a 1948 debate on budget allocations for the rum industry in Guadeloupe and Martinique, Archimède sought to peel back this new face of colonialism and lay bare its ongoing practice of inequality. She argued that the National Assembly was engaged in a "return to the former status quo, which brings back painful memories because it harks back to the colonial tax system. We have become, since that time, French departments."[28] Naming the continued colonial regime was an important step toward disrupting its persistent presence in the Antilles. What is most striking here, however, is Archimède's insistence on the Antillean territories as *départements français* (French departments) rather than as *départements d'outre-mer* (overseas departments), an insistence that characterized most of her arguments in the National Assembly. Her goal here, in arguing for a decolonial citizenship, was to situate the Antilles as an integral part of France, rather than as a bracketed outpost of the French Empire in the Americas.

Archimède was often at the forefront of putting forward a decolonial vision of citizenship that would counter the coloniality of power. She situated departmentalization on a continuum with the abolition of slavery and was hopeful that, if implemented fully, it would redress the imbalance of power concentrated in the hands of white planters and a complicit colonial administration.[29] She also condemned the continuation of a colonial regime that invested more in policing than in social and economic progress in the Antilles.[30] Through the bills and amendments that she brought before the National Assembly, Archimède spearheaded a politics of inclusion in response to this tiered system of French citizenship and ultimately charged her fellow deputies: "We want the government to remember, once and for all, that some six or seven thousand kilometers away from the metropole, there are French departments."[31] Three years later she would remind her colleagues with dismay that France continued to champion a symbolic citizenship for the Antilles with little commitment to redressing the years of stunted development wrought by colonization: "It is all well and good to repeat at each of these debates: 'You are an integral part of the French nation, your territories are French departments.' . . . But the situation is very serious in these countries."[32] Never one to mince words, Archimède chastised colleagues who sought to discredit her arguments based on procedural protocol. In one instance, when another deputy tried to silence her for speaking longer than her allotted time, she retorted, "The populations of my country will remember, Mister Minister, that you quibbled with us over a few minutes when their right to life was at stake."[33] Throughout her fiery interventions in National Assembly debates, Archimède remained hopeful that with the recognition of full citizenship would come the freedom for disenfranchised French Antilleans, particularly women, to determine their own political and economic futures through their participation in national decision-making processes.

Women in the Political Sphere

Even as Archimède ascended the political ranks from the municipal council to the National Assembly, she also remained acutely aware of the obstacles that black French women faced in the male-dominated sphere of public politics. Indeed, despite the recognition of their voice and growing political influence, women continued to face steep opposition to their presence in the electorate and their work as political actors. Archimède's contemporary, the Martinican writer and intellectual Paulette Nardal, summarized this hostility in a trenchant editorial in the journal *La femme dans la cité*: "Furthermore, those among us who, in 1948, courageously entered the fight soliciting and obtaining the seats of municipal advisors, declare themselves disgusted by the experience. . . . Facing blaring ignorance, astounding credulity, or perfidious sectarianism of certain milieus demands a rare courage, a hardened temperament, relentless health."[34]

Archimède's own experiences support Nardal's observations. She faced opposition from several quarters, including from political opponents who saw her increasingly distinguished career as a threat to the existing gender hierarchy in Guadeloupe. In 1959, when Archimède lost her seat as municipal representative of Basse-Terre, members of the opposing party paraded through the streets of her neighborhood, carrying an effigy with disproportionately large breasts and a large posterior. On another occasion, a group of opponents attacked her while she was delivering a speech at a conference and tried to strip her naked.[35] While the phenomenon of taunting a losing candidate with a caricatured puppet, known as a *bwa bwa*, was in itself not atypical, it is striking that in Archimède's case, the puppet featured exaggerated body parts rather than the distorted facial features common to such effigies. Indeed, both attacks indicate more than just differences in political ideology. They enact a specific kind of gendered violence that paradoxically seeks to erase black women's presence in the male-dominated political sphere by making them highly visible as hypersexualized objects.

Rather than view herself as an exception, Archimède recognized and challenged these structural obstacles to Antillean women's political participation. In February 1951 she sent a telegram from Point-à-Pitre to her colleague and fellow Guadeloupean deputy Rosan Girard in Paris, informing him of the low numbers of registered voters for the upcoming elections: "Majority communes 15 percent registered. Deadline extension indispensable. Signed: Archimède."[36] As Girard explained in the National Assembly, Guadeloupean voters were disenfranchised by voter registration laws that were untenable in the Antilles given the lack of basic infrastructure. Erratic power supply and a lack of photographers meant that only the privileged living in the urban centers of Point-à-Pitre and Basse-Terre could acquire the photo identification cards needed for the registration process. Guadeloupean women, particularly single mothers, were disproportionately disenfranchised in an electoral system that placed the only accepted nonphoto identification cards beyond their reach. Notably, military service cards were issued primarily to men, and only married women had access to the *livret de famille*, a civil registry noting genealogical information. The voter registration process for many single mothers therefore necessitated an expensive and often impractical journey from rural to urban areas in order to obtain the photo identification that would prove their eligibility to vote.

Despite their acquisition of citizenship, women in the Antilles still lagged behind their metropolitan counterparts in access not only to the electoral process but also to health care.[37] For Archimède, departmentalization was incomplete as long as Antillean women remained on the margins of social and economic advancements. She gave voice to their concerns, highlighting the intersecting racial and class discrimination that continued to deprive them of the social assistance and benefits that women in the metropole received: "For the past two years, women in our departments have wished to benefit from the subsidies granted to French mothers, and they do not understand the discrimination that it seems the government would like to institute."[38] As both a member and a critic of the French government, Archimède's naming of this tiered citizenship as institutionalized discrimination places Antillean women at the center of, rather than as peripheral to, the decolonial demands of departmentalization.

Equal treatment for Antillean women under French law was an uphill battle that Archimède had to fight throughout her tenure in the National Assembly due to centuries-old colonial representations of black women's sexuality.[39] In opposition to her calls for the extension of welfare benefits to Antillean mothers, French lawmakers relied on colonial stereotypes of hypersexualized Antillean women and argued that France's coffers could not keep up with the high birth rates in the overseas departments. As Archimède would later recount of her political battles: "We were opposed with all sorts of arguments and insulting allegations leveled at Guadeloupean mothers, claiming that here there was rampant overbreeding, hence the systematic refusal to extend to Antillean mothers benefits for prenatal care, childbirth, first births, and so on."[40] The specific language of overbreeding, or *lapinisme* in the original French version, is derived from the French word for "rabbit." The term connotes unbridled sexual activity and childbirth and is one example of metropolitan lawmakers' recourse to the dehumanizing image of Antillean women and their children as simply mouths to feed and a burden on the French state in order to deny them their rights as French citizens. As Félix Germain has shown, Antillean women's bodies in the postwar period were sites of political contestation, marshaled as cheap labor by the Bureau pour le Développement des Migrations Intéressant les Départements d'Outre-Mer (BUMIDOM), a government agency created to oversee the state-sponsored migration of Antilleans recruited for low-wage, unskilled jobs in France that ultimately reinforced the imbalance of power between white employers and black women as domestic workers.[41] Archimède opposed these colonial representations of Antillean women and continued to demand that France make good on its own republican narrative of equality by recognizing their humanity and eligibility as full French citizens.

Although her amendments were systematically denied when put to the vote, Archimède remained a persistent voice for French Antilleans in the National Assembly debates. In one session of the assembly's proceedings, Archimède acknowledged the disappointing results of a vote that morning that struck down one of her proposed amendments but went on, undeterred, to propose a new amendment that would include Antillean civil servants in a reform from which the government sought to exclude them. She articulated the indefatigable optimism with which she continued to represent the interests of French Antilleans: "Ladies and gentlemen, the fate reserved for the amendment that we were honored to present on article 4 could dissuade us from intervening in this debate. However, I persist in my belief that some of our colleagues are not informed on the questions that preoccupy us, and although I do not want to hurt anyone's feelings, the representatives of the government themselves do not receive the necessary information from their offices. It is for this reason that we are obliged to help them to elucidate some of the problems of the overseas departments."[42]

Archimède explains here the motivation behind her refusal to be silenced by the votes against her proposed amendments. She attributes this voting pattern to her colleagues' ignorance of the realities of life in the overseas departments and subtly critiques the failure of governmental bodies to obtain the necessary information that would allow them to make informed decisions on the lives of French Antilleans. Taking this willful ignorance as her point of departure, Archimède took up the challenge of making France's neglected citizens more visible and audible in the metropole. She sought to peel back what her contemporary Suzanne Césaire described as "the Great Camouflage" of the Antilles, to show the grim realities of stunted economic development that lay beneath the stereotypical colonial postcard image of idyllic beaches.[43]

It is undeniable that Archimède made important contributions to French Antillean politics in the early years of departmentalization as one of the first black women, along with Eugénie Éboué-Tell, to represent Guadeloupe in the French legislature. Although Éboué-Tell's political leanings were markedly more conservative than Archimède's, they converged in their criticism of France's imperial policies in the Antilles and in Africa.[44] Despite their political differences, both Éboué-Tell and Archimède made significant gains in an environment that was hostile to black women's presence in a sphere dominated by white men. Yet Guadeloupe would have to wait nearly two decades after Archimède to see another woman representative in the French government, with Albertine Baclet's short-lived tenure in the National Assembly from 1967 to 1968, and then another two decades for the election of Lucette Michaux-Chevry as a deputy in 1986. Just as the implicit promise of women's triumphant entry into politics with their acquisition of the vote was not as forthcoming as imagined, so too have the promises of departmentalization been elusive. The extensive labor strikes in Guadeloupe in 2009 suggest that the decolonial citizenship for which Archimède and others fought remains an unfulfilled promise.[45] In 1976, four years before her death, Archimède expressed her fervent wish for Guadeloupeans to continue on the path of political self-discovery and self-determination: "My dearest hope is for the liberation of my people, first of all, for their awakening to the causes of their poverty and the means to emerge from it."[46] Her words, ever hopeful, suggest that the dynamic process of decolonization, whether through the departmentalization that Césaire articulated or through the autonomy that Archimède herself would come to advocate in later years, is still an ongoing process.

Notes

1. Christiane Taubira, https://twitter.com/ChTaubira/status/692259706572795905, accessed January 27, 2016. All translations are mine unless otherwise indicated.
2. See, for example, Gary Wilder, *Freedom Time: Negritude, Decolonization, and the Future of the World* (Durham NC: Duke University Press, 2015); and Nick Nesbitt, "Departmentalization and the Logic of Decolonization," *L'esprit créateur* 47, no. 1 (2007): 32–43.
3. For the intellectual contributions of Antillean women, see, for example, Jennifer A. Boittin, *Colonial Metropolis: The Urban Grounds of Anti-imperialism and Feminism in Interwar Paris* (Lincoln: University of Nebraska Press, 2010); T. Denean Sharpley-Whiting, *Negritude Women* (Minneapolis: University of Minnesota Press, 2002); and Jennifer M. Wilks, *Race, Gender, & Comparative Black Modernism: Suzanne Lacascade, Marita Bonner, Suzanne Césaire, Dorothy West* (Baton Rouge: Louisiana State University Press, 2008).
4. Homi Bhabha, "Of Mimicry and Man: The Ambivalence of Colonial Discourse," *October* 28 (1984): 126.
5. Clara Palmiste, "Le vote féminin et la transformation des colonies françaises d'Amérique en départements en 1946," *Nuevomundo* (2014): 9.
6. For further biographical information, see Gerty Archimède and Laurent Farrugia, *Gerty Archimède: Interview* (Basse-Terre: Jeunes Antilles, 1976); the film *Gerty Archimède: La candidate du peuple*, directed by Mariette Monpierre (Les Productions de la Lanterne, 2005), DVD; and "Gerty, Marie, Bernadette Archimède," in *Base de données des députés français depuis 1789*, http://www2.assemblee-nationale.fr/sycomore/fiche/(num_dept)/186, accessed June 29, 2016.
7. See Archimède and Farrugia, *Gerty Archimède*, 16–17.
8. See Archimède and Farrugia, *Gerty Archimède*, 18. For more information on the case, see *Les 16 de Basse-Pointe*, directed by Camile Mauduech ([Paris]; Gros Morne [Martinique]: Les Films du Marigot: MP Productions; Les Films du Dorlis, 2009).
9. Archimède and Farrugia, *Gerty Archimède*, 49.
10. Archimède and Farrugia, *Gerty Archimède*, 52.
11. Archimède and Farrugia, *Gerty Archimède*, 55.
12. Gerty Archimède, *Journal officiel de la république française*, no. 115 (1950). All citations to the *Journal officiel* are available online at http://4e.republique.jo-an.fr, accessed June 20, 2016.
13. Angela Davis, *Angela Davis—an Autobiography* (New York: Random House, 1974), 215.
14. Gerty Archimède, *Journal Officiel de la république Française*, no. 110 (1948): 6057.
15. *Gerty Archimède: La candidate du peuple*; and Archimède and Farrugia, *Gerty Archimède*, 7.

16. Aníbal Quijano, "Coloniality of Power, Eurocentrism, and Latin America," *Nepantla: Views from South* 1, no. 3 (2000): 533–34.
17. Quijano, "Coloniality of Power," 536.
18. Quijano, "Coloniality of Power," 567.
19. Aaron Kamugisha, "The Coloniality of Citizenship in the Contemporary Anglophone Caribbean," *Race & Class* 49, no. 2 (2007): 22.
20. Kamugisha, "The Coloniality," 35.
21. Aimé Césaire, *Journal officiel de la république française*, no. 23 (1946): 660.
22. Césaire, *Journal officiel*, 660.
23. Wilder, *Freedom Time*, 2.
24. Nesbitt, "Departmentalization," 39.
25. Gerty Archimède, *Journal officiel de la république française*, no. 114 (1948): 6298.
26. Gerty Archimède, *Journal officiel de la république française*, no. 110 (1948): 6058.
27. Gerty Archimède, *Journal officiel de la république française*, no. 110 (1949): 6925.
28. Gerty Archimède, *Journal officiel de la république française*, no. 124 (1948): 6679.
29. See Gerty Archimède, *Journal officiel de la république française*, no. 52 (1948): 2922; and Archimède and Farrugia, *Gerty Archimède*, 42.
30. Archimède argued that the riot control forces (CRS), an overwhelmingly white police force, were granted supplementary forms of compensation that were denied teachers in the Antilles. See Gerty Archimède, *Journal officiel de la république française*, no. 11 (1950): 535.
31. Gerty Archimède, *Journal officiel de la république française*, no. 110 (1948): 6058.
32. Gerty Archimède, *Journal officiel de la république française*, no. 73 (1951): 4706.
33. Gerty Archimède, *Journal officiel de la république française*, no. 73 (1951): 4728.
34. Paulette Nardal and T. Denean Sharpley-Whiting, *Beyond Negritude: Essays from "Woman in the City"* (Albany: SUNY Press, 2009), 81–82.
35. *Gerty Archimède: La candidate du peuple.*
36. Rosan Girard, *Journal officiel de la république française*, no. 22 (1951): 1080.
37. See Gerty Archimède, *Journal officiel de la république française*, no. 73 (1951): 4574.
38. Gerty Archimède, *Journal officiel de la république française*, no. 35 (1948): 1731.
39. For further analysis of the sexualized representations of black women in French literary and popular culture, see T. Denean Sharpley-Whiting, *Black Venus: Sexualized Savages, Primal Fears, and Primitive Narratives in French* (Durham NC: Duke University Press, 1999).
40. Archimède and Farrugia, *Gerty Archimède*, 31.
41. Félix Germain, "Jezebels and Victims: Antillean Women in Postwar France, 1946–1974," *French Historical Studies* 33, no. 3 (2010): 475–96.
42. Gerty Archimède, *Journal officiel de la république française*, no. 15 (1948): 504.

43. See Suzanne Césaire and Daniel Maximin, *Le Grand Camouflage: Écrits de dissidence, 1941–1945* (Paris: Seuil, 2009), 84–94.
44. For biographical information on Éboué and information on her work as a deputy and a senator, see http://www.senat.fr/evenement/archives/D35/eboue.html. See also cartons F22/26–F22/28, Papiers personnels d'Éugenie Éboué, Fonds Éboué, Fondation Charles de Gaulle (FCDG), Paris.
45. For an in-depth analysis of labor movements and their implications for contested citizenships within the framework of departmentalization in Guadeloupe, see Yarimar Bonilla, *Non-sovereign Futures: French Caribbean Politics in the Wake of Disenchantment* (Chicago: University of Chicago Press, 2015).
46. Archimède and Farrugia, *Gerty Archimède*, 110.

PART 3 Respectability, Resistance, and Transnational Identities

7

A Black Woman's Life in the Struggle

Jean McNair in France

TYLER STOVALL

Montparnasse, May 2015. In the elegant precincts of Reid Hall, Columbia University's townhouse complex in Paris, a hundred or so people have gathered to pay homage and say farewell to an extraordinary black woman. Those assembled form a diverse assembly, French and American, male and female, young and old, black and white, their very diversity a rich testimony to the varied and complex life of Jean McNair. I was one of several people who spoke that day, giving witness in both French and English to the tragedies and triumphs of Jean McNair's life and her contributions to France, America, and the modern world. Ours was but one of several memorials to commemorate her life, including a service at the French National Assembly in February.[1] Some four hundred people attended her funeral in Caen, where she spent the last decades of her life in the working-class neighborhoods of Grâce de Dieu and La Guérinière. Marie-Jeanne Gobert, member of the Caen City Council, remembered Jean McNair with the following words:

> A woman with a special destiny, at a very young age she joined, along with Melvin, her husband, the Black Panthers revolutionary movement, risking her life to denounce and combat racism. After a time in prison

the couple moved to Caen. The families and the youth of Grâce-de-Dieu, often faced with difficulties in school, learned they could rely on Jean for regular and efficient help, as well as infallible devotion to their scholarly success. She helped found the association Esperance et Jeunesse, a warm space of welcome, of collective life, and of apprenticeship. Deeply humane, she was a determined woman who believed strongly in the struggle against inequality.[2]

Who was Jean McNair? Black Panther, revolutionary, hijacker, refugee, teacher, wife, mother, poet, all of the above, and more? A black woman from North Carolina who ended her life in Normandy, with many stops in between, McNair exemplified the transnational scope of black political activism in the late twentieth century. But at the same time, one must view her as a black woman of France, the country where she spent the majority of her life and raised her three children. To consider McNair's life from this perspective is to offer new insights into the history of black women in France, especially black women's political activism.[3]

In particular, McNair redefined the traditional image of the African American woman, and black Americans in general, in France. Often associated with jazz and performance, like Josephine Baker, the African American woman in France has generally symbolized exoticism and sexual allure.[4] In contrast, black expatriate political activism in Paris has largely been dominated by men like Richard Wright and William Gardner Smith.[5] McNair broke both molds: she was a political activist and intellectual who engaged in a variety of discussions and causes during her life in France. While never forgetting her American roots, she also embraced her new homeland and contributed significantly to its struggles for social and racial justice. In both France and the United States, her life as a black woman made a difference to those who knew her and to society as a whole.

To write about McNair as a black Frenchwoman is to take seriously a transnational perspective on French history and contemporary life. She spent the majority of her life in France and, as this chapter will show, had a major impact on a wide variety of people in her adopted country. Like all modern nations, France is a composite of many different peoples, both native-born and immigrants, and all their stories are the nation's story. Finally, this approach also challenges a certain American historical narrative, according to which immigrants come to the United States instead of leaving it, a narrative that implies that being American is the highest of all possible human destinies. The story of McNair illustrates the histories of both France and the United States as transnational nations, of the ties that bind them and the differences that separate them.

Growing Up in a Changing South

Jean McNair was born Jean Carol Allen to parents Gary and Olie Allen in Winston-Salem, North Carolina, on October 11, 1946.[6] She grew up in a South fiercely committed to the segregationist racial order yet at the same time beginning to feel the winds of change unleashed in the aftermath of World War II that would soon bring the revolution of the civil rights movement.[7] Remembering those early years, Jean at one point stated: "I know I'm not supposed to say it, but I'm going to say it anyway: I hated growing up!"[8] Winston-Salem, in the Piedmont area of North Carolina, had a large black community whose members were expected to know their place and faced horrible consequences if they did not. Jean Allen grew up hearing rumors about people who had been abducted by the Ku Klux Klan and were never seen again. She grew up with an awareness of the constant danger of sexual violence faced by black girls like herself.[9]

Such threats of violence served to reinforce the daily discrimination that circumscribed the lives of Winston-Salem's black citizens. At the age of six Jean had to get up at 4:30 in the morning to take a school bus past several white schools to attend a black school. Until 1963 all public buildings in the city had separate entrances for blacks, including the notorious segregated bathrooms. At the age of nine she learned about the murder of Emmett Till in Mississippi, an event that brought home all the dangers facing young blacks in the South. At the age of twelve Jean's father took her to a local civil rights demonstration, where she was shocked by the vicious hostility of the white counterdemonstrators.[10]

Such incidents underscored the depths of white racism in Winston-Salem, but they also illustrated black resistance and the increasing demands for a new day. Winston-Salem's black community had a strong tradition of community organization, including one of the oldest black Christian congregations in America. In 1892 former slaves founded the Slater Industrial Academy, an institution of higher education for blacks that would become Winston-Salem State University.[11] Jean Allen enrolled in Winston-Salem State University after graduating from the local high school, earning a degree in physical education.[12]

At Winston-Salem she met the man who would become her life's partner, Melvin McNair. Melvin, a star athlete, came from Greensboro to Winston-Salem on a football scholarship. Two years Jean's junior, Melvin fell in love with her, and the two became a couple, sharing their studies and their young lives. Also a product of the segregated South, Melvin was certainly aware of the oppression of his people, but Jean helped him channel that awareness into a political consciousness corresponding to the militancy of the times. The massive race riots that struck Detroit and Newark in the summer of 1967 underscored the revolutionary turbulence of the times, and Jean and Melvin followed these and other events in the struggle for black liberation closely.[13]

A turning point came for the two with the assassination of Martin Luther King Jr. in April 1968. Like many others across the country, black students at Winston-Salem staged a protest, leading to the shutting of the university.[14] Melvin and Jean took part in the movement, and in retaliation the university canceled Melvin's athletic scholarship, forcing him to drop out of school. No longer a student, Melvin thus lost his deferment from military service and a year later was drafted into the army and sent to West Germany. Faced with his imminent departure, Jean and Melvin decided to marry, tying the knot on August 25, 1969. Jean then accompanied Melvin to West Berlin, where their first child, Johari McNair, was born on May 7, 1970.

Into the Revolution

Life in the army presented new difficulties for both Melvin and Jean. They not only immediately became aware of the racism directed by many white GIs against black soldiers but also learned about the movement against the

Vietnam War in both West Germany and the United States.[15] Above all, they studied black movements in America, especially the Black Panthers, following closely their critique of American racism and imperialism. Shortly after Johari's birth the army informed Melvin of plans to transfer him to Vietnam, rejecting his appeals to stay in Berlin with his wife and newborn son. For Melvin and Jean, their family situation and their opposition to the Vietnam War, increasingly shared by many black GIs in Germany, prompted a fateful decision.[16] They traveled to Washington to plead with army authorities, but when that proved fruitless Melvin decided instead to desert, taking his first steps into illegality. In an America in which revolution seemed imminent, the young couple decided to devote their lives to the struggle for black liberation.

In 1970 Jean and Melvin moved to Detroit, which Jean described as permeated by "an atmosphere of fear." Still devastated by the massive riots of 1967, the city's black ghettos struggled with poverty, crime, and brutal police repression.[17] The day before Melvin and Jean arrived, city police attacked the local Black Panthers chapter.[18] Cautious because of Melvin's irregular military status, Jean and Melvin nonetheless began making contacts with others involved in the movement. They befriended three individuals in particular, George Brown, George Wright, and Joyce Tillerson, with whom they ended up rooming together in a house where they shared vegetarian cuisine and debated revolutionary black politics, culture, and spirituality. In particular, they explored their growing interest in the Black Panthers.[19] There Jean gave birth to their second child, their daughter, Ayana, on October 25, 1971.

The group also shared an increasingly desperate outlook about the ability of black people to survive in racist America. In January 1972 George Brown was shot and arrested by members of STRESS (Stop the Robberies, Enjoy Safe Streets), a special division of the Detroit police department terrorizing the city's black neighborhoods.[20] Although Brown was acquitted of any wrongdoing and freed from prison four months later, STRESS officers swore that he and his housemates would not survive the summer.[21] Faced with such threats and with the harsh campaign of repression unleashed against the Panthers and other militant groups by the police and federal programs like Cointelpro, Jean, Melvin, and their comrades became increasingly convinced that they had to escape the United States.[22] As Jean noted in the group's memoir, *Nous, noir Américains*, "For all of us, 1972 was the culminating moment of a period of frustration, of disillusion, of depression, and immense despair, born out of the living conditions forced upon our people. . . . The hypocrisies and the repressive measures of the government and the forces of order pushed us to a point where we could no longer not act."[23]

In the summer of 1972 an opportunity to do so presented itself. For the last few years, several radical activists had hijacked airplanes in the United States in order both to flee the country and to raise ransom money for political causes. On June 2 Black Panther Roger Holder and companion Catherine Kerkow successfully hijacked an airplane from Los Angeles to Algiers, where Eldridge Cleaver had established the headquarters of the Panthers' International Section. This dramatic act convinced the McNairs' revolutionary household to try something similar, and on July 31 the entire household of five adults and three small children (Johari, Ayana, and Tillerson's daughter Kenya) boarded a Delta Airlines flight bound for Miami and forced it instead to fly to Algiers via Boston. They also demanded and got Delta to pay a ransom of one million dollars, which they hoped to deliver to the Panthers in Algeria. For Jean McNair, age twenty-five and the mother of two small children, the hijacking was the major turning point in her life. It underscored her revolutionary commitment and apocalyptic vision of current events. It was also an irreversible decision, a definitive one-way flight. She would never see her homeland again.

The hijackers arrived in Algeria on August 1 and soon discovered that their image of the country as a revolutionary Third World paradise was more than a little naive. As they had in Cuba, America's revolutionary exiles found that Algeria's ideas about their roles and activities did not always correspond to their expectations. Although Algerian government representatives initially welcomed the hijackers, they insisted on confiscating the ransom money, which they returned to Delta Airlines. When the local Panthers objected, the Algerians harshly overruled them and began to restrict the activities of the International Section, stripping Cleaver of his leadership role. By September members of the Black Panther Party had begun leaving Algeria for other countries; Cleaver himself would depart for France on New Year's Day, 1973. By the beginning of that year, therefore, Jean, Melvin, and their comrades found themselves the last holdouts of the party in Algeria, having sacrificed everything for a dream that no longer seemed possible.[24]

Jean's greatest concern at this point was the welfare of her children, for she feared for their safety in Algeria. Melvin and Joyce Tillerson felt the same way, so they arranged to send their kids back to the United States: Johari and Ayana would spend the next several years living with Jean's family. For Jean and Melvin this was an extremely difficult decision, a low point: as Melvin remembered, "This was the low point of our defeat. We were going to lose those most dear to us."[25] They had left America hoping to win a better life for their children, and now they had no idea when (or if) they would ever see them again.

Once they had ensured the safety of Ayana and Johari, Jean and Melvin could give a thought to their own future. It soon became clear that, with the departure of the rest of the Black Panther Party and the increasingly hostile attitude of the Algerian government, they would also have to find a new land of exile. Cleaver was in Paris, and, following his example, they decided to make their own exodus from Algeria.[26] In May the five former hijackers left Algiers clandestinely and crossed the Mediterranean to France. This new country would be Jean McNair's home for the rest of her life.

Clandestinity and Prison in Paris

The Paris that received Jean and Melvin McNair in the 1970s was a city still illuminated by the afterglow of the near revolution of May 1968, full of *tiers-mondiste* activists and sympathizers. The McNairs' clandestine move to Paris had been facilitated in part by the French organization Solidarity, a small and diverse group of left-wing activists founded by the dynamic and mercurial Henri Curiel. Of Egyptian Jewish origins, Curiel, like the McNairs, was a political refugee from his homeland. He had been active in Communist and anti-imperialist movements in France since the 1950s, playing a leading role in the struggle for Algerian independence. He organized Solidarity to provide anticolonial militants from throughout the world support, training, and education. Curiel confirmed for Melvin and Jean the idea that hijacking and terrorism were ultimately political dead ends. He inspired Jean to read voraciously in political theory and movement history, broadening her ideas about how best to build a revolutionary new world.[27]

For the next three years, Jean and Melvin lived clandestinely in Paris, doing odd jobs and gradually learning French. In 1975 they moved in with a left-wing French family living in the Latin Quarter. With their hosts they continued their political education via endless discussions in the evenings. Jean also enjoyed living with a family with young children, a delightful reminder of what she had given up in Algeria. While she continued to miss her own children desperately and worried about the future, she nonetheless enjoyed the new life she had found in the French capital. As she wrote to a friend, "As for choosing a place to live, I frankly confess that I adore Paris."[28]

> The fact of living abroad gave us the possibility to develop our minds like we could never have done in the US. The benefit for us was not only educational and cultural, but also the opportunity to learn professional skills. Moreover, this experience liberated us psychologically. Because of racism, one is always conscious of one's race in the United States. We could never for a moment forget we were black.... Here we could relax. Can you imagine what a relief that was? Do you understand what I am saying? We all hope that our children will know what it is to live in France—there are so many possibilities for one's spirit to blossom.[29]

This clandestine existence could not last indefinitely. The McNairs gradually became aware that they were being watched, that police agents shadowed their movements throughout the city. On May 26, 1976, French police arrested four of the five hijackers in Paris. The American government immediately demanded their extradition to the United States to stand trial there. In prison, Jean and Melvin and their comrades Joyce Tillerson and George Brown anxiously awaited the decision of the French authorities. In October the Ministry of Justice held an extradition hearing to decide whether or not to send the accused back to America. Fortunately for the McNairs, the French had a long, proud tradition of granting asylum to political refugees. At their hearing they were ably represented by the radical French lawyer Jean-Jacques de Félice, who skillfully portrayed the hijackers as political rebels against racism. Moved by his arguments, the French court rejected the American demand for extradition, allowing the McNairs and their comrades to stay in France.[30]

This did not mean that they were free, however. According to international treaty, the French, having refused to extradite the McNairs, were then obliged to try them in French courts for hijacking. So the hijackers were returned to the prison of Fleury-Mérogis, outside Paris, to await their trial. For two years they sat in jail, corresponding with friends and family outside and waiting for their day in court. They worked on their collective memoir, *Nous, noirs Américains*, and hoped for the best. Meanwhile, a number of French people organized to promote their release, including movie stars Yves Montand and Simone Signoret. George Pau-Langevin, a French black woman political activist who was later elected to France's National Assembly, represented them in court. All the while, Jean thought first and foremost about her children, writing them as often as she could.

> Dear Johari and Ayana,
> Sometimes I need so badly to be with you that I absolutely must write you in order to stand the pain. It doesn't matter if you don't read this letter for years to come. Just writing you is a comfort for me.[31]

In November 1978 the case of the four hijackers came to trial. Supporters filled the courtroom, while at the same time the pilot and flight attendants of the hijacked airplane came from the United States to testify. After listening to their testimony and that of the defense witnesses who in effect put America on trial as a racist nation and spoke of the terrible discrimination suffered by African Americans, the jury voted to convict the four hijackers, but with extenuating circumstances. It sentenced each to five years in prison, with credit for time already served. Jean McNair and Joyce Tillerson were released immediately so they could take care of their children. As soon as Jean was released from prison she sent for

Ayana and Johari, who soon arrived with her mother to a joyous reunion. Friends helped her find a place to live and set up a new life. For the next two years they regularly visited Melvin in prison until he was released in May 1980. For the first time since they left Detroit eight years earlier, the McNairs were able to live together as a family.

By 1980 Jean McNair had survived nearly a decade of political engagement, upheaval, and sacrifice. She no longer had to live in fear of arrest and could live and work in peace with her loved ones close by. The years of revolutionary politics had left their mark: she had missed several years of her young children's lives, and she could not return to the country of her birth. Jean McNair could nonetheless now begin the task of building a new life in a foreign land. On June 30, 1981, she gave birth to her son Tumaini, Jean and Melvin's only child born outside America. The new baby symbolized the rebirth of the McNair family and the fact that they were now at home in France.

From Paris to Normandy

I first met Jean McNair in the fall of 1981, when I was living in Paris and researching my dissertation in French history. Appropriately enough, we met at a demonstration. During the early 1980s, hundreds of thousands of people throughout Western Europe took to the streets to protest the planned deployment of new missiles by the United States and the Soviet Union. The Euromissiles crisis mobilized Europeans against the nuclear threat and foreshadowed the imminent end of the Cold War.[32] During one of these demonstrations in Paris, I and several other American students decided to form a progressive group of US citizens in France to engage in political discussion and protest. Word soon got out, and when we took part in a subsequent demonstration we were joined by a friendly, discretely garbed black woman who introduced herself and began talking about her life in Paris.

That is how Jean and I met. At the time, Jean and her family were still adjusting to their new life in France. They had found an apartment in the working-class suburb of Thiais south of the city, and Ayana and Johari attended the local schools while Jean took care of Tumaini at home and also gave English lessons, at times by telephone. Years of political experience and study had convinced Jean and Melvin both of the importance of activism and of the dangers of violent revolutionary insurgency, and they wanted to teach these lessons to us, a new generation of American activists in Paris. We soon formed our political group, Citoyens des États-Unis, and began holding weekly meetings at a bookstore in the twelfth *arrondissement* of Paris. At these meetings we discussed a wide range of topics, including racism and oppression in the United States, the Euromissiles crisis and the Cold War, insurgent movements in Africa, Latin America, and Palestine, and many other issues. Frequently, we hosted presentations by political activists, French, American, and other, who wanted to address a group of progressive American students. Finally, we continued to take part in Parisian demonstrations, displaying an American alternative to the dominant Reaganism of the era.

I spent a year in Paris and then returned regularly during the summers for the next several years. During this period, I got to know Jean well, spending lots of time with her, Melvin, and their family. I passed many hours in the family home in Thiais, at times staying over, because it was a long way back to my apartment in Montmartre. I can remember babysitting young Tumaini more than once and talking with Johari and Ayana as they grew up. In 1981 I particularly remember being a guest at their house for Christmas, the first time in my life I did not go home for the holiday.

I remember Jean McNair as a woman of boundless energy. Long before the world knew the term "multitasking" she was a master at it. How she managed to take care of three children, teach English lessons, and manage the household (she was also a wonderful cook) I will never understand. One of my most vivid images of Jean is of her holding Tumaini in one arm and feeding him breakfast while at the same time giving an English lesson to a client on the telephone. In addition to all this, she took an active role in political life, going to our weekly meetings and many others, as well as demonstrations and other political events. In Jean's life, home and politics were not separate spheres: one of the great pleasures of visiting the McNairs was the wide range of interesting people one always met there, political activists and intellectuals from a wide variety of backgrounds and perspectives. Their home was a classic French salon in the Paris suburbs, and Jean welcomed everyone with good food and conversation.

During those years, Jean continued the political evolution that began when she first came to France. She remained committed to progressive politics in general and black liberation in particular. Unlike some former revolutionaries, notably Eldridge Cleaver, she never turned her back on the movement nor renounced her radical past. At the same time, years of revolutionary activism and clandestinity had taught her the importance of caution and circumspection. By the time I got to know her, Jean had come to regard revolutionary politics as futile and ultimately a trap. Like so many other youthful revolutionaries, she evolved toward an emphasis on peaceful and gradual social change, something that represented a shift in tactics more than goals. In discussing politics, Jean voiced strong opinions but also knew how to listen to and respect the ideas of others. Her own activism and her life in Paris had given her a cosmopolitan vision, an interest in a wide range of issues, and a commitment to social justice for all peoples of the world.

Finally, a profound spirituality played a central role in Jean McNair's political vision. Like so many African American progressives, in particular, so many black women, Jean's belief in political change was anchored in her faith in God and in a view of humanity that reflected the moral and ethical teachings of the great religious thinkers. There were times when, talking with Jean, I could feel the ordinary concerns of the world fall away, replaced by her desire to see and nurture the divine in every man and woman. Anger at injustice and hopes for a better world guided her politics, but faith gave her the strength that made this commitment possible.[33]

In 1986 the McNairs decided to leave Paris for Caen, where Melvin obtained a position working as a counselor in a youth center in the city, a position that came with housing. Jean in particular regarded their departure from Paris with some regret: she had a lot of ties in the city where she had lived for over ten years, and she feared the absence of the cosmopolitan communities, including American expatriates, so present in the French capital. Like many immigrant and refugee women in France (and, for that matter, like many Parisians in general), Jean worried about being isolated in the provinces. Yet the new life in Normandy offered solid advantages for the McNair family. The *banlieue parisienne* where they lived presented some social dangers, especially as Ayana and Johari were now entering their teen years. So off they went to the Norman capital, probably the most pro-American region of France, thanks to the D-Day landings two generations earlier.

After the McNairs moved to Caen I saw them less frequently, finding it hard to squeeze in visits during my (usually rapid) trips to France. My rare opportunities to see them revealed a family that was settling into a new and in some ways very different phase of their lives. In Caen, Jean and Melvin settled into the Grâce de Dieu (grace of God), a sprawling housing project in the southern part of the city. Like Thiais in the Paris suburbs, it was a working-class area with a large immigrant and multicultural population.[34] In France, the 1980s represented the beginnings of a major debate about the crisis of *la banlieue*, the sprawling and ethnically diverse suburbs of Paris and other cities that suffered from not only unemployment but also racial discrimination and alienation.[35] As my uncle John, a dentist in Detroit, noted at the time, such places did not seem all that different from American ghettos. Jean and Melvin may have fled Detroit, but they had not escaped it; in France they found new opportunities to fight for social and racial justice.

For Jean and Melvin both, their top priority was helping the youth of Grâce de Dieu, young people with few educational or professional opportunities who were trapped in isolated and underserved housing projects. Whenever I would visit for the weekend they would immediately put me to work with the youth who always surrounded them, usually by giving English lessons or talking to them about French and American history. Jean created an association, Esperance et Jeunesse, that provided tutoring, academic support, and fellowship to the young people of Grâce de Dieu. At a time when so many in France viewed the "second generation immigrant" youth of the suburbs as a social problem, Jean focused on their potential, correctly seeing in them the future of the nation.[36]

The fate of young people was a great triumph but also a great tragedy for Jean McNair. Johari and Ayana came of age during the family's early years in Caen and began to carve out their lives as adults. They had spent most of their childhoods in France but had also gone "back home" to North Carolina every summer to spend time with Jean's and Melvin's families.[37] Perfectly bilingual and at home on both sides of the Atlantic, unlike their parents, Johari and Ayana could choose in which country they wanted to build their futures. Ayana fell in love with a young Frenchman, eventually marrying and choosing to remain in France. In contrast, Johari decided to move back to America. As Jean later noted, he had never really felt at ease in France and had always missed his grandfather back in North Carolina: "He went back to take care of everybody, because I couldn't. And in a way, he sacrificed himself."[38] In Winston-Salem, Johari got involved with violence and guns, and on September 3, 1998, shortly after having been paroled from prison, he was shot and killed by another young man. He was twenty-eight years old.

How does one deal with the death of one's child? I saw Jean McNair for the last time in February 1999. I was giving a talk at the American Embassy in Paris and was amazed to see Jean, Melvin, and Tumaini (now a strapping teenager) in the audience.[39] We greeted each other, and then Melvin told me the horrible news about Johari, whom I still remembered as a boy. Reeling from the shock, I remember looking at Jean and wondering what I could possibly say to her that would make any difference how she could survive something like this. To this day, I do not know.

I believe that for Jean, Johari's death brought home to her all the reasons she chose to flee America, the worst possible example of what could happen there to a black family. Far away in Caen, she became like all the other African American mothers who have had to bury their young sons, victims of senseless gun violence.[40] It reaffirmed the rightness of her life in France, because if Johari had not returned to America, he would probably, like Ayana and Tumaini, be alive today. At the same time, Jean's exile meant that she could not be there in North Carolina to guide and protect her son through the risks of black life in America. All her work with disadvantaged youth in France had not, and could not have, saved Johari's life.[41]

At the same time, his death gave that work more meaning than ever before: Jean knew what could happen to young people at risk and remained determined to do what she could to prevent such senseless loss. She continued her work with Esperance et Jeunesse, as well as her interest in political affairs in both France and the United States. In one of the most striking events of her life, she and Melvin arranged a reunion and reconciliation with William May, the pilot of the Delta airplane they had hijacked in 1972 and had last seen at their trial in Paris. May came to Caen with his adult daughter, and they talked long about that seminal event and the different paths their lives had taken since. The meeting with William May illustrated the extent to which that now distant event continued to shape Jean's life. For years, she and Melvin pursued legal action to try to win the right to return to America, but when it became clear that they could only do so by agreeing to serve jail time in the United States, they rejected that possibility, deciding that, for better or for worse, their lives were in France.

Jean McNair died in Caen on October 24, 2014, at the age of sixty-eight. She is now buried in a cemetery in Caen next to the grave of her son Johari. Jean lived to see Ayana and Tumaini mature into young adults, find partners and careers in France, and make her a grandmother. She also lived to see her work with the young people of Grâce de Dieu and other parts of Caen bring her recognition from public officials in the city and throughout the region. She did not live to return to the United States nor to see the end of the racism that had led her to flee her native land. On the contrary, in the era of Black Lives Matter in the United States and the continued rise of the National Front in France, such issues remain more salient than ever on both sides of the Atlantic. Jean McNair's life was full of tragedies, but also achievements. While she certainly made a difference, the struggle against racial and social injustice to which she dedicated her life remains as relevant today as ever.

In December 2014 I traveled to Caen to visit Melvin for the first time in over a decade and to offer him my condolences in person. He took me to visit the graves of Jean and Johari, side by side, and we talked about Jean and old times in general. At dinner that evening in a local restaurant the young waiter asked who Melvin was, saying he seemed familiar, that he'd read about him in a newspaper article somewhere. Melvin told him about his exile from America and his life in Caen, whereupon the young man responded, "The Black Panthers? Wasn't that a baseball team?" *Sic transit gloria mundi.*

The story of Jean McNair's life is the story of all those she touched, the author of this essay included. She was a black woman from America who found in France not the fame and fortune of a Josephine Baker, nor even the political ex-patriotism of a Richard Wright, but rather new ways to engage in the struggle against racism. She came to France when the old idea of an antiracist nation had enough viability to ensure her a refuge, but at the same time, with the growth of domestic racial conflicts, that refuge no longer seemed tenable. During her life in Caen in particular, Jean McNair took part in mentoring the multicultural youth of the housing projects, in her own way helping to build the France of the future. She became a woman of France much more than most expatriate Americans, at the end of her life speaking English with a decidedly French accent. In the modern era, black women have long stood at the forefront of progressive political action in the United States.[42] The example of Jean McNair shows this was true in France as well.

Notes

My thanks to all those who helped me with this article: Maia Wechsler, Waldo Martin, Paola Bacchetta, and above all Melvin McNair.

1. "Caen: Melvin McNair avec les habitants de la Grâce de Dieu à l'Assemblée Nationale," *France 3 Normandie*, February 2, 2015.
2. *Liberté-Caen*, October 27, 2014, https://actu.fr/normandie/caen_14118/necrologie-jean-mcnair-est-decedee_2786817.html.
3. T. Denean Sharpley-Whiting, *Negritude Women* (Minneapolis: University of Minnesota Press, 2002); Trica Keaton, *Muslim Girls and the Other France: Race, Identity Politics, and Social Exclusion* (Bloomington: Indiana University Press, 2006).
4. Phyllis Rose, *Jazz Cleopatra: Josephine Baker in Her Time* (New York: Vintage, 1991); T. Denean Sharpley-Whiting, *Bricktop's Paris: African American Women in Paris between the Two World Wars* (Albany: State University of New York Press, 2015).
5. James Campbell, *Exiled in Paris: Richard Wright, James Baldwin, Samuel Beckett, and Others on the Left Bank* (Berkeley: University of California Press, 2003).
6. Telephone interview with Melvin McNair, July 20, 2016.

7. Juan Williams, *Eyes on the Prize: America's Civil Rights Years, 1954–1965* (New York: Penguin, 2013).
8. *Melvin and Jean: An American Story*, directed by Maia Wechsler (Red Triangle Productions and What's Up Films, France, 2012).
9. Danielle L. McGuire, *At the Dark End of the Street: Black Women, Rape, and Resistance—a New History of the Civil Rights Movement from Rosa Parks to the Rise of Black Power* (New York: Vintage, 2011).
10. Melvin McNair, Joyce Tillerson, George Brown, and Jean McNair, *Nous, noirs Américains, évadés du ghetto*, preface by Marie Cardinal (Paris: Éditions du Seuil, 1978).
11. Cheryl Streeter Harry, *Winston-Salem's African American Legacy* (Charleston SC: Arcadia Publishers, 2007).
12. On black student movements, see Martha Biondi, *The Black Revolution on Campus* (Berkeley: University of California Press, 2012).
13. On the race riots of the 1960s, see U.S. Kerner Commission, *Report of the National Advisory Commission on Civil Disorders* (New York: Bantam Books, 1968); Max Arthur Helman, *Summer of Rage: An Oral History of the 1967 Newark and Detroit Riots* (New York: Peter Lang, 2013).
14. Winston-Salem played an important role in black liberation struggles during the 1960s. It was the first city in the South to form a chapter of the Black Panthers. See Judson L. Jeffries, *Comrades: A Local History of the Black Panther Party* (Bloomington: Indiana University Press, 2007).
15. See Maria Höhn and Martin Klimke, *A Breath of Freedom: The Civil Rights Struggle, African American GIs, and Germany* (New York: Palgrave Macmillan, 2010).
16. On the history of the antiwar movement, see Clara Bingham, *Witness to the Revolution: Radicals, Resisters, Vets, Hippies, and the Year America Lost Its Mind and Found Its Soul* (New York: Random House, 2016); Simon Hall, *Peace and Freedom: The Civil Rights and Antiwar Movements in the 1960s* (Philadelphia: University of Pennsylvania Press, 2006).
17. Sidney Fine, *Violence in the Model City: The Cavanaugh Administration, Race Relations, and the Detroit Riot of 1967* (East Lansing: Michigan State University Press, 2007).
18. Waldo E. Martin Jr. and Joshua Bloom, *Black against Empire: The History and Politics of the Black Panther Party* (Berkeley: University of California Press, 2014).
19. Elaine Brown, *A Taste of Power: A Black Woman's Story* (New York: Anchor, 2015).
20. On the history of STRESS, see Heather Thompson, *Whose Detroit? Politics, Labor, and Race in a Modern American City* (Ithaca NY: Cornell University Press, 2004); Joe T. Darden and Richard W. Thomas, *Detroit: Race Riots, Racial

Conflicts and Efforts to Bridge the Racial Divide (East Lansing: Michigan State University Press, 2013).

21. Brendan I. Koerner, *The Skies Belong to Us: Love and Terror in the Golden Age of Hijacking* (New York: Crown Publishers, 2013), 192.
22. See Ward Churchill and Jim Vander Wall, *Agents of Repression: The FBI's Secret Wars against the Black Panther Party and the American Indian Movement* (Boston: South End Press, 2002).
23. McNair et al., *Nous, noirs Américains*, 270–71.
24. Koerner, *The Skies Belong to Us*, 212–14.
25. McNair et al., *Nous, noirs Américains*, 108.
26. On Eldridge Cleaver's life in exile and his return to America, see Eldridge Cleaver, *Soul on Fire* (Waco TX: Word Books, 1978).
27. "Henri Curiel, Citizen of the Third World," *Le monde diplomatique*, English edition, April 1998; Joel Beinin, *The Dispersion of Egyptian Jewry: Culture, Politics, and the Formation of Modern Diaspora* (Berkeley: University of California Press, 1998).
28. McNair et al., *Nous, noirs Américains*, 276.
29. McNair et al., *Nous, noirs Américains*, 272.
30. Koerner, *The Skies Belong to Us*, 247–48.
31. McNair et al., *Nous, noirs Américains*, 287.
32. Leopoldo Nuti et al., *The Euromissiles Crisis and the End of the Cold War* (Stanford CA: Stanford University Press, 2015); Diana Johnstone, *The Politics of Euromissiles: Europe's Role in America's World* (London: Verso, 1984).
33. Judylyn S. Ryan, *Spirituality and Ideology in Black Women's Film and Literature* (Charlottesville: University of Virginia Press, 2005); Charles Marsh, *The Beloved Community: How Faith Shapes Social Justice from the Civil Rights Movement to Today* (New York: Basic Books, 2006).
34. "Des habitants parlent de leur vie à La Grâce-de-Dieu," *Ouest-France*, November 5, 2015.
35. Alec Hargreaves, *Immigration, "Race," and Ethnicity in Contemporary France* (New York: Routledge, 1995).
36. Keaton, *Muslim Girls*; Susan Terrio, *Judging Mohammed: Juvenile Delinquency, Immigration, and Exclusion at the Paris Palais of Justice* (Stanford CA: Stanford University Press, 2009).
37. In doing so, they participated in an old African American tradition of blacks in the North sending their children south during the summer to live with their grandparents. See James Gregory, *The Southern Diasporas: How the Great Migrations of Black and White Southerners Transformed America* (Chapel Hill: University of North Carolina Press, 2005).

38. *Melvin and Jean: An American Story*.
39. It is worth noting that in coming to my talk, the McNairs took a real risk, because since the U.S. Embassy is technically American soil, they could have been arrested. It was an act of great courage and friendship.
40. See Marita Golden, *Saving Our Sons: Raising Black Children in a Turbulent World* (New York: Doubleday, 1994).
41. On gun violence and African American young men, see Ta-Nehisi Coates, *Between the World and Me* (New York: Spiegel and Grau, 2015).
42. Angela Y. Davis, *Women, Culture, and Politics* (New York: Vintage, 1990).

8

Am I My Sister's Keeper?

The Politics of Propriety and the Fight for Equality in the Works of French Antillean Women Writers, 1920s–40s

JACQUELINE COUTI

While stressing French Antillean black women's contribution to modern black humanism and internationalism in the early twentieth century, scholarly debates often challenge their feminism and political activism for being neither as radical as their European counterparts nor as sufficiently anticolonial.[1] Such discussions may obscure the fact that the fight for European women's rights often excluded black women. There remains a need to redefine scholarly understanding of black women's activism and its confrontation not only with institutional power but also with patriarchy and popular culture.[2] This essay questions these women's politics of propriety: the ways in which class influences conceptions of respectability and how these notions in turn affect ideas of race, gender, and sexuality. Such an approach facilitates a better understanding of black women's fight for equality.

To this end, I examine how the Guadeloupean Suzanne Lacascade and the Martinican sisters Paulette and Jane Nardal reevaluate notions of race, gender, and politics by critiquing the racist and sexist construction of blackness taking place in France from the 1920s through the 1940s. They reject the exotic embodiment of Caribbean womanhood known today as the *doudou*: both a sexual object and a desiring archetype.[3] Ideas of female decency are central in their struggles for equality and women's rights. Their lofty endeavors, contrasted with "lowbrow" constructions of race and gender produced by savvy women like performer Josephine Baker and novelist Mayotte Capécia, exposed classist leanings. All these women experienced and understood oppression in different ways, and for none of them was it easy to avoid doing the bidding of white patriarchy. Their diverse approaches and representations of black womanhood in connection to white and/or black patriarchal ideas expose the obstacles that black feminism had to overcome in the French Caribbean when dealing with feminine images inherited from a colonial discourse that both women and men had assimilated as their own.[4]

Colonial Heritage

As Bernard Moitt highlights in his work on the French Antilles, coerced coitus was integral to the plantation system in the Americas.[5] This colonial heritage generated the myth of black women as sexually available to white men. Angela Y. Davis also engages this legacy: "Their experiences during slavery—hard work with their men, equality within the family, resistance, floggings, rape—had encouraged them to develop certain personality traits which set them apart from most white women."[6] One of these personality traits was the ongoing need to negotiate sexual propriety. Issues of class and respectability in the Black Women's Clubs in North America of the 1890s often exposed structural differences and tensions between poor and wealthier elite black women.[7] Yet Davis notes that all members manifested "a collective consciousness of their sexual victimization" and desire to fight such oppression.[8]

In this context, I propose that propriety and sexual restraint have nothing to do with a mere moralistic and traditionalist approach but instead represent the assertion of control over one's own body not only for African American women but also for French Antillean women.[9] Similarly and to a greater extent than their white counterparts, both African American and French Antillean women were not exclusively claiming sexual freedom from their spouses. As previously mentioned, the plantation system has created a mythology around the availability of black women's bodies for sexual exploitation. Therefore, African American and French Antillean women were specifically seeking the right to be liberated from and unthreatened by any unwelcome sexual objectification. I thus wish to stress how for French Antillean women, politics of propriety and classist biases can also express resistance to dominant power and popular culture in continental France from the 1920s through the 1940s.

During the interwar period, Suzanne Lacascade and the Nardals exemplified how French education gave certain women from the elite of color or the black middle class the analytical toolkit to critique French dominant power.[10] Indeed, these writers' access to education did not extend to the majority of French Antilleans, who were generally illiterate due to societal inequalities. Due to the social, historical, and cultural contexts of French Caribbean societies, scholars often split the population in these communities into three ethnoclasses. The groups in which phenotypes are associated with socioeconomic status were *blancs* (white members of the bourgeoisie), *mulâtres* (mixed-race individuals of the middle class, who were often light-skinned), and *nègres/noirs* (blacks from the proletariat).[11] The division between people of African ancestry is permeable, however, and can be misleading in some cases (one might think of Frantz Fanon, a dark-skinned individual belonging to the elite of color). This *grande bourgeoisie* distinguishes itself from the *petite bourgeoisie*, whose condition improved only under the Third Republic.[12] The laws that allowed some enslaved workers to be freed before the 1848 abolition gave birth to this wealthy elite of color, which cherished its privileges. Suzanne Lacascade's novel represents the women of that ethnoclass. The Nardal sisters came from the *petite bourgeoisie*; their parents were civil servants in the colonial administration.[13] Hence, this essay also addresses how classist biases could have both clouded and enlightened these women's views.

Politics of Propriety and Activism: Desexualization of the *Mulâtresse*

In the 1920s the two literary critics using the pen name Marius-Ary Leblon described Suzanne Lacascade's novel *Claire-Solange: Âme-africaine* (1924) as "a delectable plea on behalf of *mulâtresses*."[14] Their language echoes the contemporaneous sexualization of females in the colonial and patriarchal discourse. In 1979, however, Maryse Condé described Lacascade's novel as the first serious attempt at female literary promotion of black consciousness and feminism through racial essentialism; other scholars followed in Condé's footsteps.[15] However, Lacascade's promotion of black womanhood does not concern darker-skinned women from the lower classes; rather, she focuses on the elite. The ways in which this novelist polices the sexual objectification of *mulâtresses* (light-skinned black women) highlight a politics of propriety that complicates ideas of race, gender, and equality.

In the novel, Claire-Solange is a young *mulâtresse* from Martinique. Her father, Étienne Hucquart, is a Frenchman, an officer in the colonial service, who married the now deceased Aurore Duflôt, a well-off Creole of color, against his family's will. Claire-Solange belongs to the powerful *grande bourgeoisie* of color, which fought for social advancement and against prejudices afflicting its members before the 1848 emancipation act. She resents the fact that white Creoles in 1914 still discriminate against her ethnoclass, and she initially fears that the Hucquart family will also reject her.[16]

During her 1914 visit to France, Claire-Solange realizes that her father's parents do not reject her but instead do something worse: they see her through the demeaning lens of exotic colonial literature. Her father's sister-in-law, Mrs. Pol Hucquart, portrays him as a victim who "allowed himself to be smitten by the laugh, the dark eyes, [and] the voluptuous and effortless beauty of mulatto women" (13). Mrs. Pol Hucquart also depicts Claire-Solange's mother as "la créole des romans" and projects the restrictive patriarchal and colonial construction of femininity of color as a sexualized fantasy born out of literature—a *doudou* (15). A scolding Claire-Solange refutes this exotic objectification. Her disappointed cousin Jacques Denzel initially deplores her astounding coldness and antagonism: "What an ice queen for a girl from the Antilles" (30). At the beginning, her icy and prickly demeanor display not sensuality but instead her cultural and political agenda and her rejection of all things French.

While she belittles the motherland as ungrateful for ignoring the worth of the colonies, Claire-Solange glorifies her African roots and links her black maternal lineage to aristocracy, insisting that one of her foremothers was a fierce princess (67). Hence she embraces an elitist and respectable idea of blackness. Claire-Solange's stance matters, as she praises her African matrilineal line over her European patrilineal line to subvert white patriarchy and colonialism: "I am African . . . African by atavism and despite my paternal heredity! African, like one of my foremothers, whose native name no one knows and whom the slave trade discarded as a slave in the Caribbean, the first of her race" (66).

Her gendered commentary subtly echoes the novel's dedication to both African foremothers and Creole grandmothers. Her words highlight the gruesome black feminine experience in the forced displacement that gave birth to the African diaspora in the Americas. Nonetheless, the question is raised: Can Claire-Solange embrace an aristocratic African heritage only to counteract the ways in which Frenchmen sexualize *mulâtresses*? Given the coercive sexual relations that thrived in the plantation system and the subsequent related myth of black women as oversexed, it should come as no surprise that a politics of propriety informs Lacascade's fight for equality.

Lacascade's novel praises a nonsexualized but nurturing black womanhood that is diasporic in nature. With her use of *agapē* as superior to *erōs*, Lacascade modernizes an old Christian and European tradition to feed a politics of propriety that promotes maternal bonds and blackness. Her approach delineates both the difference between spiritual and carnal thinking and the preeminence of mind over the body. It mirrors the Christian tradition, particularly in Catholicism. There *agapē* stands for pure and divine love devoid of carnality and is more celebrated than physical love and passionate desires (*erōs*). Her strategy exposes the tension and paradoxes within an individual who holds dear both an African heritage and an Occidental style of education. However, for Lacascade, women with African ancestry should be considered equals rather than second-class citizens. Hence, Claire-Solange extols the resilience of Martinican *mulâtresses* from the elite who are now widows displaced to France by the 1902 eruption of Mount Pelée. Their commendable fight for survival makes them worthy citizens for an ungrateful French nation. Nonetheless, Claire-Solange reveals class biases when she portrays their new life as breadwinners as a loss of status (54–56). In addition, unlike the white

Creole novelist René Bonneville in *Le triomphe d'Eglantine* (1897), Lacascade does not extend her exploration of praiseworthy motherhood to poor Martinican women.

Instead, Lacascade further develops the motif of nurturing womanhood with the horrors of World War I, which renews Claire-Solange's French patriotism: "In wartime, one's heart belongs to one's country," she acknowledges (148). She praises devoted French Antillean soldiers for swiftly coming to rescue a weakened France (177). Following in their footsteps, Claire-Solange becomes a nurse; consequently, she embraces "her new destiny: to alleviate pain, entertain, and strengthen" French soldiers (189). The notions of benevolence and sacrifice suggest that the nation inspires such sentiments in the "true" citizen.[17] Nonetheless, Lacascade's motif of *agapē* remains a double-edged sword that brings her novel back to colonial and racial muddy waters.

Claire-Solange's Martinican aunt, Émilienne, highlights this when she explains how her niece in love may resemble their "black great-grandmothers close by white men weakened by fever and intemperance, and who would have perished without the dedication of black women" (80). She praises a peculiar feminine contribution to colonization, as only these charitable and strong black women, embodiments of *agapē*, can repair the broken white colonists who are nothing without them. However, Lacascade's rendition of this sacrificial love brings back the colonial motif of the *mulâtresse*'s solicitude for bedridden white men as lauded with some degree of condescension by the Baron de Wimpffen (1748–1819) in the eighteenth century and Lafcadio Hearn (1850–1904) in the nineteenth century.[18]

The motif of solicitude also recalls how despite her best efforts, Lacascade's text is not devoid of sensuality. On the penultimate page, one cannot miss the (carnal) passion in Claire-Solange's vibrant love declaration to her fiancé. Here, while talking about her spiritual "African pity," she reveals to Jacques her desire for him: "I hand it over to you, dear, warmed by the sun, fragrant, burning with passion. . . . My pity . . . [i]t is a need, a passionate longing for— . . . It is a great hunger that only you can satiate" (200). On the next and last page of the novel, the image of an African woman who tenderly takes care of her husband appears tamer and more respectable.

However, for the careful reader, this reference does little to extinguish the images of desire that Claire-Solange has ignited on the previous page. The concluding paragraphs of *Claire-Solange* remind the reader of the sensuality that may still bubble beneath the guise of respectability.

Claire-Solange may respond to exoticism and colonialism with a politics of propriety that does not always elide sensual leanings; she speaks for the wealthy *mulâtres* who demanded recognition by France as equal citizens. At the end of the novel, her selfless marriage to a crippled Jacques incarnates the salvation of France by Antillean intervention. As a political allegory, Lacascade's romance illustrates a reversal of power that hails the *mulâtresse*'s and the colonies' worth. France becomes an ailing husband saved by black *agapē*. While Lacascade attempts to dismantle the sexualization of the *mulâtresse*, she is ensnared in another colonial stereotype: a nurturing figure dedicated to whiteness. Suzanne Lacascade's novel may not fit later ideas of feminism and anticolonialism, but she still grapples with institutional power and challenges racial and gender oppression. This novel epitomizes the difficulty in rejecting colonial stereotyping; the motif of the nurturing woman of color may be seen as an act of resistance or as an impediment in the fight for equality for all.

Middle-Class Apologia for *La femme noire*: Exoticism and Respectability in Question

Paulette Nardal was an eclectic writer whose promotion of race and black femininity were already seen in the 1920s with her short story "En exil" ("In Exile," 1929), in which she depicted a praiseworthy old Martinican *négresse* (dark-skinned woman) facing hardship.[19] It is true, as Shireen K. Lewis states, that "Nardal's piece is perhaps one of the few sensitive portrayals of a black woman in literature written in French at this time."[20] However, like Lacascade, Nardal uses a politics of propriety that begs for examination. The nonsexualized portrayal of the elderly and ailing Elisa, a poverty-stricken domestic plagued by rheumatism, differs markedly from the seductive *créole des romans*, to borrow Lacascade's terminology. Nardal praises this *négresse*'s resilience in a sunless and soulless Paris bent on crushing her spirit; with its frigid weather and racist comments shouted at her by young male students in the street, the city is not a home. She saves money to return to Martinique but remains too poor to do so.[21] Elisa daydreams about her island and misses the communal gatherings with friends during which, as she explains, "the whole Martinican folklore goes by. African tales adapted to the Antillean soul."[22] The notion of adaptation stresses the creolization of the descendants of enslaved Africans, now Antilleans living in a different cultural milieu.

Hence, to believe, like Lewis, that "Elisa's sense of self is therefore based on a communal black identity rooted in traditional Africa" overlooks the Creole characteristics of Elisa's selfhood and the salience of class in this story.[23] Nardal's ideology mirrors the metropolitan negrophilia of the time; Elisa's cultural background symbolizes a "pure" black Martinican soul devoid of the alienation generated by European civilization. "En exil" creates a tension from an idealized vision of African and Martinican blackness from the working class of the countryside. Nonetheless, Nardal does not focus on the plight of this underprivileged Martinican *négresse* primarily to denounce racial and socioeconomic inequality. Instead, she uses Elisa to extol Martinican culture, implying that everything is better back in "douce Martinique." Nardal does not explain the reasons that may have led to Elisa's exile, such as the arduous living conditions for poor women in the difficult economic situation of the islands. Due to the renewed sexist aspects of the Second Empire (1852–70), rural women were even more dependent on former masters, (romantic) partners, and religious institutions.[24] Under the Third Republic, abject poverty still plagued the proletariat and did nothing to improve the condition of underprivileged women.[25] With the portrayal of Elisa, Nardal's vision of womanhood, though less elitist than Lacascade's, is not about empowering poor *négresses*.

In the 1930s Nardal privileged the activism of educated women from the black intelligentsia living in Paris. In her 1932 bilingual article "L'éveil de la conscience noire" (The awakening of black consciousness), she laments that, in comparison to black American writers who addressed issues of race awareness and blackness earlier, male writers from the French Antilles are lagging. She then argues that enlightened women were pioneers who fostered such racial awareness. She insists that black female students have had to overcome many obstacles, while she explores the history of their race to prove that the black African diaspora comes out of a worthy civilization: "The coloured women living alone in the metropolis, until the Colonial Exhibition (1931), have certainly been less favored than coloured men who are content with a certain easy success. Long before the latter, they have felt the need of a racial solidarity which would not be merely material. They were thus aroused to race consciousness."[26]

Perceiving Paris as a colonial, racist, and sexist space, a place of estrangement, Nardal affirms that black women (French Antillean students) faced more hurdles than black men. She is therefore criticizing black men who embrace patriarchal ideas that privilege men over women. Though black men were oppressed by the colonial system, educated individuals gained an increased social status in military professions and as civil servants. Nardal thus implies that despite the challenges black men may have encountered, they were still more privileged with their "succès faciles."

One may assume that by "succès faciles" Paulette Nardal means research and working opportunities. However, in my view the African American anthropologist Eslanda Goode Robeson, wife of Paul Robeson (a civil rights activist, singer, and actor), offers a way to read this notion of easy success as sexual prowess. Robeson reveals intriguing aspects of the discrimination that was thriving in Paris within the student communities with members from the French colonies in Africa and the Caribbean: "The Negro boys often have great success, and are sometimes lionized by the French girls; the mulatto is often successful too. But the Negro girls of the better class, often proud and sensitive, have a difficult time; their own boys are more interested in making conquests in the new fields, and leave them sadly alone; and French boys are not interested in them, excepts as friends."[27]

Not considering propriety as a way to prevent sexual objectification, Robeson highlights the predicament of respectable dark-skinned women from the middle class in a stereotypical fashion. For her, these discarded good black girls lack romantic partners due to their modesty, while black men (dark-skinned and light-skinned alike) enjoy life due to their sexual success with white women.[28] Holding Robeson's comments up next to Nardal's not only exposes the complex effects of class, race, and gender but also points to an unspoken sex war. These scholars convey a restrained critique of black patriarchal ideas that highlights how men from the colonies participated in the oppression of black women. However, their remarks do not address the ways in which the French colonial project has altered these black men's patriarchal visions of gender and sexuality.

Nardal also notes that French Caribbean authors, black and white, "talk about their island as if they were its lover."[29] Nardal critiques them for perpetuating colonial and exotic discourses as they construct their homeland as their object of affection or lust. Such a sexualized trope suggests that female bodies, like the island space they live in, are there for the taking. Nardal's discussion implies that French Caribbean literature both emulates metropolitan literature and feeds the sexualized expression of the colonial project. Yet, contrary to Lacascade, Nardal here does not vigorously critique white exotic literature. Indeed, her focus on racial consciousness led her to praise the Greek-born Lafcadio Hearn for his representation of the French Antilles, race and ethnoclasses, and Martinican culture.[30] Like many Martinican scholars, she ignores his sexualization of women of color and his racialized and, at times, racist vision. As she explains, her project is not about denigrating French/white culture but about promoting the cultural creations of the African diaspora.[31] Thus, ironically, her dedication to blackness inhibits what some might now consider a more appropriate criticism of exoticism.

Insidious Masculine Reverie: The Peril of Sexualized Exoticism

Ten years younger than Paulette Nardal, Jane seems to have been more willing to spread around her critique of the exotic and sexual construction of the black female body. In "Pantins exotiques" ("Exotic Puppets," 1928), the younger sister did not spare contemporaneous white writers with exotic leanings. She reviewed Paul Morand's collection of short stories *Magie noire* (1928) to denounce how black women, no matter their class and citizenship, are restricted to sexualized stereotypes. The younger Nardal also condemned French critic Léon Werth, especially his inability to conceive black individuals, especially black women, as anything other than "illusions deeply anchored in the French mind and fallen from literature to the realm of the public."[32] She particularly denounced literary stereotypes concerning the black dancing body. This quote from Werth's *Danses, danseurs et dancings* (1925) exemplifies the type of characterization that Nardal objected to: "This is when I caught sight of the black woman. I'm not certain she was not at first adorned with a poetry of the sort found in books. Maybe she was first a literary negress, princess and sultana. Novels of the islands and the tales from the *Thousand and One Nights*. But it is not my fault if this lithe grace has passed through into literature, or rather if it has become a kind of sexual poetry, innate in us."[33]

Werth's gaze reduces a *négresse* dancing in a ballroom to the gracefulness of her flexible body, which then feeds a "sexual poetry" that Lacascade had already derided in 1924. His comments evoke Lafcadio Hearn's passion for a female "population of the Arabian Nights." In his *Two Years in the French West Indies* (1890), Hearn often fuses two archetypal objects of desire: the Orientalist odalisque and the tropical woman of color. Hearn describes a *mulâtresse* as a "Byzantine virgin" and adds that "there was an Oriental something in her appearance difficult to describe; something that made you think of the Queen of Sheba."[34] His inability to differentiate between two distinct sexual archetypes of feminine otherness displays the reductive aspects of European exoticism in the late nineteenth century.

However, though Werth's 1925 commentary emulates this previous masculine discourse, Werth, contrary to Hearn, extols the dark-skinned and mesmerizing *négresse* whose face was "a beautiful block of shadow." She transports her dancing partner to an exotic seashore somewhere in the French Caribbean or Africa.[35] Jane Nardal does not find his ode to the *négresse*'s beauty and grace flattering and instead sees her reduced to her physicality. Nardal further exposes the dangers of this so-called glorification of black femininity without intellect, particularly of a black dancer on the model of Josephine Baker at that time (before her involvement in the French resistance during World War II).

For the younger Nardal, Baker's jazz performance amplifies the problematic dissemination of French colonial stereotypes, often sexual in nature, that promote black women's status as second-class citizens with no brains. Like her sisters Paulette and Andrée, Jane was wary and critical of the sexualized aspects of jazz: "And the blasé artists and snobs find in them [African American performers] what they seek: the savory, spicy contrast of primitive beings in an ultramodern frame of African frenzy unfurled in the cubist decor of a nightclub. This explains the unprecedented vogue and the swell of enthusiasm generated by a little *câpresse* who was begging on the sidewalks of St Louis Mississippi [*sic*]."[36]

Jane's remarks indicate how African American entertainers such as Baker nurtured Parisians' negrophilia, the craze for Negro arts, and their thirst for modern primitivism and sexual exoticism. Nardal asserts that the interest in the exotic other was a conscious decision to consume the exotic and sexualized other for entertainment.[37]

Nardal's commentary, however, is not devoid of class biases. She first characterizes the low origins of the performer as a *câpresse*, a black woman whose skin is more chocolate than honey, begging on the streets of St. Louis, in order to demystify the craze surrounding her and mock her admirers. It is telling that she uses the term *gueuser* (to beg), which expresses a poverty tainted with ignominy, instead of the more neutral *mendier*, as *courir la gueuse* also means to seek sexual encounters. Neither the use of Baker's low social status nor the term *câpresse* seems accidental either. The latter indicates a racial taxonomy that puts the artist in a lower category. Nardal questions Baker's morals to underscore that this artist is not a middle-class *femmes de lettres*, thus emphasizing that what her fans lust for is sheer baseness. Initially, Nardal brings to the fore not so much La Baker's early poverty as her French audience's desire to flirt with controlled lewdness and lowbrow culture. For Nardal, Baker may be a successful and shrewd entertainer, but she is no intellectual.

Nardal's sense of respectability leads her to insinuate that Baker, as an imported and foreign artist, with her oversexualized persona, plays with fire among other American Negroes doing the same thing. Indeed, Baker epitomizes not merely what Brent Hayes Edwards terms "a kind of universal feminine colonial other" but an utterly sexualized version of the colonized woman.[38] As a commodified *méta-mulâtresse*, she is the latest manifestation in popular culture of the sexualized woman of color at the disposal of the dashing Frenchman. For instance, she played a Martinican laundress-cum-singer in *Zouzou*, transformed into a mesmerizing *doudou* (1934), and a young Berber from Tunisia in *Princesse Tam Tam* (1935), a Pygmalion-like tale. In both movies, despite her frantic adoration, the woman of color, unlike Lacascade's Claire-Solange, cannot be considered an equal and so cannot be loved, thus demonstrating the French prerogative to accept or refuse interracial love.[39]

Jane Nardal's class biases are in plain view when she mocks a writer like Paul Morand representing a black artist/performer. She sarcastically states that, with "the conquest of the artist accomplished, it remains for him to undertake the conquest of the bourgeois, of the intellectual. We will wait for that conquest as some European attributes to the 'literary' Negro a few innate qualities."[40] She places performers such as Josephine Baker below the bourgeois/intellectuals. The intellectual and bourgeois of color have escaped objectification because their existence in real life has not yet been accepted or conceived in literature. Only black sex sells. Only black sex associated with triumphant white masculinity and vilified black patriarchal ideas can give birth to a best seller, as suggested by the success of Mayotte Capécia's *Je suis martiniquaise*.

Climbing the (Social) Ladder: Impropriety and Inconvenient Truth

The Martinican Lucette Céranus Combette took advantage of the negrophilia persisting in the 1940s to write and publish her first novel, *Je suis martiniquaise* (1948), in France under the pen name Mayotte Capécia. Focusing on the historical information that scholars such as Christiane Makward and, more recently, Myriam Cottias and Madeleine Dobie have provided not only dispels the mystery around Combette but also stresses the salience of socioeconomic betterment in her activism. Combette lived her life with courage and resourcefulness; coming from the lower strata of Martinican society, she held many jobs before becoming the writer Mayotte Capécia. While she understood what it meant to be *nègre* in Paris, she also realized that, despite her African heritage, her beauty and light skin worked in her favor.[41] She was celebrated in the literary world and was in contact with contemporary celebrities, including Josephine Baker.[42] For Makward, however, *Je suis martiniquaise* is a collaborative work between the illiterate Combette, mother of three, and French ghostwriters who helped her advance her life.[43]

In her interviews, Capécia consistently argued that she wanted to call attention to the difficult condition of *femmes de couleur* in Martinique and show that they could suffer just like white women from continental France and were no less respectable, which seems to indicate a racial feminist consciousness.[44] Nonetheless, her endeavors also highlight the extent to which impoverished and formally uneducated people often need to be "schooled" about their oppression to effectively undermine institutional power. Should it be surprising that formerly poor women such as Baker and Combette were initially more invested in their own survival than in engaging with race promotion or racial equality? As Donald Macedo asks, how could "one dialogue without any prior apprenticeship with the object of dialogue and without any epistemological curiosity?"[45] In their fight against racial and/or social inequality, women with African ancestry coming from diverse walks of life often offer conflicted responses to that question.

Indeed, the invention of the persona Mayotte Capécia exemplifies how in any given structure of power, as James Scott puts it, "those obliged by domination to act a mask will eventually find their faces have grown to fit that mask. The practice of subordination in this case produces, in time, its own legitimacy."[46] Too often, people who interacted with Capécia relegated her to the role of the *doudou*. Male journalists and literary reviewers were particularly condescending and prejudiced and continually emphasized her beauty and exotic graces.[47] As Capécia, Combette, who could not afford to lose the support of her patrons, had to navigate murky waters.

Capécia's first novel, about a proudly self-reliant *mulâtresse* looking for respectability in Martinique before deciding to leave it with her "white" baby for an idealized France, illustrates this ambivalence. This protagonist first becomes the owner of a successful *blanchisserie* (laundry) in which she employs other black women.[48] The novelist both highlights a feminine will for self-determination against black patriarchy and attempts to show how assimilation to metropolitan whiteness is the best protection against local oppression. Her protagonist, Mayotte, though aware of her oppression, cannot recognize all of her oppressors in her quest for social advancement.

Her *blanchisserie* eventually becomes a metaphor for her desire to "cleanse" herself from what she considers the failings of blackness. She vilifies only black men who resemble her father: womanizers, gamblers, and abusive partners. Mayotte believes that only marrying a white man can guarantee her respectability and well-being. As a little girl, she decided "she could only love a white man, a blond with blue eyes, a Frenchman" (59). Her first and last sexual encounter with a *nègre*, which she describes in somewhat titillating detail as she "felt transported into an unknown world" (104), persuades her to control her libido to seek the "reformation" that metropolitan whiteness may provide. She often despises other black women for their loose morals, sexual availability, and lack of ambition (121, 123, 130). Here her self-restraint merges with the "activism" of Lacascade and the Nardals. However, her self-deprecation and questioning of her African ancestry indicate that, like the *méta-mulâtresse* played by Josephine Baker, Mayotte is not worthy of white love. Even before meeting the father of her child, she knows that "white men do not marry black women" (131). Her white navy officer lover abandons her and their son. Her romance remains a cliché in that it evokes the motif of the failed interracial love in the eighteenth-century song "Adieux foulard" and the exotic and eroticized postcards that extolled amorous relationships between white sailors and *doudous* during the Vichy regime.[49]

In the early 1940s Martinique was a doubly oppressive space due to both the preexisting colonial order and the new Vichy regime, which intensified racial discrimination. However, *Je suis martiniquaise* blames only an oppressive black patriarchy without probing the colonial system and the white patriarchy that influenced it. This oversight could imply either a lack of proper analytical tools and skills or a morally questionable willingness to reinforce the prejudiced stereotypes of the French colonial discourse. Believing at the time that Capécia belonged to the alienated elite of color, the Martinicans Jenny Alpha in 1948 and Frantz Fanon in 1952 opted for the latter. They vilified the novelist's portrayal of blackness and promotion of whiteness.[50] Unlike Maryse Condé, who later praised Capécia for exposing a particularly unsavory truth about black masculinity, Alpha and Fanon considered their compatriot a betrayer of her race.[51] They thus dismissed the pertinence of her critique of black patriarchal ideas and belittled the femininity she claimed to represent. Keeping in mind Combette's illiteracy and modest origins, I stress instead how Capécia's flexible idea of propriety and her faltering or absent capacity for social analysis remind us that the fight for black women's rights should be inclusive and cannot overlook the significance of class and education in addition to race and gender.

Conclusion

Lacascade's and the Nardal sisters' struggle for equality rejected racial and gendered prejudices while at the same time imposing an idea of proper femininity that may not appear radical today but was much more so in their context. Their quest for respectability may also seem to express a traditional and bourgeois way of thinking with exclusive leanings, yet for them, in the interwar period, between wantonness and virtue, were there any other options? As for the "lowbrow" projects of Capécia and Baker, those projects may call attention to the women's effective, though ambiguous, strategies of survival, the necessity to educate the masses, and the possible condescending and oppressive aspects of this educational endeavor if mismanaged. Regardless of how their positions may look through the lens of twenty-first-century understandings, all the women described here offer a challenging rewriting of black activism, the fight for equality, and the feminism of color that emphasizes their political and cultural values. They link the personal to the political while denouncing patriarchy and colonial discourse for their promotion of black women's purported inferiority. Willingly or in spite of themselves, though, they also expose the roadblocks that feminism from the French Caribbean had to overcome, such as the absence of a sense of sisterhood and the need for internal cooperation and inclusiveness.

Notes

1. On these women's contributions, see Shireen K. Lewis, *Race, Culture, and Identity: Francophone West African and Caribbean Literature and Theory from Négritude to Créolité* (Lanham MD: Lexington Books, 2006); Tracy Denean Sharpley-Whiting, *Negritude Women* (Minneapolis: University of Minnesota Press, 2002); Brent Hayes

Edwards, *The Practice of Diaspora: Literature, Translation, and the Rise of Black Internationalism* (Cambridge MA: Harvard University Press, 2003); Christiane Makward, *Mayotte Capécia ou l'aliénation selon Fanon* (Paris: Karthala, 1999); Myriam Cottias and Madeleine Dobie, *Relire Mayotte Capécia: Une femme des Antilles dans l'espace colonial français* (Paris: Armand-Colin, 2012). On the debates concerning their activism, see *Small Axe* 9, no. 1 (2005), in the section "Book Discussion" dedicated to *The Practice of Diaspora*, in particular Brent Hayes Edwards, "Pebbles of Consonance: A Reply to Critics," 134–49; and Tracy Denean Sharpley-Whiting, "Erasures and the Practice of Diaspora Feminism," 129–33.

2. On black women's activism and institutional power, see Patricia Hill Collins, *Black Feminist Thought: Knowledge, Consciousness, and the Politics of Empowerment* (New York: Routledge Classics, 2008), 217.
3. For a recent study of this motif, see chapter 3 of Jacqueline Couti, *Dangerous Creole Liaisons* (Oxford: Oxford University Press, 2016), 121–60.
4. On black feminism's particular challenges, see Audre Lorde, *Sister Outsider: Essays and Speeches* (Berkeley: University of California Press, 2007), 61–71, 110–14.
5. Bernard Moitt, *Women and Slavery in the French Antilles* (Bloomington: Indiana University Press, 2001), 99–100.
6. Angela Davis, *Women, Race and Class* (New York: Vintage Books, 1981), 26.
7. Davis, *Women, Race and Class*, 128–48; Evelyn Brooks Higginbotham, *Righteous Discontent: The Women's Movement in the Black Baptist Church, 1880–1920* (Cambridge MA: Harvard University Press, 1993); and Erin Chapman, *Prove It on Me* (Oxford: Oxford University Press, 2012).
8. Davis, *Women, Race and Class*, 183.
9. On class and lack of solidarity between women in Martinique between 1848 and 1852, see chapter 1 of Gilbert Pago, *Les femmes et la liquidation du système esclavagiste* (Petit-Bourg, Guadeloupe: Ibis rouge, 1998), 19–33. For classist biases and respectability in the 1890s, see Myriam Cottias, "Un genre colonial? Mariage et citoyenneté dans les Antilles françaises (XVIIe–XXe siècle)," in *Genre et postcolonialisme: Dialogue transcontinentaux* (Paris: Édition des archives contemporaine, 2011), 67–70.
10. For a recent discussion of the Nardal sisters' politics of respectability, see Rachel Anne Gillett, "Jazz Women, Gender Politics, and the Francophone Atlantic," *Atlantic Studies* 10, no. 1 (2013): 109–30.
11. Armand Nicolas, *Histoire de la Martinique*, vol. 2, *De 1848 à 1939* (Paris: L'Harmattan, 1996), 245.
12. Nicolas, *Histoire de la Martinique*, 120, 128.
13. Among the Nardal children were eight sisters. For more information, see Jil Servant's documentary *Paulette Nardal, la fierté d'être négresse* (2004).

14. George Athénas and Aimé Merlo, two cousins born in La Réunion, wrote under this pen name. See Marius-Ary Leblond, *Écrits sur la littérature coloniale* (Paris: L'Harmattan, 2012), 185. Unless otherwise stated, translations are mine.
15. Maryse Condé, *La parole des femmes: Essai sur des romancières des Antilles de langue française* (Paris: L'Larmattan, 1979), 29; Sharpley-Whiting, *Negritude Women*, 16. For a more recent study, see chapter 1 of Jennifer M. Wilks, *Race, Gender and Comparative Black Modernism* (Baton Rouge: Louisiana State University Press, 2008), 26–67.
16. Suzanne Lacascade, *Claire-Solange: Âme africaine* (Paris: Eugène Figuière, 1924), 37. Hereafter cited parenthetically in the text.
17. Benedict R. Anderson, *Imagined Communities: Reflections on the Origin and Spread of Nationalism*, rev. ed. (New York: Verso, 2006), 141.
18. Alexandre Stanislas, baron de Wimpffen, *Saint-Domingue à la veille de la révolution (souvenirs du baron de Wimpffen)*, ed. Savine Albert (Paris: Louis-Michard, 1911), 76–77; Lafcadio Hearn, *Two Years in the West Indies* (New York: Harper and Brothers Publishers, 1890), 332.
19. Paulette Nardal, "En exil," *La Dépêche Africaine*, no. 19 (December 1, 1929): 66.
20. Shireen K. Lewis, "Gendering Négritude: Paulette Nardal's Contribution to the Birth of Modern Francophone Literature," *Romance Languages Annual* 11 (2000): 69.
21. Nardal, "En exil," 6.
22. Paulette Lacascade, "In Exile," trans. Sharpley-Whiting, *Negritude Women*, 117.
23. Lewis, "Gendering Négritude," 70.
24. Pago, *Les femmes*, 192.
25. Nicolas, *Histoire de la Martinique*, 117.
26. Paulette Nardal, "L'éveil de la conscience de race chez les étudiants noirs," *La Revue du monde noire*, no. 6 (April 1932): 29, 30. I am using Paulette Nardal's translation.
27. Eslanda Goode Robeson quoted in Edwards, *The Practice of Diaspora*, 155.
28. On this masculine sexual prowess, see Jennifer Boittin, "Reverse Exoticism and Masculinity," in *Colonial Metropolis: The Urban Grounds of Anti-imperialism and Feminism in Interwar Paris* (Lincoln: University of Nebraska Press, 2015), 111–32.
29. Nardal, "L'éveil de la conscience noire," 28, my translation.
30. Nardal, "L'éveil de la conscience noire," 28.
31. Nardal, "L'éveil de la conscience noire," 31.
32. Jane Nardal, "Exotic Puppets," trans. Sharpley-Whiting, *Negritude Women*, 108.
33. Léon Werth, *Danses, danseurs et dancings* (Paris: L. F. Rieder et Cie), 117–18.
34. Hearn, *Two Years*, 38, 314.
35. Werth, *Danses, danseurs et dancings*, 118–19.
36. Gillet, "Jazz Women," 13; Nardal, "Exotic Puppets," 109. In the original, Jane Nardal confuses Mississippi with Missouri.

37. Jennifer Boittin's rebuke of Elizabeth Ezra's notion of the "colonial unconscious" in her *The Colonial Unconscious, Race and Culture in Interwar France* (2000) is useful in understanding the lust for the other as also a "conscious embrace of the colonial" and not something hidden in the psyche. See *Colonial Metropolis*, 3.
38. Edwards, *The Practice of Diaspora*, 162. On the genealogy of Josephine Baker as the symbol of the colonized woman, see Boittin, *Colonial Metropolis*, 1–35.
39. For more, see Tyler Stovall, "The New Woman and the New Empire: Josephine Baker and Changing Views of Femininity in Interwar France," http://sfonline.barnard.edu/baker/stovall_01.htm.
40. Jane Nardal, "Pantins exotiques," *La Dépêche africaine*, no. 8 (October 15, 1928): 2.
41. The word *nègre* is from one of Combette's notebooks, quoted in Cottias and Dobie, *Relire Mayotte Capécia*, 57. See Capécia's interview with the journalist Léo Larguier, quoted in Cottias and Dobie, *Relire Mayotte Capécia*, 56.
42. Cottias and Dobie, *Relire Mayotte Capécia*, 51, 53.
43. Christiane Makward, "Histoire des textes II," *Mayotte Capécia*, 181–208.
44. Also from an interview of Mayotte Capécia, quoted in Cottias and Dobie, *Relire Mayotte Capécia*, 56.
45. Donaldo Macedo, "Introduction to the Anniversary Edition," in *The Pedagogy of the Oppressed* (London: Continuum, 2000), 19.
46. See James C. Scott, *Domination and the Arts of Resistance: Hidden Transcripts* (New Haven CT: Yale University Press, 1992), 10.
47. Cottias and Dobie carefully transcribed some of these interviews; see *Relire Mayotte Capécia*, 56.
48. Mayotte Capécia, *Je suis martiniquaise* (Paris: Corrêa, 1948), 131. Hereafter cited parenthetically in the text.
49. See the collections of the Departmental Archives of Martinique and the Ethnographic and Historical Museum of Martinique for similar postcards.
50. Alpha's essay was first published in *Présence africaine* 5 (1948), quoted in Makward, *Mayotte Capécia*, 39. See also Frantz Fanon, *Black Skin, White Masks*, trans. Charles Lam Markmann (New York: Grove Press, 1967), 34.
51. Maryse Condé, *Le roman antillais*, vol. 1 (Paris: Nathan, 1978), 14, 48; see also "Order, Disorder, Freedom, and the West Indian Writer," *Yale French Studies* 83, no. 2 (1993): 121–35.

9

Between Respectability and Resistance

French Caribbean Women Confronted by Masculine Domination during the Second Half of the Twentieth Century

STÉPHANIE MULOT AND NADINE LEFAUCHEUR

Any analysis of French Caribbean women's resistance and their struggle for equality also involves studying what is happening in the private sphere, in domestic life, and in intimate moments between partners. Guadeloupe and Martinique are infamously known for their higher rates of single parenthood; the frequency of gender-based violence; and the continued male practice of having multiple sexual partners, which puts women in competition with each other.[1] For these small island societies, where it is difficult to escape from the gaze of neighbors and other people's opinion, the straitjacket of moral and religious norms restricts the possibility of female emancipation.

Multiple generations of women have learned how to endure oppression based on their race, sex, social class, and age, all while being taught by Christian precepts and societal expectations how women should act to be deemed respectable. While these expectations about "respectability" govern women's education and adult life, the expectation that they also have to "pull through" has often given them the strength to resist the situations they faced in a world controlled by men. In the French West Indies, as in every country of the Caribbean, women have to deal with the ordinary practice of male multipartnership, which appears to be inevitable and which puts women in a world of competition with its own rules.

Based on interviews conducted during the 1990s and from 2009 to 2014, this chapter seeks to analyze how women can exercise resistance in private, intimate spaces while under strong societal scrutiny.[2] We focus first on the rules for respectability that traditionally govern female socialization. Next, we present extracts from life stories that testify to the efforts of women to liberate themselves from various facets of masculine oppression. Finally, we take a look at the current evolutions in the situation of French Caribbean women.

Female Socialization and Respectability

Inspired by Peter Wilson's work, multiple studies of the late twentieth century have shown that both female "respectability" (sense of decency) and male "reputation" (as womanizers) reinforce heterosexual norms of socialization in the Caribbean.[3] Our observations confirm that rules about female respectability across classes have played a fundamental role in the lives of French Caribbean women for the last century; to some extent, the same rules still dictate how most girls are educated. These rules aim to control girls' conduct, bodies, and freedom. (Unlike girls, boys are granted a great deal of freedom, regardless of their social class.)[4] These rules, which seek to guarantee conformity to social and moral norms, put a high pressure on a girl's life choices and experiences.

Discretion and Control of the Female Body

As is usually the case in rural societies or relatively small communities, conformity and social discretion are the most sought after aspects of girls' education and female respectability in the Caribbean. Not being the focus of gossip, not disgracing oneself or one's family—the rules affecting girls and women testify to the strength of societal, religious, and community control and the power of neighborhood gossip. In these island universes, networks of circulating information, or *milans* (gossip), can earn someone either a good or a bad reputation. This social control is further reinforced by churches, especially Protestant churches and churches where members' identities are primarily connected to their membership.

Ideas about discretion for women traditionally placed emphasis on the control of the body: a woman's appearance can be just as important as her behavior or language. The clothing, hair, and outward presentation of women (and the children they raise) must be cared for properly. Women must be dressed correctly, always wearing clothing that has been well ironed. Having neat and smoothed hair (*maré*), as well as straightening hair if it is naturally frizzy, has long been and is still important to avoid being seen as neglected. Adult women are also supposed to wear makeup every day, do their nails, and wear gold jewelry (inherited from family members or given by one's partner), especially when they belong or claim to belong to the middle classes—although to be athletic and to watch one's weight and diet have recently gained more importance as a sign of social respectability for women, while the fashion of African American nappy hair has spread. Obedience to these commandments creates the image of respectability, while not respecting these rules may lead to being sidelined and avoided by others. When parents, neighbors, or friends make critical remarks about a person's appearance, such criticism functions as a formidable moral and societal sanction against the individual.

A Sexuality Based on Passivity and Reproduction?

Societal expectations about bodily control also require control over sexual behaviors and conjugal relationships. Even though virginity at the time of marriage is a religious value that most women today have been emancipated from, not having many sexual partners still remains a sign of respect for women. On the contrary, having several partners, especially simultaneously, and making children with many fathers are seen as an inability to "respect oneself." Furthermore, socially authorized sexual practices differ according to whether they occur within or outside a legitimate romantic relationship. To avoid being considered "dirty," a "rat," *une femme ochan* (promiscuous), or, worst of all, a slut, someone no man would marry, women who value their respectability must avoid appearing too sexually active. Despite these restrictions on women's sexual behavior, the need to preserve a conjugal relationship when faced with strong competition from other women may also compel women to consent to unwanted sex acts in order to prevent their spouse from taking a mistress. (To avoid having to participate in such acts, some wives alternatively accept that their husband may seek out other women, and these wives devote themselves entirely to their children.)

The need for women to "respect themselves" obviously does not extend to giving respect to their own sexual desires. Most importantly, women must not question the respectability of their family and loved ones. Contrary to what happens for women, the heteronormative rules of male domination authorize Caribbean men to have an active and free sex life, combining the pride of possessing a respectable spouse with the pleasure of having one or more mistresses with whom men can share illegitimate sexual desires. These societal rules also allow men to disengage from familial obligations, leaving women responsible for domestic and child-rearing burdens.

Avoiding Single Motherhood and Giving Preference to Marriage

Still today, most women want the most respectable model of femininity both for themselves and for their daughters: to be a married woman, faithful (even if her husband is not), whose children share the same father, to whom she is married. Raising children outside of a stable relationship (and especially a married relationship) is always a subject of concern, especially in middle-class or very religious families. Being a single mother and having children with different men is stigmatized as a failure to adhere to standards of respectability and conjugal legitimacy. Despite this, such circumstances are very common (more than half of all families with children today) and regarded as a Caribbean reality, a consequence of the supposed inability of Caribbean men (since they are, above all, womanizers) to engage in a conjugal and paternal role. These situations of single motherhood are rarely chosen but are sometimes the result of women who have attempted in vain to force a man to stay by having a child with him, and sometimes they are the "second choice" of women who wanted a child and have chosen to rely upon their own strength or the support of government funding for single parents rather than on the help of an "irresponsible" father.

While most women would like to be married, the "right to marry" is not accessible to all women. Even though, after the abolition of slavery in 1848, this "new right" was usually seen as a welcome development, often only women from the most favored social situations had (and still have) the opportunity to begin their conjugal life with a ceremony before the priest and the local mayor. To move from being a "visited partner" to a concubine and from a concubine to a wife, a woman may have to wait until enough time has passed for the man to be sure that he really wants to stay with her and to have enough savings to settle the family in a house and to pay for the wedding. Many women, especially the poorest women, were and still are lost in this process. They have become involved and had children with different partners in the hope that these men would provide milk, bread, or a name to the children with whom these women have already been abandoned.

Wives and concubines also sometimes have chosen and still choose to face infidelity, violence, desertion, or the death of their partners by creating a single-parent family, sometimes in a matrifocal family structure.[5] In a show of resistance, these women turn the stigma of their situation into a mark of maternal and family merit. They are capable of sacrificing themselves to provide a home, food, clothes, and education for their children whose fathers are "absent."

A secondary form of respectability is therefore based on resistance, endurance, bravery, courage, sacrifice for children, and the ability to cope with the trials of life while enduring the abandonment or escapades of partners, thereby holding on despite life's challenges (*kimbé, tchimbé*). This second responsibility makes mothers, especially women who have failed to achieve or maintain full female respectability through their conjugal married status and a stable conjugal life, proud and upright women (*fanm doubout*) who become central pillars in the lives of their families and children (*potomitan*).[6]

Intimate Resistance and Adaptation to Rules of Respectability

Not all French Caribbean women have a violent or "runaway" husband. Not all are abandoned by the fathers of their children. Nevertheless, these aspects of male dominance are the most frequently mentioned grievances in the stories collected in Martinique, as well as in the testimonies of Guadeloupean women published in the early 1980s.[7]

What should a "self-respecting" woman do when betrayed by her partner either through violence or because he seeks out other women? Should she leave him, or should she do everything to save her relationship, her family, and her status as a respectable woman? How can a person remain "respectable" when she finds herself alone as a single mother? Can someone refuse the role of a *potomitan* mother? As can be seen in the life stories collected from women born between 1939 and 1970 who faced these situations during the second half of the twentieth century, the answers to these questions vary depending on a person's age, social status, and individual history.

Refusing to Have a Large Family

Mirette (born in 1939) was the ninth of eleven children. She resisted social pressure and the desires of her husband by declaring after the birth of her first child that she no longer wanted any more children. "My parents," she explained, "suffered too much with eleven children. For me, having children was a hassle. I never came to terms with my family history, and I never wanted other children." After five years of resistance, Mirette (herself a midwife who, according to her account, cries upon seeing pregnant women) agreed to have a second child. Yet it would be her husband (a teacher) who would have to take care of the little girls: "I would say to him, 'Our child is crying,' and he would get up. I am glad to have found a husband who took over without grumbling." Mirette would have no other children, and she never regretted it: "No regrets! I did not have the time, eh, for family."

Representing the next generation of women, Jocelyne (born in 1957) agrees: "After the first child, for me, it was over. My husband insisted on having another one. I took my time." With or without the consent of their partner (and sometimes their priest or pastor) and using modern or traditional methods of birth control (regardless of their legality), many women from these generations have, like Mirette and Jocelyne, resisted multiple pregnancies. While their mothers had an average of seven children (and sometimes up to fourteen), the women interviewed in the Faire family survey only had two or three. This "silent revolution" allowed women to work outside the home after having children, increasing their negotiation power in their conjugal relationships.

Resisting the Unfaithful or "Runaway" Partner

Burdened with multiple children and without any personal income of their own, the women of Mirette's mother's generation were forced to endure their partners' infidelity, explained Mirette: "Women took care of the children, and men brought the money, so when men would speak, everyone would obey." At the same time, however, "they did not accept. They suffered!" Mirette also argued that times had changed: "The submissive woman no longer exists. Women have moved past submission. They stood up. Now, young women are not like us: if things aren't going the way they should, they can separate themselves from the men."

Mirette herself never considered leaving her husband, because he was "a very good husband and a very good father." Moreover, during their generation, women, especially women from privileged classes, were already forbidding their husbands to "sleep around" or be blatantly unfaithful. Georges (a senior manager born in 1937) and Stéphane (a wealthy merchant born in 1949) both were divorced by their wives when knowledge about the men's sexual exploits became public. ("I am Antillean; it is in my genes," Georges argues.)

For Mirette, a Seventh-Day Adventist, "having sex before marriage was the ultimate sin." Thirty years later, Clara (born in 1966) was not a virgin on her wedding day. At the age of seventeen she and her sister tried to hide birth control pills in the house, and their discovery became a family tragedy: "When my father learned that I had had sex before marriage . . . it was a big deal! My father even cried out of desperation! We had lost our honor!" After marriage, Clara had to deal with her husband's infidelity: "I quickly lost hope in our relationship. He was fickle. He told me that things would change after the marriage. We got married in August, and by December he had a girlfriend." She did not understand why her second pregnancy made her husband "very angry" until she learned that he had conceived another child "outside."[8] She suspected that professional obligations were not the only reason why he would come home late from work and finally no longer accepted her ex-husband's mistresses or children conceived out of wedlock: "I was a bit of an accomplice, because I wanted the children to have their father, so I closed my eyes for a while. I was looking for excuses because I was not ready to leave him. And then I asked him for a divorce, because the situation had deteriorated and I could not stand it." Moreover, she rejected the gendered relationship of their marriage and their children's education: "It's a backward vision of the role of father when he is there to provide financial support to his family and the rest of the work is given to the mothers. . . . I did not want to raise my son like that. I never told my son, 'You are a man, so you don't do dishes.' I never told my daughter, 'You are a girl, so it is up to you to do everything.' No, I always told my children that we are all the same, and we all do the same things." Despite this, given the financial problems that Clara encountered after leaving her husband, she sometimes wonders if she would have done better to ignore the infidelity.

Faced with the infidelity of their husbands and the existence of children fathered out of wedlock with other women, Lélène (born as Clara in 1966) and Jocelyne (born in 1957) also refused to respect their husbands' choices but found ways to preserve the economic and parental aspects of their relationships. After learning that her husband had fathered a daughter with another woman, Lélène forced him to live in the same house as her for nine years, but with "him downstairs and me upstairs." Only after following a "very very difficult personal path" was she able to forgive him. For financial reasons, Jocelyne refused to leave her high-paying job to follow her husband when he moved to mainland France, since "things had happened that made his departure welcome." Despite this, she refused a definitive separation, because they wanted to remain "a united parental couple." To this end, her husband still participates in all decisions concerning their children and is "always available to them, despite his absence," thanks to phone calls almost every week.

Andrée (born in 1949) places less emphasis on her companion's infidelity than on his respect for his paternal obligations, favoring her own respectability as a woman who has all her children with the same man: "I wanted to have children. At twenty-four, I said to myself, 'I am ready.' I decided to have a child." A very free person, she asked a neighbor to conceive a child with her. Later, when she wanted other children, she asked him to live with her. She refused to give heed to her companion's sexual exploits, focusing instead on the importance of not conceiving children with different men: "For me, it's all about respect and righteousness. I never wanted to have children with different men." If the father plays his role well and cares for his children, it doesn't matter what else he does. "If he needs to leave, he leaves. After having children with me, he had other children. I know it. I don't know if he's dealing with it. It doesn't interest me. I know that at home everything is going well. My life is mine: it is tidy and clear. You have to be patient. Not all women are patient: if it goes wrong, it's over! Not me."

When a man fathers a child out of wedlock with a woman who does not have sufficient means to take care of it, his wife may sometimes agree to raise the child as her own. This may be imposed upon her by the husband, who may want to unite all of his children under one roof for his own respectability as a "responsible father." At the same time, it can also be a way for the "betrayed" woman to overcome shame by focusing on what is best for the children while simultaneously demonstrating her solidarity with other mothers and her own benevolence. Lélène, after having long refused, finally "adopted" her husband's daughter as her own.

Escaping Domestic Violence

Violence often accompanies infidelity.[9] "When he didn't have another woman, he was nice. It felt like he became mean when he betrayed me. He was violent. Because he's the kind of guy who doesn't like when I ask, 'Why are you leaving? Why are you going there? Why are you doing this?' He doesn't want that. He had to show he was the man. That's it: he had to be a man," analyzes Valérie (born in 1957), who was severely abused by her partner.[10]

When supported by their families, some women are quick to flee from a violent partner, such as Sarah (born in 1945) and Vanessa (born in 1966). But getting out of a situation of domestic violence is often a long and difficult process.[11] Here again, the methods of resistance vary according to the woman's generation and individual circumstances, as Jeanne's example demonstrates. Born in 1970, she was thirteen when she saw her mother nearly "beaten to death" by her father. For Jeanne's mother, a housewife and mother of five children without any financial autonomy, it was "a kind of bravery to suffer without letting anyone know. For her, it was more important" to endure everything rather than divorce, said Jeanne. Despite this, Jeanne's mother was unable to hide what was happening after news got out to the neighborhood. At the insistence of her daughter ("If you don't leave, I will run away!"), Jeanne's mother finally "activated the machinery" that led to divorce and (according to her daughter) to "emancipation and a wonderful life!"

Strengthened by this experience, Jeanne was certain that such a thing would never happen to her. Unfortunately, when she was a student in mainland France she met a man who exercised a strong influence over her. Jeanne "allowed" the verbal, physical, and sexual violence that happened to her, learning to consider them as "almost normal." "He said that my behavior forced him to do things to me. I didn't understand, but I was always trying to improve. I never questioned why he was beating me. I learned to do everything his way so that I wouldn't bother him. I learned to live under pressure." The violence became worse, and finally she understood that she should have left this man before having children with him. However, like many women, she found herself "bound hand and foot because of them." It was her own infidelity—a brief and secret liaison with a colleague—that gave her "some breathing room" and ultimately (in her words) led her "to reflect on my life, its meaning, and what I wanted for me." After having refused to follow her companion when he moved back to the French Caribbean, she eventually joined him so as to not "separate the children from their father." "I remember telling him, 'I will come, even if we split up once I am in Martinique. But at least we will be in the same place, and you will be able to see your children.' If I had refused, he would have come back to France, and that would have been even more hell." Despite this, hell was nevertheless unleashed in Martinique. Jeanne hoped to be able to "hold on" until her children (four to seven years old when they moved to the island) came of age. After four years of violence and depression she was compelled, after having seen "fury, hatred, and bloodlust" in the eyes of her companion, to run away under cover of night on Christmas Eve with curlers still in her hair. She left her children with him: "After all of the blows, with a back like a zebra and lacerated thighs, I said to myself, 'Save your skin!'" A few days later, she would crash her car into the gate of a police station so that police officers would be forced to recognize that her companion was trying to run her off the road. Housed in a shelter for victims of domestic violence, Jeanne struggled to "pay her bills" and recover the custody of her children, who initially rejected her. Her sisters criticized her, refusing to acknowledge what they called her conjugal "failure." Her father, on the other hand, personally acquainted with "the way a violent man thinks," supported her: "He told me quite firmly, 'You will not go back to him.'" Despite everything, Jeanne sometimes wonders if her companion would have changed in the same way that her father had changed and if it would have been better to "endure." Claiming that she is a "rebellious woman," she refused, however, to yield to her former companion, who offered her a much easier life if she would just accept having "to obey."

In Response to the Abandonment of Fathers: Becoming Potomitan

Raising children alone, "sacrificing" for them, and "holding on" in the face of adversity, exhaustion, poverty, and stigmatization: such is the fate of many French Caribbean women. They rarely chose such a fate, especially when sex education was limited to advice like "Don't come back with a big stomach!" Martha (born in 1940) was impregnated by a married neighbor when she was twenty years old. She has overcome her anger toward the father but asks herself, "I did not want it, but it was already there. What could I do?" Marie-Josèphe (born in 1966) and Yveline (born in 1959) raised their daughters after having learned, like many others, that their children's fathers were married or already had a family. "I wanted to get married, and so far I haven't been able yet!" regrets Marie-Josèphe. Yveline, who wanted five children, decided that "there would not be two. I didn't want to have a child with one man and then another with a different man and so on."

Societal disapproval can be strong, especially if the woman is a minor, if there are several fathers, or if there is a difference in social class. This was the case in the 1960s for Viviane (born in 1940), the third sibling of thirteen children. She explains that her family "emerged from a peasant environment" and joined the lower middle class when her father became "a driver for a military officer." She also explained that she had been completely rejected for having two children with married men: "People never accepted, given my parents' status, the situation they had on their hands. . . . It was a terrible condemnation, at all levels. Everyone quarantined me. They didn't understand how I could have let myself go . . . having children out of wedlock and without any conjugal home." After a period of depression, she decided to take control of her destiny, and she traveled to mainland France to start a new life with her children.[12]

"I was looking for love, but I only found children." Such is how Marie (born in 1947, probably as the product of rape) summarizes her life. Ill-treated by her mother and grandmother, she was very ignorant of sexual matters and became pregnant at the age of twenty while working as a domestic for the local *béké*. After a "quick" relationship with a delivery man, she watched him marry another girl, while a third woman gave birth to another of his children a month after Marie. Pregnant the following year from another "quick hit" with a different partner, she learned that a woman had committed suicide after discovering that Marie was pregnant with "her man's" child. Marie decided to flee to the other end of the island with her two children and eventually ended up living there for four years with the father of her third child. This man did not care for her while they lived together nor after he left: "I have always managed by myself, by the sweat of my brow. I've always worked, but when the children arrived I was focused on them: 'Get undressed! Take a bath! Put on clean clothes and do your homework for school!' In the morning they are ready with neat hair. Their milk is ready, their little dresses. . . . I did what I could. It is only now, when I think back to it, that I say to myself, 'Oh, I have suffered! I have suffered!'"

Most of these "abandoned" women base their honor on "doing everything they can" for their children and being a single mother *potomitan*. This is true for Yveline, who refused to have additional children to avoid becoming "a woman who has children with everyone," as well as for Marie, who was alone at age thirty with three children from different fathers. The musician Jacob Desvarieux, lead singer and guitar player for the group Kassav, said the following regarding his mother (born in 1920): "A *potomitan* is what holds the roof of the house up. It's what stops people from being exposed to the weather. It's the person who protects others, and my mother was that person. What I mean is that, until I was an adult, she did everything she could to protect me: providing food every day, helping me get dressed and go to school. . . . The most important thing for her was that her child never ended up in a mess, and for that she was ready to do anything, no matter the sacrifice."[13]

Gender Inequality: A Rising Challenge

In the second half of the twentieth century, when most of the women surveyed gave birth to their children, French Caribbean women found different ways to resist the violence and infidelity of their spouses, refusing to be assigned to traditional roles like mother, housekeeper, and educator. Women also turned the stigma of being a single mother into a *potomitan* medal of honor. These many ways of resisting did not abolish patriarchal male domination and usually cost women dearly. Women increasingly wonder if the respected status of *potomitan* is actually a trap that locks them into a precarious situation while simultaneously allowing male vagrancy and the "absence" of fathers. These women denounce culturalist or naturalist alibis that help to reproduce male oppression by convincing women that they must obey gender norms in order to avoid rejection by their families and society. Persuading oppressed people that such treatment is to their benefit is a classic tool of subjugation.

The culturalist alibi is often used to explain that Caribbean men, because they are Caribbean, cannot be faithful. This argument compels some women to search for a white partner from mainland France in order to minimize the risk of violent and unstable romantic relationships. But supporters of the culturalist argument assert that white men and metropolitan men are just as unfaithful as the West Indians; these men are just better at hiding their behavior. The culturalist point of view is also used to justify the courage, sacrifice, and resistance of women, whose identity is connected to that of the *potomitan*, a totemic figure that represents all Caribbean women worthy of the name. On the other hand, for supporters of the naturalist alibi, both the practice of men having multiple sexual partners and the "valor" of French Caribbean women can be attributed to genetic coding. By invoking an African heritage that possibly involved polygamy, naturalist apologists can claim that "men have it in their blood" and that women are "naturally" programmed to be resistant and *potomitan*. These alibis, despite being questioned today on internet forums about television series or in spoken word competitions between *slammeurs*, nevertheless persist as an effective way to avoid challenging the power relations that govern society.[14]

New Models?

In recent decades, declining fertility rates, higher rates of educational achievement and training, and higher numbers of women in skilled administrative jobs have resulted in many Caribbean women achieving financial autonomy. At the same time, women have strengthened their relationship to men, the ability to negotiate within romantic relationships, and the power to denounce male behavior.

Female respectability remains a dominant value, but with new developments in mobility, tourism, new communication technologies, and social media, new models of behavior are being proposed and often adopted.

The French Caribbean women interviewed for these projects all observed that many things had changed since their youth and, more importantly, that women changed while also changing society: "As soon as women began to work and be independent, everything changed. Everything changed. Now women have revolted," says Paula (born in 1968). An evangelical, she believes that old customs of submission "were not good. The husband dominated and believed that everything was allowed. [But] if the Bible says that the father is the head of the household and the husband is in charge of the wife, it is not in the spirit of domination but in the sense that the husband should take care of his wife and children." Marie-Josèphe is of the same mindset, saying that "things evolve. Men were so macho! They were 'Their Lordship!' It's changed!" By accessing wage labor, "girls created a kind of rebellion," confirms Lélène while feeling sorry for the boys who suffered from these developments. While Andrée thinks of herself as "patient" and seemingly indifferent to the extramarital affairs of her companion, she nevertheless recognized that "young women no longer accept when their partners come and go like that, being with someone, leaving, coming back, going with someone else." Leïla (born in 1962), having lived in Paris, emphasized the role of migration and tourism in the evolution of French Caribbean society: "When you have traveled, you see things differently." Andrée agrees: "Before, there was a significant difference between life in mainland France and life here. Now, not so much."

The oldest women rejoiced that they were finally seeing "men investing time in being a father" (Mirette) and "getting the job done" (Claudine, born in 1945). But the younger women surveyed are more sensitive to the difficulty of finding companions who respect them and with whom they can share feelings and activities: "Men no longer respect women. Everything is about sex, and there is no respect," says Clarisse (born in 1975). At the same time, Sophie (born in 1976) says, "We cannot trust men, and that does not change very quickly. They are creating too much suffering." Martine (born in 1969) believes that "it is very rare to find a couple with a normal life," while Clara is saddened by what she sees: "When I look at society or my friends, I see a bunch of women running after something they can't catch. . . . When I look at my grandfather, my father, or my husband, I see a situation that is always repeating itself. There are only a few couples that I know where there is a feeling of osmosis. A couple that works well together, well, there aren't many!"

Women "stand up," and men cannot follow (or do not want to follow) unless they are motivated by a strong sense of love or by strong ethical or religious convictions. The women interviewed felt that it was important to raise girls and boys "the same." But the obstacles and contradictions are also shared by the women themselves. It is not easy to escape one's education. Clara explains her attitude toward her current relationship: "I was raised with the image of an authoritative man. My partner is different, understanding, faithful, and we can count on him. But sometimes I reproach him for being too sweet." Stéphanie (born in 1963) is trying to persuade the young mother of Stéphanie's son's two children that he is still too young to commit and still needs to "frolic." Saddened by the fact that her son had "reduced his sister to his servant," Jeanne concludes, however: "Oppression is beginning to go away. There is a good segment of society that is beginning to see things differently. So it is up to us as moms to be vigilant and instill the right values in our sons."

In the end, these are the challenges facing Caribbean societies and women in their struggle for equality: ending gender-based double standards (like the glorification of the runaway man and the *potomitan* mother), as well as the emotional, educational, and economic consequences of absent fathers and domestic violence.

Notes

1. In Guadeloupe and Martinique, 25 percent of thirty- to sixty-five-year-old women are single parents, versus 3 percent of men of the same age and 10 percent of women in France. See Lise Demougeot, "Femmes et hommes en Martinique: Regards sur la parité aux différents âges de la vie," in *INSEE Analyses Martinique*, no. 17 (March 2017), https://www.insee.fr/fr/statistiques/2650384; and Demougeot, "Femmes et hommes en Guadeloupe: Regards sur la parité aux différents âges de la vie," in *INSEE Analyses Guadeloupe*, no. 19 (March 2017), https://www.insee.fr/fr/statistiques/2650552. In Martinique, 23 percent of women face frequent psychological violence, 7 percent face forced sexuality, 2.6 percent have experienced physical assaults, and 1 percent have experienced death threats. See Nadine Lefaucheur and Elizabeth Brown, "Relations conjugales et configurations parentales à la Martinique," *Politiques sociales et familiales* 106 (2011): 1–16. More than 26 percent of men have several relationships in the same year in Guadeloupe, 22 percent in Martinique, and 12 percent in France. See Sandrine Halfen et al., *Les connaissances, attitudes, croyances et comportements, face au VIH/sida aux Antilles et en Guyane en 2004* (Paris: ANRS-ORSIF, 2006).

2. The 1990s interviews are included in Stéphanie Mulot, "'Je suis la mère, je suis le père!': L'énigme matrifocale; Relations familiales et rapports de sexe en Guadeloupe" (PhD diss., Paris, EHESS, 2000). The interviews from 2009 to 2014 were part of two surveys conducted under the responsibility of Nadine Lefaucheur by the research group Genre et Société aux Antilles (Laboratoire Caribéen de Sciences Sociales, formerly Centre de Recherches sur les Pouvoirs Locaux dans la Caraïbe, Université des Antilles): "Sortir de la violence conjugale: Obstacles et ressources" (2009–10) and "Faire famille à la Martinique" (2013–14). See Nadine Lefaucheur, ed., "Genre et violences interpersonnelles à la Martinique," *Pouvoirs dans la Caraïbe* 17 (2010–11); and Lefaucheur, "Modes de constitution et dynamiques des configurations familiales à la Martinique," 2016, http://colloque.aidelf.org/documents/1569.docx. Life stories were collected by Roger Cantacuzène, Joëlle Kabile, Paola Lavra, Léoncine Ozier-Lafontaine, Clara Palmiste, Myriam Thirot, William Touzane, and Mylenn Zobda-Zebina.
3. Peter Wilson, "Reputation and Respectability: A Suggestion for Caribbean Ethnology," *Man* (1969): 37–53.
4. Nadine Lefaucheur and Stéphanie Mulot, "La construction et les coûts de l'injonction à la virilité en Martinique," in *Boys Don't Cry! Les coûts de la domination masculine*, ed. D. Dulong, C. Guionnet, and E. Neveu (Rennes: Presses Universitaires de Rennes, 2012), 207–29.
5. Stéphanie Mulot, "La matrifocalité n'est pas un mirage créole," *L'homme* 207–8 (2013): 159–91.
6. In 2009, 41 percent of the one thousand women surveyed in the "Gender and Violence in Martinique" survey lived with a partner (two out of three were married), and 25 percent had a "friend" or a "visiting partner"; 22 percent said that their husband or partner was the first and only sexual partner they had. Among the single mothers (29 percent of the women surveyed), 35 percent had a visiting partner, 42 percent were separated or divorced, but 23 percent had never lived with a man for at least six months (Lefaucheur and Brown, "Relations conjugales," 9–23).
7. France Alibar and Pierrette Lembeye-Boy, *Le couteau seul . . . Sé Kouto sèl . . . La condition féminine aux Antilles*, vol. 1, *Enfance et adolescence*, vol. 2, *Vies de femmes* (Éditions Caribéennes, 1981–82).
8. Children who are fathered by a married man (or by a man who lives regularly with a woman) with another woman are usually called *timoun dewô* (outside children).
9. Nadine Lefaucheur, "Situation des femmes, pluripartenariat et violences conjugales aux Antilles," *Informations sociales* 186 (2014): 28–35.
10. Léoncine Ozier-Lafontaine and Nadine Lefaucheur, "Histoires de couples, histoires de violence," *Pouvoirs dans la Caraïbe* 17 (2010–11): 125–60.

11. Joëlle Kabile, "Mais pourquoi ne partent-elles pas?," *Pouvoirs dans la Caraïbe* 17 (2010–11): 161–98.
12. The life story of Viviane was collected in 1979 by Marie-Françoise Le Drian. See Nadine Lefaucheur and Marie-Françoise Le Drian, "Histoires de Marie Lambert," research report (1980); Nadine Lefaucheur, "Maternité extra-conjugale et reproduction sociale," *Annales de Vaucresson* 26 (1987): 181–98.
13. In Mehdi Darlis, *Manman, 43 témoignages en hommage à la femme créole* (Pointe-à-Pitre: Jasor, 2015), 93, 97.
14. On *slammeurs*, see Nathalie Almar, Roger Cantacuzène, and Nadine Lefaucheur, "Pratiques culturelles, production des identités et questionnement des frontières de genre," in *Questions de genre, questions de culture*, ed. Sylvie Octobre (Ministère de la Culture et de la Communication, France, 2014), 75–99.

PART 4 The Dialectics between Body, Nation, and Representation

10

Media and the Politics of "Re-presentation" of the Black Female Body

SARAH FILA-BAKABADIO

In John Akomfrah's documentary *The Stuart Hall Project*, Stuart Hall suggests that he has multiple identities.[1] He is a Jamaican man, an immigrant, and a scholar. Hall discovered that he had built his identity out of these many representations. In Britain his immigrant identity coexists with his colonial, gender, and social identities. He names this process "the reconfiguration of the old."

One could use this analysis to understand visual representations of black women in contemporary France.[2] As the French continue to struggle over the relationship between republican *laïcité* (secularism) and the presence of multicultural and hyphenated identities, more and more images of black female bodies have appeared in the media within the last fifteen years. Whether produced by the cosmetic industry or by black media entrepreneurs, black female bodies are "reconfigured." They combine colonial imageries and stereotypes of African and Caribbean women to represent black women in contemporary France. The media invents a composite body that does not reverse stereotypes but codes them in different terms. For that reason, the black female body continues to be a site of tension and political struggle.[3] Indeed, the representation of black bodies, particularly black female bodies, is entangled with the black populations' outcry for better social and political visibility in contemporary France. I call this phenomenon to "re-present," which means inventing new images of a specific subject (in this case, black women) to modify its social, political, and historical significance.

In the eighteenth century, the black female body was first presented to the French as a slave body later epitomized by the Hottentot Venus. This primary exposure generated signs, discourses, and images that perpetuated the commodification of the black female body.[4] Throughout French history, this phenomenon was repeated over time. However, black populations in contemporary France are now re-presenting: they are attempting to present blackness in their own terms. To be sure, the black female body is entangled with a historical, social, and political conundrum that the 1960s and 1970s women's struggles and current debates on diversity have not addressed. Indeed, contemporary debates about black communities in France ignore the question of visual representations of black women. This phenomenon persists despite new magazines about black women that attempt to redefine black female agency and reconfigure imperial and male-dominated visions of the black female body. In this essay, I explore current depictions of black women in leading French women's magazines, as well as the process of re-presenting black women in magazines that focus exclusively on black women.

Out with the Old?

In *Black Skin, White Masks*, Frantz Fanon refers to "être noir au monde" (being black to the world) as a separation between a black self and an "estranged body" turned into a cover, a "shell" that its inventor, the oppressor, gradually thickened, preventing the black man from seeing who he truly is.[5] While Fanon discusses this process in pathological terms, Achille Mbembé reminds us that being black means having to constantly move between otherness and the self, between forced invisibility and the affirmation of being. It means creating blackness in one's own terms despite the aforementioned condition. Two points emerge from Fanon's analysis. The first one is that black people worldwide have long worked on visibility as a primary tool for recognition. It meant, as the founders of the negritude movement emphasized, exposing the concealed and reversing the stigma to reinvent oneself.

March 2016: a black model is for the first time on the cover of *Elle*, the most widely read French female magazine. Unlike other magazines like *Vogue* and the conservative *Madame le Figaro*, which had already presented international black models such as the Ethiopian Lya Kebede and Alicia Keys, the African American performer, *Elle* reluctantly entered the debate about the invisibility of black bodies in the press. This woman is like other models: young and skinny. She embodies an anonymous Photoshopped vision of womanhood. Her only specificity is her skin color: she is a light-skinned black version of global beauty standards developed by the cosmetics industry. Her features and morphology do not show the diversity of womanhood. She is merely a "colored" variation of a unique and universalized aesthetic code. *Elle* is ambiguous here. Following French racial definitions, this woman would be categorized and identified as "mixed," not black. In 2016 *Elle* finally hired a model of color but did not go as far as hiring someone categorized as black. Instead, it entered the field through the idea of *métissage*, in which hair texture and skin color tell the reader about the persistence of two forms of prejudice. On the one hand, mixed-race people are a form of "in-between" racial selves who could, at times, be acceptable and used as symbols of blackness; on the other, darker-skinned black people are still excluded from the mainstream press.

In 2012, although black journalists, models, and antidiscrimination activists asked *Elle* to better represent racial diversity, the magazine still resisted moving beyond the norms of some universalized whiteness that never fully represented French society.[6] This cover was a crack, not a breach, in the uniform vision of beauty. Within the next weeks, Julia Roberts, Sophie Marceau, and white models were back, reminding black readers that the absence of their bodies in the magazine is still the norm.

Elle's attitude is grounded in a colonial history that not only built whiteness as the unique visual reference but also coded the "other" bodies as "other spaces."[7] In mainstream media, blackness or black people are "zones of nonbeing" whose visibility is problematic whenever it moves away from the margins.[8] *Elle*'s attitude confirms the relentless impact of colonial imagery on our contemporary representations of blackness. Indeed, as Tina Campt mentions, past images shaped a visual lexicon that allows us to think: "We think we see, we think we recognize and therefore know."[9] French popular culture is filled with clichés that composed visual preconceptions of black womanhood shaped during colonial times: women half-naked, standing in front of explorers' cameras; paintings of so-called lascivious African females. These bodies first appeared as dissenting ones that, following the Hottentot Venus, existed through their physicality. They were exposed, scrutinized for scientific purposes, or subjected to the French gaze.

The French discovered black women in images that advertised the greatness of the French Empire. Posters from the *agence des colonies françaises*, stamps, postcards, and photographs from explorers celebrated the enduring civilizing power of France and turned bodies into territories that should be conquered. Each body symbolized a continent or a region. Dressed in traditional outfits (or naked), these bodies helped the French identify geographically and culturally distant places. Women regularly appeared on posters for the traveling colonial exhibitions and the *villages noirs* that toured France in Nantes, Strasbourg, and Orléans. They appeared as powerful amazons dominating tiny black men or as housewives burdened with "savage" traditions who could potentially be freed by the motto *liberté, égalité, fraternité*.

In 1922 a poster from the Imprimeries Mourlot for the colonial exhibition in Marseilles embodied the French perception of black women. Mourlot depicted three characters: two black women and an Asian one. A black woman stands side by side with the Asian girl. She holds the corners of a French flag that floats in the air to protect the women from "savages." They stand on the shores of Africa. Asia meets Africa as subalterns who apparently accept—if not recognize—that France "brought peace and civilization to her 60 million indigenous people."[10] Standing bodies are the symbols of their insertion into the French crucible, which merges diversity into an idealized color-blind republic. On the fringe of the image, the second black woman embodies Africa. She is a female counterpart of the Noir Banania, an excessively smiling and muscular male figure dressed in an outfit that mixes traditions from East and West Africa (male and female clothing, cowries, turban, and a fly whisk). Like the black females in Pierre-Henri Ducos de La Haille's frescos at the Palais de la Porte Dorée in Paris, she is disproportionately smaller than the other characters. Her size signals an internal hierarchy between those who accepted "civilization" and others who remained "backward." Like other colonial designers, Mourlot naturalized black bodies presented along with land resources and animals to illustrate an exotic yet appealing Africa that became visible because of France.

This female version of the *tirailleurs sénégalais* entered the daily lives of the French via a colonial marketing that associated the black body with washing powders, cigarettes, milk, or cocoa; Palmolive, La Perdrix soap bars, Félix Potin's lithographs of Clown Chocolat, and the soap Lessive de la Ménagère coded black characters into the French visual lexicon. What they all have in common is that they have been literally whitewashed, and women were the ones doing that whitewashing. Whether a white woman was cleaning a black child or a black woman was bleaching her "negro" child, women were in charge of making sure children conformed to French norms of civilization, progress, and modernity, in other words, whiteness. Ads replicated clichés about black female physicality derived from scientific racism. Black women appeared as stout women who combined some masculine strength and an exuberant femininity symbolized by large breasts and pelvis.

Black women also symbolized ugliness.[11] In the *Histoire naturelle de l'homme et de la femme*, naturalists and anatomists Georges Cuvier and Georges-Louis Leclerc de Buffon linked territory and beauty as they spanned the physical differences of humanity. According to Buffon, Indian women from the Malabar Coast were beautiful, black and African women were dark and ugly, and some, like the Hottentots, bore a "monstrous" anatomical deformation later labeled stereatopygia.[12] In 2001 the South African historian Zine Magubane considered that the Hottentot Venus had more to do with class issues than with biopolitics, but she was wrong. Colonial images of black women used race and physicality to distance black womanhood from Frenchness.[13]

Colonial images created both estrangement and false proximity. Estrangement emerged from the overdetermination of physical features interpreted as signs of the marginal. Proximity appeared as French people were confronted by these images on a daily basis and therefore felt their eyes had captured the "essence" of a black person, a phenomenon Campt calls the "transparency of the visual."[14] In other words, "I can see it, so it is." Accordingly, fixed racial and gender markers (kinky hair, flat noses, thick lips, large buttocks and breasts, etc.) represent accurate attributes of blackness. They are constructions made out of perceptions, curiosity, and imaginaries that developed a phenomenology of the black body based on racialized appearances and "epidermal encasement."[15]

Here my point is not to linger on the many images colonialism generated but to emphasize that, in debates about black populations in France, this visual heritage has been the first presentation of black females. Colonial images created notions of black womanhood; it developed a visual lexicon through which the black female body is imagined. Even among black populations, many think that large buttocks are attributes of African women. This heritage has not been consistently deconstructed to allow French society and the press to reflect on the representation and lack of representation of black identities. Indeed, as *Elle* demonstrates, the erasure of blackness is still the norm. The press avoids discussing the racialization of black bodies; it ignores the specifics of intersectionality.

In with the New?

Amina, the first Francophone magazine for black women, was born in 1972. The cover was extracted from the now famous *roman-photo* that identifies the magazine. A young nurse was in the forefront, thinking about the doctor standing behind her. A caption allowed readers to read her mind: "Do you love me . . . ?" This was the beginning of the first re-presentation of the black female body in the French public sphere. The black woman was first a romantic teenager who hoped to meet the love of her life. She was a mother-to-be and the keeper of the household. She was a figure whose complexity will again appear through others' eyes, particularly male eyes.

Amina was born out of a historical and geographical detour that connected the colonial and postcolonial eras. It was created in the former capital city of Afrique Occidentale Française (AOF, French West Africa),

Dakar. The monthly magazine was the achievement of Michel de Breteuil, the son of a French entrepreneur who settled in Senegal in 1933. Breteuil's father created the Société Africaine de Publicité et d'Édition Fusionnée (SAFEP), a press group that developed news magazines in the French African colonies. At the dawn of the postcolonial era, Breteuil decided to conquer new markets: female and sports magazines. Referred to "the black woman's magazine," *Amina* presented "desirable" black female bodies: athletes, local designers, and artists became role models for women who were initially referred to as African, Malian, or Congolese but not as black. *Amina* replicated the typical sections of female magazines (fashion, beauty, society) and added an African twist by localizing its stories and portraits in various countries of the former French Empire. Each story contributed to the formation of a modern vision of the African woman: socially engaged, juggling work and family while preserving traditions. *Amina* developed archetypes similar to those of other women's magazines (focus on slender models, Paris-based fashion, the imperative of bodily transformation through makeup and diet, and the need to fit in the role of women as mothers and spouses in traditional African society).

From 1972 to 2001 *Amina* was the only large-scale magazine representing black women in France and in Francophone Africa. It was easily available in newsstands in Dakar, Yaoundé, Paris, Marseilles, and even Fort de France. Black women used it as a reference guide to imagine and reinvent themselves as postcolonial subjects. Yet the context from which it originated deeply impacted its contents. Indeed, despite a genuine interest in African cultures and peoples, *Amina* proposed an archetypal image of womanhood that needed to visually conform to Western standards of beauty. Paris and France remained the undisputed standard for high arts, fashion, and modernity. Africa embodied traditions. Still, *Amina* circulated images of black women within Africa, allowing women to discover other cultures. Bodies identified countries; they typified cultures (Mandingo, Pulaar, etc.) and generated a cartography of beauty practices in postcolonial Africa, including the diversity of clothes, head-wrapping techniques, and beadwork or braiding styles meant to represent the specifics of each new nation. But this vision was not devoid of colonial representations.

The magazine celebrated the diversity of cultures but interpreted some African aesthetic practices as "traditional," thereby perpetuating stereotypical visions of Africa.

In 1976 the magazine relocated its headquarters in Paris and developed Caribbean and French editions. It regularly discussed local and global social issues like excision, the gender glass ceiling, and the emergence of black communities in France. Yet it avoided questioning the visual heritage of colonialism. Black women were re-presented. Their images were silent exposés of consigned bodies whose meaning was determined by their relationship to the same dominant group: white Frenchmen. They continued to be disruptive spaces for which beauty could only appear when it conformed to Western standards.

Amina allowed black female bodies to be visible in the French public sphere. It contributed to a visualization of black womanhood, but it never interrogated why a fair-skinned woman should be more desirable or why having "bad hair" is not only a styling issue. It did not explore the aesthetic and normative "apparatuses" that generated racial categorizations and influenced black women's self-representations.[16] It did not discuss the role of images in the internalization of racial prejudice, nor did it refer to intersectionality to explain the multiplicity of black women's identities and experiences. Rather, Caribbean, African, and Afro-French became the "articulated parts" of an unnamed operating racial category: black.[17]

This first re-presentation of the black female body in contemporary France goes with a second one: an African American one. In the early 1970s, like the investors who founded *Essence,* Breteuil was interested in exploring an economic niche. Interestingly, this economic incentive affected the representation of black women. Despite the SAFEP backing, *Amina* needed funding to support the dozen freelance journalists who wrote about forty articles each month. Publicizing the new collection of a tailor in Yaoundé or *centres de la beauté noire* in the Parisian Château Rouge and Château d'Eau was not enough to allow the magazine to exist and expand. International trademarks like L'Oréal and Estee Lauder originally refused to invest in an all-black magazine. Apparently, they thought that the black beauty market did not exist in France or in Francophone Africa.

Until the mid-1980s, *Amina* mainly received financial support from African American cosmetic companies like Softsheen-Carson, Naomi Sims, Palmer's, and Flori Roberts. But with funding came reconfigurations of the black French woman's body based on American aesthetic codes. Indeed, they replicated aesthetic codes developed in the 1920s by Madame C. J. Walker, who used the transformation of the female body as a tool for economic empowerment.[18] In each of *Amina*'s one-hundred-page issues, ads from TCB, Optimum Care, Ambi, and Ultra Sheen recalled Walker's preparations: body butters, relaxing creams, hair conditioners, bleaching soaps, brushing powders, and hair-growth balms featured prominently. The products and slogans were the same as those of the 1920s, when Walker reassured dark-skinned customers that they could be attractive too.

American trademarks exported a visual rhetoric that responded to a governmentality of bodies that crystallized with slavery and segregation. They proposed a black aesthetic that had empowered African Americans in the United States. Indeed, in a white supremacist climate, straightening one's hair, thanks to Dark and Lovely's lye-free conditioner, offered African Americans a positive image.[19]

As effective as this strategy was in the United States throughout the twentieth century, these images reflected the lived experiences of people who were forced to confront racism as their main political, social, and ascriptional uniting feature. In France, from slavery in the Caribbean and La Réunion to colonization in Africa, racism or notions of racial similarity have never been uniting factors. Antiblack racism emerged from various forms of political violence entrenched in different laws (the Code Noir, Code de l'Indigénat), legal statuses (slaves, *libres de couleur*, colonized subjects, migrants, so-called second-generation), and diverse social practices. Therefore, the multiplicity and flexibility of histories, identities, and cultures (Martinican, Congolese, Réunionese, Afro-French, diasporan, etc.) frame a multiscaled pattern of race that has only recently been addressed.

Nonetheless, commercial images of black women introduced *Amina*'s readership to race. It allowed readers to make a connection between race and nation. Simultaneously, the African American influence helped insert black women in France into a race-based global visual referential and solidified their position as a racial minority in France, a phenomenon that is still debated.

Re-presenting Again

The black feminine press in contemporary France often ignores the legacy of the colonial period and embraces, uncritically, an African American vision of black womanhood. Since 2001 *Amina* has been competing with new magazines. Indeed, there are at least twelve black magazines in France. The African American and celebrity-focused *Miss Ebène* and *Black Beauty*, *Culture Femme*, *Divas*, and *Première Dame* and the Vogue-like *FashizBlack* are among the most popular ones. Although these magazines praise black aesthetics, they encourage women to transform themselves via wigs, weaves made with Indian hair, and fake lashes. Imitations of Michelle Obama's style, Rihanna's outfit, or Beyoncé's "empowered" womanism color their pages. However, few black French women appear in these magazines; actress Aïssa Maïga, journalist Audrey Pulvar, and former minister of justice Christiane Taubira are the few homegrown role models.

Like magazines in the United States during the twentieth century, most of these magazines were founded by black men who targeted an economic niche without caring about promoting gender and racial equality. In 2001, when Almamy Lô and Achille Tobbo, two French African entrepreneurs, created *Miss Ebène*, "the magazine of the modern woman," they did not think about its social and political impact. Rather, for the sake of profits, they used models who conformed to Western standards. Funded by American partners, Lô and Tobbo literally imported images and codes from the United States. Articles on celebrities like Halle Berry, Kanye West, Serena Williams, and Solange Knowles appeared with ads from Black Up and Cover Girl. In other words, the magazine invited readers to imitate African Americans by mimicking their styles. But the ordinary life and concerns of black women in France were barely mentioned. Lô and Tobbo, like the founders of *Black Beauty*, never considered searching for local models who could represent the experiences of black women in France. Yet their economic endeavor is quite successful. In 2015 *Miss Ebène* sold more than 20,000 copies, while *Amina* peaked at only 7,555 copies.[20]

In 2001 Tobbo declared that *Miss Ebène* would provide positive images of black people.[21] However, these images come from the American cosmetics industry. They do not include black French women. The magazine praises African American popular artists but shuns Francophone African and Caribbean stars like Fally Ipupa, Elie Kuame, Owl, and Inyü, a band that mixes their African and French cultures to create a new "Afropolitan" musical genre. Black French subjects only appear occasionally. They figure in the press when a major film features a black actor like Omar Sy or to refer to the yearly beauty fairs like Boucles d'Ebène, where local trademarks such as Noire Ô naturel compete with international trademarks like Iman Cosmetics.[22] *Miss Ebène*'s re-presentation of the black body embodies the African American vision of blackness; it does not connect people of African and Caribbean descent to France.

Other magazines have tried to oppose this still male-oriented and African American vision of the black woman in France. *Culture Femme* and *Kabibi*, magazines recently founded by black women in France, fall into this category.[23] They seek to represent the black French woman's experience in her own terms. But unlike *Miss Ebène* and *Amina*, they seem to be fully aware that the black feminine press is a small and fragmented market.

Kabibi illustrates how contemporary black media entrepreneurs explore the cultural and social experiences of African and Afro-descendant women in France. The magazine informs readers about cultural trends in Francophone and Anglophone Africa, discusses the evolution of African social practices like the *tontine* (informal communal savings account), and promotes young designers from Africa and from the African diaspora in Europe. It was founded in 2010 by a Kinshasa native who insists on publicizing the works of artists and designers. Within the last six years, *Kabibi* has promoted the Congolese (DCR) fashion designer Tina Lobondi, who lives in London; the French Congolese shoe designer Natty Ngoy; Medhi Slimani, the Moroccan designer of the "made in Africa" sneaker; and the Paris-based furniture designer Myriam Maxo. Celebrities like Aïssa Maïga and Lupita Nyongo'o are mentioned but are seldom the magazine's focus. As in *Culture Femme*, the incentive to gain readership. Articles on sterility, sexual abuse, labor relations, religion in the family, regional identities, and money matters fill the pages. Models are young and about to be famous, not yet Photoshopped. In discourses and in visual productions, from the featured designers to the artists and the journalists, the magazine celebrates *métissages* and diversity in Africa and the African diaspora. It presents black French womanhood as a combination of African, French, and European identities. *Kabibi* offers a contemporary vision of distinct and diverse African and diasporan identities associated with a France-based racialized minority ascription. It does not represent an imagined, abstract, or imported notion of black womanhood.

However, *Kabibi* is influenced by African magazines. Following Nigerian and South African female magazines like *Arise*, *Kabibi* moves Africa away from its consignment as a land of origins. Instead, Africa appears as a place where dynamic cultural, artistic, and aesthetic production can rejuvenate the practices of African people in Europe. While *Miss Ebène* exposes some global blackness built in a circulation between France and the United States, in which black French femininity is a derivative of an American one, *Kabibi* explores a transnational sense of belonging that mixes various cultures, ascriptions, and histories. It questions race as an essentialized tool that constrains the existence and positionality of the black female in France. As it weaves South African fashion, Afro-American cosmetic practices, and French habits into numerous articles, the magazine reinvents the black female body, placing it at the center of a cosmopolitan geography of belonging where references, images, and discourses jointly explore diversity and commonalities.

Conclusion: Negotiation

Images matter. Images structure our vision of the world and of others. The black female body entered French society via images from the French colonial gaze and, recently, via the black feminine press. Images have framed black women's social, political, and aesthetic positionality. Images often present black women in a complicated manner. That said, the black feminine press participates in the repositioning of black women from the margins of a white-based beauty market to a new multiethnic one that allows black, Arabic, or Asian women to imagine what they want to look like. Consequently, "women of color," particularly black women, develop their own visual rhetoric. Through notions of blackness imported from the United States, Africa, and the Caribbean, as well as references to black celebrities and global/transnational black cultures, the black feminine press reinvents the black French female body in its own terms.

This emerging market expands Stuart Hall's interrogation on the self. Out of his reflection on negotiated identities, he came across the body as a site for this negotiation. He understood that his body was the space for the encounter of the old and the new. It is the space for the reconfiguration of exogenous and past images as much as for the collection of new ones from the diaspora and for the production of composite images that represent his cultural and historical "here" (Britain) and "there" (Jamaica). The same goes for images of black women's bodies in France. They are sites of negotiation between the colonial past and the contemporary era, which is marked by a growing interest in connected selves, traveling identities, and transnational identities.[24] The next step might be to engage in a critical (and maybe a black French feminist) discussion on intersectionality so that re-presenting would mean not only visualizing again but also embodying black womanhood in contemporary France.

Notes

1. John Akomfrah, *The Stuart Hall Project* (London: Smoking Dogs Film, 2013).
2. The expression "black women" here should be understood as women categorized as black. For convenience, I will use this expression throughout.
3. For a discussion focusing on the representation of the black female body in previous decades, particularly the interwar period, see Brett Berliner, *Ambivalent Desire: The Exotic Black Other in Jazz-Age France* (Amherst: University of Massachusetts Press, 2002).
4. See T. Denean Sharpley-Whiting, *Black Venus: Sexualized Savages, Primal Fears, and Primitive Narratives in French* (Durham NC: Duke University Press, 1999).
5. Frantz Fanon, *Peau noire, masques blancs* (1952; Paris: Gallimard, Folio Essais, 1971), 60. For "shell," see Achille Mbembé, *Critique de la raison nègre* (Paris: La Découverte, 2013), 67.
6. On January 13, 2012, a heated debate arose between beauty bloggers, journalists, and readers, on the one hand, and *Elle*, on the other. A staff journalist, Nathalie Dolivo, used a series of clichés to describe "black fashion power." *Elle* first refused

to address the racist orientation of the article. A few weeks later, the chief editor clumsily apologized both for the article and for the lack of concern with its black readership. Sonia Rolland, Rokhaya Diallo, Noémie Lenoir, Audrey Pulvar, and China Moses, "A quand une femme noire en couverture de 'Elle'?," *Le Monde.fr*, January 31, 2012, http://www.lemonde.fr/idees/article/2012/01/. The only recent example of racial diversity is Christiane Taubira, then minister of justice. She was on the cover of the magazine in November 2013. However, it had more to do with her political achievements and the racist attacks she had to stand up to than with the representation of blackness in the public space.

7. Michel Foucault, "Of Other Spaces" (1967), *Diacritics* 16, no. 1 (1986): 22–27.
8. Lewis R. Gordon, "Through the Zone of Nonbeing: A Reading of *Black Skin, White Masks* in Celebration of Fanon's Eightieth Birthday," *C. L. R. James Journal* 11, no. 1 (Summer 2005): 1–43.
9. Tina M. Campt, *Image Matters: Archive Photography and the African Diaspora in Europe* (Durham NC: Duke University Press, 2013), 127.
10. Slogan on a poster for the 1931 colonial exhibition in Paris titled *C'est avec 76.900 hommes que la France . . .* , B. Milleret.
11. Georges-Louis Leclerc de Buffon, Georges Cuvier, et al., *Histoire naturelle de l'homme et de la femme: D'après nos plus grands naturalistes / Buffon, Cuvier, Lacépède, Viret, etc.* (Paris: Armand-Aubrée, 1834), 221.
12. Leclerc de Buffon et al., *Histoire naturelle*, 222.
13. Zine Magubane, "Which Bodies Matter? Feminism, Poststructuralism, Race, and the Curious Theoretical Odyssey of the 'Hottentot Venus,'" *Gender and Society* 15, no. 6 (December 2001): 816–34.
14. Campt, *Image Matters*, 127.
15. Fanon, *Peau noire, masques blancs*, 90.
16. Michel Foucault in Giorgio Agamben, *What Is an Apparatus and Other Essays* (2006; Stanford CA: Stanford University Press, 2009), 2.
17. Stuart Hall, "Race, Articulation and Societies Structured in Dominance," in *Sociological Theories: Race and Colonialism*, ed. UNESCO (Paris: UNESCO, 1980), 305–45.
18. On Madame C. J. Walker's role in the black beauty industry, see Susannah Waker, *Style and Status: Selling Beauty to African American Women, 1920–1975* (Lexington: University Press of Kentucky, 2007).
19. Amina Mama, *Beyond the Masks: Race, Gender and Subjectivity* (London: Routledge, 1996), 11.
20. *Miss Ebène* prints about 75,000 copies and affirms selling about 25,000 each year. *Amina*'s sales have gradually declined: 8 percent in France and 10.3 percent worldwide

in 2015. It prints about 40,000 copies worldwide but only sold 19,000. Source: Association pour le Contrôle de la Diffusion des Médias.

21. Statement included in the first issue of *Miss Ebène*. It replicated part of John H. Johnson's 1989 description of *Ebony*: "In a world of despair, we wanted to give HOPE. In a world of negative Black images, we wanted to provide POSITIVE Black images. In a world that said Blacks could do few things, we wanted to say they could do EVERYTHING" (John H. Johnson and Lerone Bennett Jr., *Succeeding against the Odds: The Autobiography of a Great American Businessman* [Chicago: Johnson Publishing Company, 1989], 1).
22. Boucles d'Ebène was created in 2005. It celebrated its ten-year anniversary in 2015, turning the fair into a European gathering for beauty, culture, cuisine, media, and design.
23. *Culture Femme* was created in 2005. It stopped publishing in 2007 because of a lack of funding, reappeared in newsstands in 2012, and disappeared again in 2014.
24. See Stuart Hall, "Cultural Identity and Diaspora," in *Everyday Theory: A Contemporary Reader*, ed. Becky McLaughlin and Bob Coleman (New York: Pearson, 2005), 295–307.

11

Shaking the Racial and Gender Foundations of France

The Influences of "Sarah Baartman" in the Production of Frenchness

ROBIN MITCHELL

Writing about how black women negotiated the boundaries of patriarchy and racism in France is a compelling project, even more so when one understands that 1848, the final end of slavery in France, represented a reimagining of racial and gender identities, one that had begun well before that time period.[1] Yet if black women (or representations of them) have been discussed, they are usually viewed in a vacuum, with little analysis of how they fit together historically or what they can tell us about France over longer periods of cultural and national reinvention. The following narrative, purported to be from the mouth of a black woman named Sarah Baartman, is only one example of the production of the black female body via a white male hand. At the same time, Baartman becomes a useful example to use in understanding how the French "produced themselves" via a subjectivity and then a citizenship based upon whiteness and maleness, one that was both hypervisible and invisible in the definitions of Frenchness. By investigating Baartman's early discursive importance in France proper, I hope to illuminate important correlations between the production of black female bodies, French subjectivity, and French citizenship. When I refer to the production of these bodies, I mean the manipulation and (mis) appropriation of so-called black female identities by white French men. It is critical that we understand these processes of delegitimization so that we are able to see why subsequent struggles for black female equality in France have been so fraught. This essay argues that black women were useful in, and exploited for, articulating what it meant to be French. I highlight this by examining how one contemporary French writer appropriated the life and the voice of arguably the most famous—or infamous—black woman in France in the first half of the nineteenth century, a young South African named Sarah Baartman.

At first glance it might appear that not much more can be gleaned from the dizzying number of writings already about Baartman.[2] Indeed, Clifton Crais and Pamela Scully in *Sara Baartman and the Hottentot Venus: A Ghost Story and a Biography* offer the most thorough and nuanced historical study of Sarah Baartman to date.[3] Yet Crais and Scully sometimes assign too much agency to Baartman herself, neglecting the ways that the cultural production of Baartman by white French men worked to alleviate their own lack of control after the loss of the Haitian Revolution. Among other Baartman scholars, a serious reflection on the intersection of race, sexuality, and nation seems to elude Crais and Scully.[4] Indeed, Z. S. Strother's "Display of the Body Hottentot" represents a strong historical study of Sarah Baartman. Yet Strother claims that to her contemporaries, Baartman was seen as neither "black nor sexy." Moreover, Strother states that the gaze at Baartman was, in effect, "antierotic." I disagree; it is clear that some observers found her to be "unsexy." However, race was critical in her overall construction; furthermore, the so-called scientific gaze allowed all gazes directed toward her to *seem* antierotic and thus acceptable. In addition, Strother notes that Baartman could "never actually threaten the viewer with the sexual power of a 'Venus.'" Again, I disagree; the anxiety over interracial relationships and the fanaticism in developing racial categorizations belie that argument (deemed necessary by the proliferation of multiracial children produced in the French colonies, for instance), hence the need to make her seem so sexually repulsive.[5]

I, on the other hand, hope to shed light on the intersection of race, sexuality, and nation by discussing her rhetorical presence in France in a new way. Historians such as David Bell have addressed French national identity in the eighteenth century, and there is scholarship on nationalism in the late nineteenth century, specifically affected by the trauma of the Franco-Prussian War.[6] But there is little for the period immediately following the Haitian Revolution through the second abolition of slavery in France in 1848. This is particularly curious given the collective hand-wringing and self-examination that normally follow a loss of such magnitude—especially since this loss came at the hands of so-called racial inferiors. I link Baartman to Haiti and the ongoing crisis of French identity after that devastating loss, and I highlight how white French men shored up white male subjectivity at a time of crisis via a type of racial and gender mimicry. These anxieties are critically tied to feelings and questions about national identity and belonging.

On January 1, 1804, after more than a decade of fighting, the French sugar colony of Saint-Domingue declared itself the Republic of Haiti, though France would refuse to acknowledge this significant development until the 1830s. This loss, together with the occupation of revolutionary France by European armies, meant that a once-conquering nation had now become a conquered one. Haiti represented an economic loss, a political defeat, and a weakening of cultural prestige. Dismissively called the "troubles" by many contemporary French men and women, the Haitian Revolution brought notions of citizenship and national identity into question. As Krishan Kumar writes, "Nations are formed of national memories, of the stories of great men and great deeds. . . . But it is not just triumphs and glory but also, and perhaps more so, defeats and trials that make the nation."[7] The defeat in Saint-Domingue and the subsequent loss of the colony had both tremendous economic and geopolitical impacts on France.[8] In a nation of well over twenty-five million, there were never more than a few thousand black women in early nineteenth-century metropolitan France, yet images of and discussions about them appear repeatedly across several milieux.[9] This process occurred first through the manufacturing of black female identity as savage and hypersexual, a phenomenon rooted in the French encounter with African people in France's black colonies. It continued on French soil. In both spaces, black women embodied a threat to French national integrity and purity.[10]

We know little of the real Sarah Baartman, not even her actual name. She was born fifty miles north of the Gamtoos River in the 1770s. According to musicologist Percival Kirby, Baartman was smuggled out of South Africa in April 1810 by Hendrik Cesars without knowledge of the governor.[11] Aboard ship or perhaps prior, Cesars entered into a partnership of sorts with surgeon Alexander Dunlop, who sold his "stake" in Baartman in London. Dunlop, Cesars, and Baartman sailed from Cape Town and arrived in Chatham, England, in July that year.[12] The contract—if indeed there was one—stated that she was to be given a portion of the proceeds from her exhibition and repatriated to South Africa after a period of two years.[13] But Dunlop died in July 1812, and Cesars's whereabouts were unknown. It appears Baartman traveled with various shows until Henry Taylor took her to France.[14] By then, she had ceased being Sarah Baartman and had become the pejorative "Hottentot Venus."

Arriving in Paris in September 1814, a decade after the proclamation of independent Haiti and only months after Napoleon's abdication, Baartman offered a titillating cultural distraction from French imperial defeat. She was used in France in ways that were quite different from those in London, where she had been a mere spectacle of exoticism. Her display, treatment, and representation embodied continuing French anger and anxiety over the loss of its first colonial empire.[15] In literature, plays, photography, art, and other forms of cultural expression, the French used Baartman to depict their country as a conquering nation and to resolve pervasive anxieties after the defeat in Haiti. Their sense of dislocation is revealed in the mechanisms they deployed to appropriate her voice and body. She was also repackaged and sold as an important reminder—perhaps even a cautionary tale—for returning aristocratic émigrés and newly arrived colonial refugees. Furthermore, her availability to be viewed meant that one could use her body, either for fantasy or as a substitute to articulate those fantasies, without personal accountability. She seemed to invite the gaze, even as she allegedly repelled the viewer—flagrant public seminudity, which she was said to have endorsed, was proof of her corruption. Since Baartman existed both in flesh and in discourse, the distinctions between the two are often murky. But while she is a subject for me, she was an *object* for them. For this reason, I reiterate that none of the writing to which I now turn—and that claims to be from Baartman—is actually her own.

One of the more extreme efforts to manipulate Baartman's identity flowed from the pen of Charles-Joseph Colnet (1768–1832). Colnet was a former royal exile, a journalist, a poet, a bookseller, and a well-known writer of French satire. A longtime contributor to the *Journal de Paris* and the *Gazette de France* and an outspoken critic of Napoleon, he made a habit of speaking about the juiciest and most topical happenings of the day. In November 1814 a series of fake satiric letters written by Colnet appeared in the *Journal de Paris* (he signed them simply with a *C*). They would be republished as a consolidated letter in 1825, when Colnet chose the best work from his journals for a book titled *L'hermite du faubourg Saint-Germain*.[16] The first purported letter from Baartman to spring from Colnet's pen appeared on November 7, 1814, in the *Journal de Paris*. Titled "Sartjee ou la Vénus hottentote a [*sic*] son cousin," it began, "My friend, I am happy here as I was bored in London. The Paris air suits kind women. . . . It is agreed that everyone rushes to see Sartjee. These people are not disgusted."[17] These musings had one thing right: although her time in Paris was brief, she cast a large metaphorical shadow.[18] That Baartman claimed to have been "bored" in London is absurd, since a highly public court case brought about by British abolitionists to determine her slave or free status would have been anything but "boring." That she makes mention of the fact that the French people are not "disgusted" by her is a nod to that court case, undertaken on her behalf (and during which people were disgusted for a variety of reasons), and it foreshadows that the French, in fact, were also disgusted by her. That understanding by Colnet's readers—of which Baartman is made to seem unaware—will become achingly clear.

In the letter, "Baartman" believed that even if the French sometimes "forget their natural lightness" and were sometimes prone to melancholy, "they are lively, irascible . . . and their vengeance is not cruel." That was true, with the exception of "certain individuals who had abused their privilege as powerful men to oppress and harm others."[19] Clearly directing her second letter at Napoleon Bonaparte and those who followed him, she asserts, "They have been run off in shame, much milder punishment for those who, for a long time, have undone themselves in matters of honor." "Baartman" ends her letter with the following praise of the French, who allowed Bonaparte to escape ultimate punishment: "This trait alone was enough to critique to you a nation of which many good things could be said if one set out to illustrate its good qualities rather than its poor ones" (Letter 2). As the fictive Baartman writes, "The chief of glory of these brave men, the man their courage and good fortune elevated to the highest point of glory and power," saw his role "more philosophically," losing "the most beautiful empire in the world, and he is enjoying the best of health" (Letter 2). This "most beautiful of empires"—France's glorious First Empire—had been lost, including, of course, the wealth-producing Saint-Domingue. Colnet here channels this rancor directly at Napoleon. As ousted leader, he becomes an easy scapegoat for a myriad of military and thus imperial failures.

Colnet as Baartman threw down the gauntlet, for France was fighting for its political and cultural future. But as she also admonished her "cousin," "too many bad things have been said about the French" (Letter 2). France might have real problems, she writes, but at least it is populated by honorable "warriors," not "idle" ones like the Hottentots and Marmotes (Letter 2)—warriors who were fearless to the point of recklessness, sometimes fanatically worried about advancement in rank, and so committed to displaying their bravery that those who came home unwounded or even alive felt the shame of letting down their country. If Colnet/Baartman's letter is to be believed, French men certainly need, if not saving, then at least a stern talking to. Here her focus turns to Frenchmen, the war, the role of journalists, and the potential failures of the French nation. On the one hand, they care about defending France; on the other, personal advancement colors their judgment. Racialized others, like "Hottentots and Marmotes," were at least fearless. What had happened to Frenchmen?

This anxiety concerning French male effeminacy and weakness also played out in Baartman's musings. These tensions would have been even more apparent following a staggering military loss like the one in Haiti. Baartman's letters included the salacious details of a sex scandal brought on by an angry husband whose effort to shame his wife backfired. The court decided that it was his lack of virility and masculinity that had led his wife astray; furthermore, his own impotent (and visible) actions prevented even the possibility of finding another woman. As the imaginary construct of Baartman portrays him, "The husband hardly dares to show his face in public, and it is no surprise: women would tear his eyes out to avenge the honor of their sex" (Letter 1). Furthermore, he was publicly admonished to show more confidence and less jealousy in the future. It is clear that the wife had strayed. It is also clear that everyone knew it. But the shame lay not with the adulterous wife or the duplicitous suitor but with the whiny and incompetent husband. Another message: a woman can step out of acceptable gender roles briefly, but only to ensure suitable behavior—a proper marriage, for instance, or to cheat if her husband is not manly enough to put a stop to it, or, worse still, to tear apart a weak man who dared insult her. But while Frenchwomen keep the men in line, the problem that some men *need* to be kept in line remained.

The rhetoric of the ineffectual French man simultaneously impacted representations of white French women—often portrayed as shrewd, surreptitious, and silly. While white French men were unsuccessfully fighting a war (for something actually worthy of men: France's very future as a major European power), French women, according to the faux Baartman's first letter, were engaged in an inexplicable war of their own: a "war of hats." Whereas French women wore theirs so high that one "must stand on tiptoe" to touch the top, English women wore theirs so low that they were barely able to see. Patriotism is bungled in French women's hands: in order to prove their national loyalty, they "coif themselves to frighten in order to better prove [that loyalty]" (Letter 2). So acrimonious did the ludicrous altercation between French and English women become that it threatened to start an actual war—the government almost had to intervene.

The highly gendered subject matters in the two letters pitted frivolous but powerful French women, competing with each other in fashion, against honorable, ambitious, but broken French men. From this perspective, it is possible to discern Colnet's rather misogynist critique: French masculinity was at risk because the women were fighting their own war—in their tall hats. To make matters worse, French women were refusing cultural directives to stay in the private sphere where they belonged. Men's actual warfare (and their subsequent defeat) is displaced to misbehaving women and their towering *chapeaux*, reminding French men of their own emasculated military and social status. The fact that this ridiculous cultural "war" was happening against the British Empire is telling of recurring French fears of being eclipsed by England. The rallying call for French nationalism was against a common enemy, but such patriotism was bungled in French women's hands. Fashion trends were usurping national concerns. The fictional Baartman's critique was not only a call for the regulation of white French women's capricious and misguided attempts to protect the nation but an indictment of the situation that necessitated such behavior. Baartman tells her cousin that this latest fad compelled her to tell her new French friends to stop this foolishness and to adopt Hottentot fashion, again placing her in a position of commenting on French behavior. Baartman's position outside French society allowed Colnet to tell his compatriots to also "stop this foolishness."

Given that Colnet was such a critic of Napoleon (under surveillance by the Paris police, no less), it is perhaps unsurprising that he would hide his identity. What is telling is that he chose to veil himself behind the persona of a black woman. Colnet (re)invented the black female Baartman to protect himself and to criticize his opponents by telling the stories of white French men and women behaving badly. In this new version of history, masterminded by Colnet, Baartman both "saves" the nation from inept men such as Napoleon and reinscribes a Frenchness based upon "true" virile white French masculinity. In the end, the fictional Baartman's missive to her cousin allowed the aristocratic Colnet to make fun of the men who flaunted their military service and honor, even in the nation's defeat. Because he placed his missives in the mouth of a black woman, Colnet's words would have stung more deeply. The obvious unsuitability of Baartman to be making such observations allowed Colnet to shame his compatriots while hiding behind her darkness.

Colnet's fake letters using Baartman hit upon issues of politics, economics, culture, and class, and they highlight how fraught new and rapidly changing definitions of Frenchness could be in the aftermath of the Haitian

Revolution. We can still see some larger factors that stood out, even with additional examples, well into the nineteenth century. The Haitian Revolution produced economic, political, cultural, and class disasters for France. My work highlights one early way that France manufactured paths of inequality for women of African descent (in this case, Sarah Baartman) by proxy. This was done by crafting depictions of women like her as patently un-French, setting the stage for later representations that were further invigorated by the French colonial project. White French inhabitants saw her presence in France as much-needed confirmation of their own racial superiority. This in turn reminded them (in the midst of the ongoing dialogue about Haiti) that if recapturing Haiti was possible, then a strong France was still possible. Baartman allowed France to see itself as a conquering nation again at a time of military and economic weakness and now bereft of its most important colony. One way to do this was to use her to speak about the very struggles of equality and identity that the French loss in Saint-Domingue precipitated. One such project set black women like Sarah Baartman (excluded from the French body politic based upon both her race and her gender) so far outside the boundaries of French civilized behaviors that only a strong French colonial empire (and fervent colonial subjects) could control women like her.

White French men had already prostituted Baartman for money. Here she is prostituted as antithetical to what French national identity needed to be while it attempted to shore up white subjectivity at a time of crisis. White insiders could critique their own society while they were hidden behind another body, making the racial and gendered transvestism all the more potent because of supposed insider knowledge. Black women like Baartman remained essential in forwarding the discourse about race, gender, sexuality, and class in France. My work, then, even as it addresses previously excluded bodies, should be seen as part of an ongoing conversation about Frenchness and French national identity, since Monarchy, Revolution, Republic, and Empire each required separate visions of Frenchness. They were not the same visions, nor did they remain static. Investigating the significance of black women illuminates heretofore overlooked, yet important, correlations between the depiction and manipulation of black female bodies, on the one hand, and French subjectivity and citizenship, on the other. The traumatic loss of Saint-Domingue was displaced in a manner and onto a racialized body that simplified a far more complex range of experiences and identities. I do not mean to imply that whites were not "raced" or racialized. Their reluctance to see themselves as such or to acknowledge their hegemonic position does not make it less so. It actually strengthens my argument that Frenchness required unacknowledged whiteness as a racial identity. Nowhere is this better exemplified than in the story of Sarah Baartman. These linkages afford us new avenues of interpretation and discovery.

Notes

1. I look at these issues more deeply in my forthcoming book project, "*Vénus noire*: Black Women, Colonial Fantasies, and the Production of Gender and Race in France, 1750–1850," currently under contract with the University of Georgia Press.
2. See Claude Blanckaert, ed., *La Vénus hottentote: Entre Barnum et Muséum* (Paris: Publications Scientifiques du Muséum National d'Histoire Naturelle, 2013); Henri de Blainville in "Sur une femme de la race hottentote," *Bulletin des sciences par la société philomatique de Paris* (1816): 183–90; and Georges Cuvier, "Extrait d'observations faites sur le cadavre d'une femme connue à Paris et à Londres sous le nom de Vénus Hottentotte," *Mémoires de Muséum d'Histoire Naturelle* 3 (1817). See also Anne Fausto-Sterling, "Gender, Race and Nation: The Comparative Anatomy of 'Hottentot' Women in Europe: 1815–1817," in *Deviant Bodies: Critical Perspectives on Difference in Science and Popular Culture*, ed. Jennifer Terry and Jacqueline Urla (Bloomington: Indiana University Press, 1995). Bernth Lindfors offers useful information on Baartman and other blacks in "'The Hottentot Venus' and Other African Attractions in Nineteenth-Century England," *Australasian Drama Studies* 1 (1983); and Lindfors, "Ethnological Show Business: Footlighting the Dark Continent," in *Freakery: Cultural Spectacles of the Extraordinary Body*, ed. Rosemarie Garland Thomson (New York: New York University Press, 1996). See also François-Xavier Fauvelle-Aymar, *L'invention du Hottentot: Histoire du regard occidental sur les Khoisan, XVe–XIXe siècle* (Paris: Publications de la Sorbonne, 2002).
3. Clifton C. Crais and Pamela Scully, *Sara Baartman and the Hottentot Venus: A Ghost Story and a Biography* (Princeton NJ: Princeton University Press, 2009).
4. Percival Kirby deserves credit for bringing Baartman to historical attention, particularly as early as he did; however, he must also be recognized as continuing a strategy of (re)making her into a public spectacle ripe for the titillated gaze. Thus

his writings, however important, must be read both cautiously and critically. See "The Hottentot Venus," *Africana Notes and News* 6, no. 3 (June 1949): 55–62; Kirby, "La Venus hottentote en Angleterre," *Æsculape* 16 (January 1952); Kirby, "More about the Hottentot Venus," *Africana Notes and News* 10, no. 4 (1953); Kirby, "The 'Hottentot Venus' of the *Musée de l'Homme*, Paris," *South African Journal of Science* 50, no. 12 (July 1954); and Kirby, "A Further Note on the 'Hottentot Venus,'" *Africana Notes and News* 11, no. 5 (December 1954).

5. Z. S. Strother, "Display of the Body Hottentot," in *Africans on Stage: Studies in Ethnological Show Business*, ed. Bernth Lindfors (Bloomington: Indiana University Press, 1999).
6. David Avrom Bell, *The Cult of the Nation in France: Inventing Nationalism, 1680–1800* (Cambridge MA: Harvard University Press, 2001). See also Eric J. Hobsbawm, *Nations and Nationalism since 1780: Programme, Myth, Reality*, 2nd ed. (Cambridge: Cambridge University Press, 1990). For many historians, the Revolutionary Decade forms an almost impenetrable barrier, with scholarship falling squarely on either side (or narrowly within). By contrast, my work looks at how the efflorescence of colonial slavery and plantation society and the culture production of race and gendered discourse in Saint-Domingue on the eve of the Revolution offer categories of understanding that will be reiterated in the Napoleonic and Restoration eras.
7. Krishan Kumar, "English and French National Identity: Comparisons and Contrasts," *Nations and Nationalism* 12, no. 3 (2006): 3.
8. Historians of Saint-Domingue and modern-day Haiti have provided compelling histories detailing the importance of the Haitian Revolution in the history of France. They have illuminated how the Revolution redefined and restructured notions of citizenship, as well as France's part in the larger Atlantic World. This work builds upon and incorporates this scholarship, asking how knowledge of Haiti can tell us something more about France itself. For some general histories, see Laurent Dubois, *Avengers of the New World: The Story of the Haitian Revolution* (Cambridge MA: Harvard University Press, 2004); Dubois, *A Colony of Citizens: Revolution & Slave Emancipation in the French Caribbean, 1787–1804* (Chapel Hill: Published for the Omohundro Institute of Early American History and Culture Williamsburg Virginia by the University of North Carolina Press, 2004); Dubois, *Les esclaves de la république: L'histoire oubliée de la Première Émancipation, 1789–1794* (Paris: Calmann-Lévy, 1998); and Joan Dayans, *Haiti, History, and the Gods* (Berkeley: University of California Press, 1995). For accounts of the intersection between race and citizenship, see John D. Garrigus, *Before Haiti: Race and Citizenship in French Saint-Domingue*, 1st ed. (New York: Palgrave Macmillan, 2006); Garrigus, "Sons of the Same Father: Gender, Race and Citizenship in French Saint Domingue, 1760–1792," in *Visions and Revisions of Eighteenth-Century France*, ed. Jack R.

Censer, Lisa Jane Graham, and Christine Adams (University Park: Pennsylvania State University Press, 1997); Elizabeth Colwill, "Sex, Savagery, and Slavery in the Shaping of the French Body Politic," in *From the Royal to the Republican Body: Incorporating the Political in Seventeenth- and Eighteenth-Century France*, ed. Sara E. Melzer and Kathryn Norberg (Berkeley: University of California Press, 1998); and Stewart R. King, *Blue Coat or Powdered Wig: Free People in Pre-revolutionary Saint Domingue* (Athens: University of Georgia Press, 2001). See also David Patrick Geggus and Norman Fiering, eds., *The World of the Haitian Revolution* (Indianapolis: Indiana University Press, 2009); David Barry Gaspar and David Patrick Geggus, eds., *A Turbulent Time: The French Revolution and the Greater Caribbean* (Bloomington: Indiana University Press, 1997); David Patrick Geggus, *The Impact of the Haitian Revolution in the Atlantic World, the Carolina Lowcountry and the Atlantic World* (Columbia: University of South Carolina, 2001); Geggus, *Haitian Revolutionary Studies* (Bloomington: Indiana University Press, 2002); and Doris Lorraine Garraway, ed., *Tree of Liberty: Cultural Legacies of the Haitian Revolution in the Atlantic World* (Charlottesville: University of Virginia Press, 2008).

9. The number of citizens may have been as high as twenty-eight million by 1789. Pierre Boulle's work allows us to have more complete information about how many blacks were in France at the eve of the French Revolution; he has determined that as of 1777, the actual figures were approximately 765 nonwhites registered in Paris and a total of 2,239 individual nonwhites in France. See Pierre H. Boulle, *Race et esclavage dans la France de l'Ancien Régime* (Paris: Perrin, 2007), 109.
10. See, for example, Jeremy D. Popkin, *Facing Racial Revolution: Eyewitness Accounts of the Haitian Insurrection* (Chicago: University of Chicago Press, 2007).
11. Kirby, "More about the Hottentot Venus," 125. Court documents take pains to reassure that she personally went and asked for permission to leave. Crais and Scully argue that while there were attempts at a contract, it was a contract between Dunlop and Cesar in the Cape, not between either of them and Baartman. Also, they assert she was listed as being "free." See Crais and Scully, *Sara Baartman*, 54–57.
12. Crais and Scully, *Sara Baartman*, 57, 59, 61.
13. On the possibility of a contract, see Kirby, "More on the Hottentot Venus," 125. On that contract's terms, see T. Denean Sharpley-Whiting, "The Dawning of Racial-Sexual Science: A One Woman Showing, a One Man Telling, Sarah and Cuvier," *FLS: Ethnography in French Literature* 23 (1996): 117. Solly and Moojen's deposition states that she was to be "Caesar's nursery maid." See "Transcripts of the Sworn Affidavits filed during the Trial of 1810," deposition of Zachary Macaulay, Thomas Gisborne-Babington, and Peter Van Wageninge, October 17, 1810, Record PFF 747 (KB1/36/4, fol. 117), Public Records Office, National Archives, London, England, under "Saartjie Baartman on Display" (accessed January 24, 2014). Solly's

and Moojen's depositions claim the period of servitude to be six years. See "The Following Is the Result of the Examination of the Hottentot Venus—27th Nov. 1810," 43. Bullock's sworn statement claims two years. See "In the Kings Bench," William Bullock, November 21, 1810, Record PFF 723 (J18/462), Public Records Office. The court documents claim the period was for five years.

14. Crais and Scully, *Sara Baartman*, 119.
15. Crais and Scully, *Sara Baartman*. In their quest to find the woman behind the representation, the authors write: "We will always know more about the phantom that haunts the Western imagination, a phantom so complete that it has nearly become a living, breathing person, than we do about the life of Sara Baartman, the human being who was ultimately destroyed by an illusion" (6).
16. Charles Joseph Colnet du Ravel and Alexandre Desenne, *L'hermite du faubourg Saint-Germain, ou observations sur les moeurs et les usages français au commencement du XIXe siècle* (Paris: Chez Pillet Ainé, Imprimeur Librairie, 1825), 2:50–67.
17. Charles Joseph Colnet du Ravel, "Sartjee ou la Vénus hottentote, a son cousin," in Colnet and Desenne, *L'hermite*, November 7, 1814, Letter 1, 1:50–67. Hereafter cited in text. It is noteworthy that the so-called letters from Baartman echo the beginning of Montesquieu's *Persian Letters*.
18. There were also so-called interviews and other satires using Baartman. One was a fictional journal entry in *La Quotidienne*: "Nouvelles: On dit que la Vénus hottentote va faire un journal," March 5, 1815. The other was a "private exhibition and fictional conversation" in the *Journal des dames et des modes*, January 25, 1815, 37–40. I discuss these letters and these other false narratives in much greater detail in my forthcoming manuscript.
19. Colnet, "Sartjee ou la Vénus hottentote," November 19, 1814, Letter 2. Hereafter cited in text.

PART 5 Black Women Critique the "Empire"

12

Discourse on Immigration

Fatou Diome's Commitment to Human Rights in *The Belly of the Atlantic*

JOSEPH DIÉMÉ

"In the past, just after the Second World War, the French welcomed lots of people with open arms because they needed workers to rebuild the country. They hired immigrants from all over the place who agreed to go and risk their lives down the coal mines to escape poverty. . . . Successive waves of African immigrants have all ended up in slums. . . . Their children, who've grown up with the refrain 'Liberty, Equality, Fraternity,' no longer have any illusions once they realize, after a long battle, that their hard-won naturalization doesn't improve their opportunities."[1]

In the above excerpt, the female protagonist is visiting Niodior, her native Senegalese island. She interrupts young men gathered under the palaver tree who are passionately discussing migrating to France.[2] Defiantly, this female protagonist, who is not authorized to take the floor in this male-dominated sphere, speaks up to report on the living conditions of African immigrants in France. My essay situates *The Belly of the Atlantic*, a best-selling novel by Franco-Senegalese writer Fatou Diome, in the context of growing anti-immigrant rhetoric and legislation in Europe, stressing its contribution to the diversity of voices arguing about whether European borders should be open or closed to immigrants coming from the Global South. Originally published in French and translated in multiple languages, the novel suggests that illegal migration of African subjects to France is the by-product of France's relationship with Africa since the end of the Second World War. It also focuses on the lives of African migrants in France, offering a story that differs from the usually pejorative description of African lives in the French Republic. In the novel, Salie, a Senegalese woman residing in Strasbourg, France, plays an important role in the process of rethinking African experiences in France. Her multilayered experiences force readers to acknowledge that colonial relations still structure French relations with African people. Giving a voice to African female subjectivities in postcolonial France, *The Belly of the Atlantic* offers a new paradigm to emancipate postcolonial subjects from the "mental shackles" of French socioeconomic and cultural hegemony over Africa.

The *Indigènes* of the Republic

Fatou Diome has written nine novels touching on the themes of immigration, racism, national identity, neocolonialism, and globalization.[3] Diome is a household name in France, where she appears regularly on French television. She often questions the inequitable status quo between Europe and Africa, calling for social justice in Africa and throughout the globe. *The Belly of the Atlantic* was published in 2003, just two years before the November 2005 riots. These riots show that the people of the *banlieue* (suburbs)—people of color, in particular—will react to unfair treatment (poverty, unemployment, academic failure, and racism). The riots allowed the world to discover French ghettos, which have an odd resemblance to the plantation system. Indeed, the French inner cities, in both their architectural form and the stigmatization of their inhabitants, display many similarities with plantation societies, which Edouard Glissant describes as space capturing bodies and preventing social mobility. Accordingly, "crossing was strictly forbidden: impossible to leave without permission or unless authorized by some ritual exception, such as Carnival time. Chapel or church, stockrooms for distributing supplies or later the grocery story, infirmary or hospital: everything was taken care of within a closed circle."[4] Both the plantation and the ghetto are designed to be self-sufficient and completely separate from the dominant culture—the white culture.[5]

As Diome suggests in the quote above, Africans and their descendants living in the metropole have been subjected to a second-class status since the colonial period. This allegation amplifies the claim that African immigrants and their descendants are the new *indigènes* of the republic. From that perspective, we can view the riots as a symbol of resistance to colonial relations. As Didier Lapeyronnie notes, "The 'inner cities' are not a territory conquered and occupied by the army, and the colonizers did not come to settle and 'exploit' the resources and people living in a state of subordination and dependence justified by racism. Needless to say, the experience of discrimination and segregation, and the feeling of being defined as a social problem who needs to be integrated into society evoke the colonial period. For many descendants of immigrants, this is an unacceptable situation."[6]

In *The Belly of the Atlantic*, Diome contextualizes the riots. She discusses their implication and frames them as a human rights issue.[7] This context is critical to the articulation of a counternarrative to the demonization of African immigrants by politicians, among whom the most popular is Jean-Marie Le Pen.[8] His Far Right political rhetoric, usually rejected by right-wing politicians, should not overshadow the fact that leaders of the Right have been outsourcing Le Pen's ideas into mainstream politics. In 2007 Nicolas Sarkozy ran his political campaign and won the presidency by distorting the history of African immigrants in the Hexagon. In his political campaign, he described African immigrants as people fleeing their respective poor nations to take advantage of the welfare state, thereby delegitimizing their presence and painting them as leeches of the state.

In *The Belly of the Atlantic*, Salie interrogates France's "integration policy," particularly as it applies to French citizens of African descent: "As for their integration policy, it only applies to their national football team. *Black, Blancs, Beurs*—Blacks, Whites, Arabs—is nothing more than a slogan stuck on their international showcase, like a bad Benneton ad, it's just a recipe—braised beef and butter—which the TV channels fight over for millions" (125). Diome's "insurrection" against her nation, France, follows a long tradition of activists who have stood up against the abuse of human rights sponsored by the state during slavery, the colonial period, and the modern era. She is rebelling against a sort of covert state-sponsored racism that has been at the center of many administrations, like President Giscard d'Estaing's Year of the Heritage.

Whiteness and Frenchness

France's motto—liberty, equality, fraternity—stipulates that all citizens, irrespective of their race, religion, gender, and sexual orientation, should be treated equally. However, Giscard d'Estaing, who served as president of the French Republic from 1974 to 1981, launched the Year of the Heritage, a program that was discriminatory.[9] Herman Lebovics points out that "at no time in the official Année du patrimoine were the traditions, or even the existence, of the millions of immigrants from North and sub-Saharan Africa mentioned."[10] For him, the events were a deliberate political initiative to erase France's African minorities from the national identity.

The erasure of African identities in France during the Year of the Heritage meant that "Frenchness" was imagined to be unequivocally white. Thus, under President d'Estaing, the political elite embraced an "eliminativist" definition of national identity.[11] Their idea of national identity was based on racial attributes—Frenchness was apparently the result of blood connections to mythical ancestors and shared past experiences.[12] However, this "revisionist" approach elides the fact that West Africans and France have a common history, one that predates the formation of plantation societies. Thus, as Diome also acknowledges the contributions of African immigrants in *The Belly of the Atlantic* she describes Frenchness as a "post-national, civic identity that coexists seamlessly with any number of cultural identities."[13]

The irruption of Diome on the national stage coincides with a turning point in France's history. She gained notoriety at a moment when many French citizens of African descent refused to remain silent about the reproduction of social injustices in France. Contrary to their parents, who arrived in the 1950s and 1960s and remained invisible due to language and educational barriers, blacks born and educated in France want to participate in current debates on national identity. But their voice is often silenced. Thus, Diome compensates the institutional and curricular deficit of attention to the living conditions of Africans in France by giving them a voice. She invites the nation to change.[14] Accordingly, as Homi Bhabha notes, "The nation is no longer the sign of modernity under which cultural differences are homogenized in the 'horizontal' view of society. The nation reveals, in its ambivalent and vacillating representation, the ethnography of its own historicity and opens up the possibility of other narratives of the people and their difference."[15] While speaking up for the historical representation of African immigrants in *The Belly of the Atlantic*, Diome also creates an opportunity to examine the intersection between immigration, neocolonialism, and neoliberalism in her native Senegal, a country with a rich history of transnational connections with France.

Neocolonialism, Neoliberalism, and Immigration

In *The Belly of the Atlantic* Diome circumvents esoteric academic language to explain how neocolonialism and neoliberalism impact human lives. The interactions of the characters in the novel and the description of the physical space allow readers to understand these phenomena. Diome's protagonist, Salie, has been living in France for at least a decade and visits her native island during the summer. In her village, all young people want to migrate to Europe, preferably France, at any cost. This dream is fueled by the stories told by the "been-tos" and the architecture of the postcolonial state.[16] In the novel, the character nicknamed "the man from Barbes" epitomizes the life of a been-to. The stories that he recounts under the palaver tree are in continuity with a long tradition of delusion that is reminiscent of elitist literature from the Caribbean of the plantation era. In that literature, "conventional landscape [was] pushed to extremes—the gentleness and beauty of it—[and had] the propensity to blot out the shudders of life, that is, the turbulent realities of the Plantation, beyond the conventional splendor of scenery."[17] He is considered a success story and is treated accordingly. He has been given a fast-track promotion to the status of "elder" (in the traditional route, age, experience, wisdom, and exemplary behavior are necessary criteria).

The man from Barbes does not have the traditional qualities required of an elder. He returned from France with an abundance of wealth, which he displays ostentatiously. Under the palaver tree, the audience passionately listens to him. There is a striking continuity between his psychology and the habitus of the black man who has set foot in the metropole, as described by Fanon in *Black Skin, White Masks*. Fanon notes that "after a fairly long stay in the *métropole*, many Antilleans return home to be deified. The native islander who has never left his hole, the country bumpkin, adopts a most eloquent form of ambivalence toward them. The black man who has lived in France for a certain time returns home radically transformed."[18] The latter refuses to speak Creole, speaks softly, watches his diction, and, most importantly, "will make every effort not only to roll his r's, but also to make them stand out."[19]

The testimony of the man from Barbes puts France on a pedestal the same way accounts by Caribbean migrants praised France for the economic opportunities it presented. The man from Barbes is the epitome of the colonial subject who wants "to become equal to that splendid model [the colonizer] and to resemble him to the point of disappearing in him."[20] Upon his return to his native land, the man from Barbes, now a been-to, becomes the griot of the former colonizer.[21] His "astronomical spending power [and] impressive residence [ensured] him the villagers' respect and admiration" (17, 18). In his repertoire, France equals "the Eiffel Tower and the Obelisk touch[ing] the sky, the Champs Elysées, the Arc de Triomphe, the Panthéon, Notre Dame Cathedral" (55–56). France is a country where "every couple lives with their children in luxury apartments, [and] nobody's poor, because even those with no work are paid a salary by the State: they call it benefit" (56–57). Clearly, the psychology of the man from Barbes illustrates the fact that decolonization did not eradicate colonial perceptions of France. This is further evidenced by the current political architecture of Senegal.

In postcolonial Senegal, French, the official language of the country, serves as a constant reminder of the former colonizer's presence. As Diome writes, "[The French] language wears trousers, suits, ties, shoes with laces; or skirts, suits, sunglasses and high heels" (8). The construction of contemporary Senegalese identity is still influenced by France. Senegalese subjects still think and behave like French citizens, in continuity with

France's assimilationist policy during the civilizing mission (1885–1962). Salie further unpacks the semiotics of neocolonialism:

> Hence, even the television that allows them [the youth] to see matches comes from France. Its owner [the man from Barbes] lived in France. The schoolteacher, a knowledgeable man, did part of his training in France. All those with important jobs in this country have studied in France. The wives of our successive presidents are all French. To win the elections, the nation's father first wins over France. The few rich and famous Senegalese footballers play in France. To train the [soccer] national team, they always seek a Frenchman. Even our ex-President awarded himself retirement in France, so he could live longer. Thus on the island, even if we can't tell France from Peru on a map, we're well aware it rhymes with chance. (32)

Diome encourages the reader to think about France's involvement in Senegal, a scenario that can be extended across Francophone Africa. The above quote gives credit to the many voices that have been speaking up against the negative French influence over Francophone Africa since the dawn of independence. Supposedly, France infringes on these countries' sovereignty by exploiting their resources with the complicity of the local elites. This phenomenon, which generates wealth for the elite and poverty for the populace, is allegedly referred to as *Françafrique*.[22] As François Gèse notes, "This alliance between the heart of the French state, its great industrial corporations, and the permanent heads of state of the ex-African colonies . . . constitutes—along with nuclear capability—the foundation of 'French power' in the course of the following decades. [It is] a neocolonial alliance cemented by money (of oil, uranium, raw materials, arms sales, financing of political parties)."[23]

Diome unveils a new colonization in Francophone Africa, a sort of neocolonial machine that generates a culture of dependency and perpetuates the belief that African subjects cannot survive without the assistance of the former colonizer. *The Belly of the Atlantic* offers examples of neocolonial situations: the "water pump given by our friends the Japanese, . . . the cargo of rice donated by France, France's promise to reassess Senegal's debt in the near future" (37). It paints the conditions of oppression; it describes a neocolonial situation where impoverished Africans view the West as an avenue to success. In *The Belly of the Atlantic*, the impoverishment of Africans is accentuated by the ill-advised adhesion of the Francophone elites to a neoliberal model of development.

Friends of Neoliberalism

Diome describes the impact of neoliberalism on Senegal by highlighting the profanation of the land:

> The hotels stand there, hideous on their gilt pedestals. As the state is so keen for revenue from tourism, it lets foreign investors take over the most beautiful stretches of coast and pay their staff peanuts. Steak for the powerful, the bone for the poor! So be it in the kingdom of capitalism which stretches into the shades of the coconut trees. . . . Let the hotel industry operate for the pleasure of western tourists! Don't be too particular about what they do there, and whatever happens don't upset them. You want the customers to come back. Too bad if a few lecherous visitors come only to admire the landscapes of Black buttocks instead of the Pink Lake, the island bird sanctuary, our empty grain stores, and our picturesque shanty towns. Besides, to make ends meet, some receptionists will rustle up a few cinnamon beauties on request, high-class prostitutes with honeyed smiles who are used to dancing the rigadoon. It makes a change from paperwork. (140)

Here, Diome suggests that capitalism occupies the center stage of "development" at the expense of human beings, who are merely part of the *décor*. People are mobilized to serve this ideology, which means they are easily disposable. Postcolonial Senegal seems to be at the mercy of corporations whose primary concern is profit. Such a *déjà-vu* picture is reminiscent of slavery and the colonial era, where the primary concern of the slave owner or the colonizer was to take advantage of the land by exploiting the body of the slave or the colonial subject. Similarly, *The Belly of the Atlantic* claims that during the postwar era, France took advantage of African workers and channeled them into slums.

Similar to Senegalese social critic like the filmmaker and writer Ousmane Sembene, Diome indicts neoliberalism. She laments the International Monetary Fund's and the World Bank's agenda, two agencies that are controlled by France and the United States and that exert much influence on Senegal. It is thus not surprising that the narrator, Salie, deplores how Senegal, mired in debt, is forced to open its borders to foreign investors, subjecting the country and the continent to another scramble.[24]

Neocolonialism and neoliberalism, two concepts that figure prominently in *The Belly of the Atlantic*, are the root causes of emigration. On the one hand, Senegalese citizens are conditioned to look to France to construct their own identities; on the other, they are turned into instruments for the development of the elite. But *The Belly of the Atlantic* also raises new questions. Diome questions the relevance of national sovereignty. Was the independence of 1960 a false promise? Was it not going to offer Senegalese citizens a life of dignity and prosperity? Should the nation and the majority of its people continue to be servants of capitalism? Are young people, the human resources that are critical for the development of the nation, condemned to migrate to Europe, where their predecessors are second-class citizens? In the end, *The Belly of the Atlantic* suggests that a different path is accessible. Diome's optimism is in alignment with the hope that was resonant in the social movements that have shaken the world since 2010. Instead of promoting violence that leads to social change, *The Belly of the Atlantic* advocates for a mental revolution that will attack the root causes of emigration and guarantee peace and prosperity to the postcolonial nation. This revolution is embodied in the novel by Madicke, Salie's brother.

A Paradigm Shift

In the novel, Madicke's metamorphosis represents a turning point in the psychology of the youth who want to migrate to Europe. Throughout the novel, he and the other young people were under the spell of the man from Barbes, whose stories perpetuate notions of French superiority. At the end of the novel, Madicke's change of mind is symptomatic of an emancipatory moment, a moment that "asserts not just the right of African, Asian, and Latin American peoples to access resources and material well-being of the West, but also the dynamic powers of their cultures."[25] Madicke's newfound optimism in *The Belly of the Atlantic* is echoed by the youth who protested in many regions of the world against neoliberal policies. During a phone conversation with his sister, Madicke reaffirms that his center of gravity has shifted from Paris to Dakar:

> Hey wait! I was about to say I so wish I could see them [the Senegalese national soccer team] play live at the Léopold Sédar Senghor stadium in Dakar, for example. Who's talking about leaving? Maybe some of my friends still think about it, but I am not interested anymore. I've got a lot of work in the shop; I'm always having to reorder stock. I think I am going to build an extension; it's really doing well. I even managed to hire a big TV, and we all watched the World Cup Final at my place. Listen, Grandma wants to know how you are and whether you got her parcel? She never stops talking about you. She misses you. You really ought to come home, there's so much to do here. (187)

Madicke's emancipation process takes place through several stages that need unpacking. The fact that he no longer has to go to the house of the man from Barbes to watch television means he has demystified the latter's narratives about France's "greatness." Liberated from this mental prison, Madicke looks at his homeland with a new lens. He no longer sees it through the filter of the West, symbolized by the man from Barbes. His preference to see the Senegalese national soccer team play in a local stadium named after Senegal's first president, Léopold Sédar Senghor, is a patriotic posture.[26] Home becomes as valuable as France. Madicke's patriotism is conveyed via the shop he recently opened thanks to his sister's financial help, a shop he plans to expand. Arguably, owning a shop allows him to decide what he wants to sell: he manages *his* store; he is invested in *his* country.

The transfer of Madicke's agency from the local level, the village, to the nation is a revolutionary act. Symbolically, it dismantles neocolonialism and protects the country from being overtaken by outside forces. However, it seems that Madicke's paradigm shift could not have materialized without the contribution of his sister, Salie, who lives in Strasbourg. The brother invites the sister to come home, because there is a lot of work to do in Senegal. But the *work* that Madicke refers to involves developing Senegal through a Senegalese-centered approach.

Madicke's invitation conveys the notion that the Senegalese diaspora plays a critical part in the "development" of the continent. Their return home, with the experiences and the intellectual and economic capital they have accumulated in France, will be an added value to the development of the country. Such a message has the potential to bring an end to the belief that migrating to France is an inevitable step for Senegal's development. It presents the possibility of achieving economic success at home.

The Belly of the Atlantic is a powerful testimony to Fatou Diome's commitment to the fight for human rights in her two homes: Senegal and France. Within the context of the current migration crisis between Europe and Africa, her novel is a substantial contribution to the immigration debate. In addition to highlighting the paternalistic relationship that France has developed with Senegal, Fatou Diome boldly interrogates the very nature of the systemic inequities between North and South. She suggests that France is equally responsible for creating the previous and current waves of migration from Senegal to France. She invites her audience to reflect on the origin of current anti-immigrants' narratives. As a Franco-Senegalese woman, she claims and embodies a postcolonial space that only meteoric political leaders of the caliber of Patrice Lumumba and Thomas Sankara have occupied.[27] The political undertones of her writing suggest that she is politically nonaligned and devoted to giving a voice to marginalized African subjects. Diome offers France and Senegal a roadmap to achieve liberty, equality, and fraternity, a slogan that has eluded most African subjects in France and Senegal.

Notes

1. Fatou Diome, *The Belly of the Atlantic*, trans. Lulu Norman and Ros Schwartz (London: Serpent's Tail, 2006), 17, 18. Hereafter cited in the text.
2. In precolonial Africa, the palaver tree represented an "institution" where the most important decisions pertaining to a clan, a tribe, an ethnic group, or a kingdom were made. The elders, mostly men, gathered in the shade of the baobab tree, praised for its exceptional longevity. The baobab is the emblem of Senegal. Colonial discourse

denatures the cultural significance of the palaver tree, as the colonizer thought the elders' long discussions were mere rigmarole.

3. The term *indigènes* is reminiscent of French law in the colonies. The relationship between the colonizers and the colonized was dictated by a French colonial law called the Indigenous Code, adopted on June 28, 1881, and maintained until 1962. Being called an *indigène* meant having second-class status. See Olivier Le Cour Grandmaison, *Coloniser, exterminer: Sur la guerre et l'état colonial* (Paris: Fayard, 2005).
4. Edouard Glissant, *Poetics of Relation*, trans. Betsi Wing (Ann Arbor: University of Michigan Press, 1997), 64.
5. See Euzhan Palcy, *Sugar Cane Alley* (1983; Paris: Euzhan Palcy, 2004), DVD; and Mathieu Kassovitz, *Hate* (1995; Paris: Christophe Rossignon, 1995), DVD. The two films draw striking parallels between the plantation and the ghetto.
6. Didier Lapeyronnie, "La banlieue comme théâtre colonial, ou la fracture coloniale dans les quartiers," in *La fracture coloniale: la société française au prisme de l'héritage coloniale*, ed. Pascal Blanchard, Nicolas Bancel, and Sandrine Lemaire (Paris: La Découverte, 2005), 210.
7. Laurent Mucchielli and Véronique Le Goaziou, eds., *Quand les banlieues brûlent: Retour sur les émeutes de novembre 2005* (Paris: La Découverte, 2006) enumerates a list of criteria that substantiate the claim that France has ghettos: absence of social integration, challenges of many parents and children in the school system, discrimination of all sorts due to where they live, an unemployment rate much higher than in the dominant culture, health problems, absence of political representation, and the feeling of being abandoned and even rejected by the political leaders.
8. Jean-Marie Le Pen was the founder of the National Front in 1972. It is an anti-immigrant political party.
9. Herman Lebovics, *Bringing the Empire Back Home: France in the Global Age* (Durham NC: Duke University Press, 2004), 107.
10. Lebovics, *Bringing the Empire*, 114.
11. Simon Glendinning, *Derrida: A Very Short Introduction* (New York: Oxford University Press, 2011), 74.
12. Dayna Oscherwitz, "Decolonizing the Past: Re-visions of History and Memory and the Evolution of a (Post)Colonial Heritage," in *Memory, Empire, and Postcolonialism: Legacies of French Colonialism*, ed. Alec G. Hargreaves (Lanham MD: Lexington Books, 2005), 191.
13. Oscherwitz, "Decolonizing the Past," 189.
14. Nicolas Bancel, "L'histoire difficile: Esquisse d'une historiographie du fait colonial et postcolonial," in Blanchard, Bancel, and Lemaire, *La fracture coloniale*, 90.

15. Homi K. Bhabha, "DissemiNation: Time, Narrative, and the Margins of the Modern Nation," in *Nation and Narration*, ed. Homi Bhabha (New York: Routledge, 1990), 300.
16. In Ghana a "been-to" is the title given to a person who went abroad and came back, usually rich. The status means that that person "made it."
17. Glissant, *Poetics*, 70.
18. Frantz Fanon, *Black Skin, White Masks*, trans. Richard Philox (New York: Grove Press, 2008), 3.
19. Fanon, *Black Skin*, 5.
20. Albert Memmi, *The Colonizer and the Colonized* (Boston: Beacon Press, 1965), 120.
21. In precolonial Western Africa, griots were members of a hereditary caste known for their polyvalent positions in society. As historians, they kept the history of the kingdoms and empires alive via oral tradition.
22. For more information on this topic, I recommend François-Xavier Vershave, *La Françafrique: Le plus grand scandale de la République* (Paris: Stock, 2003).
23. François Gèse, "L'héritage colonial au cœur de la politique étrangère française," in Blanchard, Bancel, and Lemaire, *La fracture coloniale*, 158.
24. See Thomas Pakenham, *The Scramble for Africa* (Boston: Little, Brown Group, 1992). In this book, the author discusses Europe's takeover of Africa subsequent to the Berlin Conference in 1884–85.
25. Robert J. C. Young, *Postcolonialism: A Very Short Introduction* (Oxford: Oxford University Press, 2003), 4.
26. In Senegal, my native country, there is consensus as to Léopold Sédar Senghor's intellectual contribution to world civilization. However, such is not the case as far as his political contribution to Senegal, as he is believed to have "sold" Senegal to France since independence by allowing France to have great control over Senegal.
27. Patrice Lumumba and Thomas Sankara were eliminated for denouncing Belgium's and France's neocolonial practices in Africa. Lumumba, the first prime minister of Congo, a former Belgian colony, was assassinated in 1961. Sankara, former president of Burkina Faso, a former colony of France, was assassinated in 1987.

13

Remapping the Metropolis

Theorizing Black Women's Subjectivities in Interwar Paris

CLAIRE OBERON GARCIA

Women of the African diaspora were crucial to the black anticolonial and citizenship rights movements of the early twentieth century, yet it has only been since the beginning of the twenty-first century that we have seen scholarship focused on their participation. Paulette Nardal, the journalist who cofounded two of the early publications to promote a black diasporic consciousness (*La revue du monde noir* and *La dépêche africaine*) complained in a private letter, "Césaire et Senghor ont repris les idées que nous avions semées. Ils les ont exprimées avec beaucoup plus de panache et de brio. Nous n'étions que des femmes. Nous avions montré le chemin aux hommes" (Césaire and Senghor took up the ideas that we had sown. They expressed them with much more panache and brio. We were just women. We had shown the path to the men).[1] These seeds were often planted in conversations in the Nardal sisters' Clamart salon, editorial offices, university classrooms, and conversations in cafés, but they may also be found documented in stories, articles, sketches, and essays that appeared in newsletters and other periodicals published in Paris during the interwar years, a landscape often dominated in the Western imagination by the experiences and literature of white men and women and black men. The artists, writers, and scholars associated with the New

Negro and negritude movements realized that the struggle for liberation and equality necessitated challenges to European American epistemologies and the development of new ones. Central to these enterprises was redefining the meaning of blackness and the connections among colonized and formerly enslaved people across the diaspora. Because of their lived experiences as black women whose access to education afforded them certain class privileges but whose race and gender marginalized them in different ways in various settings, Paulette Nardal and other black French women's writings engaged and theorized intersectionality *avant la lettre*. As they formed their black subjectivities, they articulated the connections between imperialist, racist, and patriarchal ideologies.

Groundbreaking work by U.S. and Caribbean scholars has included issues of gender in the genealogies of the New Negro and negritude movements. Shireen K. Lewis's "Gendering Négritude: Paulette Nardal's Contribution to the Birth of Modern Francophone Literature" (2000), T. Denean Sharpley-Whiting's *Negritude Women* (2002), and Brent Hayes Edwards's *The Practice of Diaspora: Literature, Translation, and the Rise of Black Internationalism* (2003) brought attention to the writing of Nardal sisters (Paulette, Jane, and Andrée), Susan Césaire, and other black French women in the development of anticolonial and civil rights movements in the first part of the twentieth century. Historian Jennifer Anne Boittin's *Colonial Metropolis: The Urban Grounds of Anti-imperialism and Feminism in Interwar Paris* (2010) looked at the relationships among white and white French women and black men in French political organizations during this crucial era. These pioneering scholars reframed anticolonial and black cultural movements as gender inclusive. In this volume, the Antillean scholar Jacqueline Couti focuses on the particular challenges black French women faced in developing vigorous and liberatory black feminist approaches to the oppressions of patriarchy and popular culture. In this chapter, I discuss how the struggle for black French women's equality included the development of black women's epistemologies as alternatives to the dominant imperial white supremacist ideologies. Central to this enterprise is the articulation of a crucial principle that only decades later would the U.S. attorney Kimberlé Crenshaw coin a term for but that had characterized and continues to shape black women's lived realities in the modern world: intersectionality.

I examine key texts by Paulette Nardal and Roberte Horth to highlight their contributions to theorizing intersectional black feminist diasporic subjectivities. You shall see that Paulette Nardal and Roberte Horth constructed emergent black female subjectivities that laid the groundwork for enacting political agency. These texts inscribe black women's experiences on the overdetermined and multivalenced spaces and places of the city of Paris, and, in doing so, they challenge social, political, and cultural narratives in which black women were invisible, marginalized, or systematically misread. These writers—architects in the development of new rhetorical and conceptual frameworks—use stories about black women's ability to navigate the spaces and places in Paris, the metropolitan capital of the French Empire, to critique and articulate black women's agency. I conclude with the view of black French women's bodies in Parisian spaces offered by Jessie Fauset, a contemporary of Nardal's and Horth's from another point in the black Atlantic diaspora who demonstrates that their feminist articulation and exploration of black women's embodied subjectivity were part of a larger discursive phenomenon.

Paris: The Belly of the Beast

W. E. B. Du Bois dubbed Paris, France's imperial metropole, "the only real white democracy."[2] During the interwar years, the capital city was characterized by multiple and often conflicting identities: the standard bearer for republican values that honored men who gave intellectual credence to racist theories in streets and monuments; a multicultural city that offered a cosmopolitan landing place for political and cultural refugees from the world over; a global intellectual and artistic center; the city that epitomized modernity; and a site of sexual, social, and aesthetic liberties for those with discretionary income or leisure time. Moving to the sounds of jazz music, Paris was a city both psychically ravaged and culturally enriched in the aftermath of the Great War; Parisian spaces embodied the frivolities and frustrations of European civilization in conflict with itself and in confrontation with modernity.

Although there had been a black presence in Paris from at least the sixteenth century, the numbers of black people who converged on the city from throughout the world during this period were unprecedented. Some were driven there by desperation or desire, others by chance. A city "as significant for its imaginary topography as for its actual landscape," Paris was a practical and ideological force to contend with.[3] The geographies of imperialism formed colonial subjects from the beginning of their lives. The distant metropole shaped the colonized subject's sense of self and objects of desire through textbooks, products consumed, and the formal and informal rules that govern social relations. The colonized woman understood early on that space and place are entangled with power. In *Space, Place, and Gender*, Doreen Massey encourages us "to think about space in terms of the articulation of social relations, a spatial form in their interactions with one another. If this notion is accepted, then one way of thinking about place is as particular moments in such intersecting social relations. . . . Thinking of places in this way implies they are not so much bounded areas as open and porous networks of social relations."[4]

The texts discussed in this chapter feature black women from the overseas territories navigating the spaces of interwar Paris to create new cartographies of the city and thus of political possibility that extend beyond the city. They make claims for recognition of the black woman as agent and citizen. To inscribe black women on Parisian spaces is to create new cartographies that challenge the ideological and material constraints that deprived black women of their humanity, equality, and citizenship rights. We must add discourses of gender to our understanding of liberation struggles throughout the diaspora.

Many of the black French women who found themselves in Paris during these years were either domestic workers or members of the first generation of women from the French Caribbean to come to Paris to earn university degrees and certificates. By the time Paulette Nardal arrived in Paris in 1920, educational possibilities had been opening up for women in Martinique for several years: "Le développement de l'école laïque à partir de la fin de XIXème siècle permet l'éclosion dans la sphère intellectuelle, de personnalités masculines et féminines, issues de la bourgeoisie mulâtre ou noire" (The development of secular schools at the end of the nineteenth century made space for an intellectual blossoming of masculine and feminine identities among the "mulatto" bourgeoisie and black classes).[5] Although according to Nardal earning degrees through correspondence courses was "très en vogue," a young Antillaise who was serious about her education "va passer quelques années en France, de préférence à Paris" (was going to pass several years in France, preferably in Paris).[6] Thus Paris plays a significant role in the black French woman's imaginary and formation.

"Une belle arme": Roberte Horth's "Histoire sans importance / A Thing of No Importance"

Paulette Nardal credited French Guianan writer Roberte Horth's brief story "Histoire sans importance / A Thing of No Importance" with expressing perfectly the conditions that led to a pivotal moment in the development of black racial consciousness.[7] Horth's story was published in the second issue of *La revue du monde noire*, the bilingual review focused on the black diaspora that Paulette Nardal cofounded and edited with her sister Jane (a classics teacher), the Haitian scholar Dr. Léo Sajous, and Dr. Clara Shepherd (a U.S. professor at the premier African American university, Howard). Nardal provides an overview of the development of racial consciousness among black writers, intellectuals, and militants of the early twentieth century in her seminal essay, "L'eveil de la conscience du race / Awakening of Race Consciousness," a piece published in the final issue of that short-lived but transformative periodical. The article, which is a call to continue the work of the review after its demise, is interesting in several respects, including its attempt to describe the foundations and future of an intraracial, linguistic, and border-crossing African diasporic consciousness. Claiming that "the coloured women living alone in the metropolis . . . have certainly been less favored than coloured men who are content with a certain easy success," Nardal's most radical statement in this essay is to locate the awakening of modern black racial consciousness in the attempts of uprooted and intellectually restless women students to make sense of their place in the world from their marginalized position.[8]

Excluded from and stereotyped by white French society and unable to fit comfortably into the established Antillean male student culture, these black women in Paris challenged the race, gender, and class expectations of Antillean bourgeois propriety, as well as the Parisian mania for turning black women into what Jane Nardal termed "exotic puppets." At once invisible and highly visible, these deracinated young women "understood the relativity of all things."[9] In other words, they could articulate and theorize the connections between patriarchy and imperialism and imagine the conditions of political, emotional, and cultural liberty.

For Nardal to locate a transformative moment in the narrative of the evolution of black consciousness among women of color whose perspectives had been honed by deracination, dislocation, and marginalization develops several theoretical points. First, it suggests that even in an educational system that prizes objectivity and requires a clear distinction between the scholar and the object studied to generate knowledge, there is room for and value in the knowledge generated by experience and positionality. This is a foundational principle of black feminism. Second, Nardal also suggests, presciently, that one can conceive of a black consciousness that is not merely rooted in a common condition defined in material terms: the women, in contrast to the men, "have felt the need of a racial solidarity which would not be merely material."[10] In other words, the women had a vision of a truly diasporic consciousness that valued the connections among black people across borders forged not only by the conditions of enslavement and colonialism but by a wellspring of cultures that had their roots, no matter how far removed in time and space, in Africa. Jennifer Anne Boittin recognizes that in this essay Nardal "marked a turning point for the intellectual preoccupations of all blacks in interwar Paris away from the working-class, material solidarity that existed before the Colonial Exposition toward an intellectual and cultural one that soon became known as négritude."[11] One of the aims of the *Revue*, articulated in the inaugural issue, was "to study and popularize . . . all which concerns NEGRO CIVILIZATION and the natural riches of Africa, thrice sacred to the black race."[12] Nardal saw the "grande DEMOCRATIE / great Brotherhood" comprising two hundred million African-descended people united across continents, languages, and class not only as an assertion of the value of black lives and culture but as a model for a modern global democracy that respects multiculturalism, a problem that the world continues to struggle with well into the twenty-first century.[13] Finally, in a black woman's rejection of dualistic, either/or identities and embracing of the "relative" nature of all ideas and relations, Nardal is here preparing the groundwork for a conceptual tool that Crenshaw fifty years later would term "intersectionality": women of color live the reality that identities within a single body are multiple and contending. Nardal points to Horth's essay in the second issue of the *Revue* as being the first to express how the black woman found herself in a position to construct a new idea of race consciousness that recognized the mutual constitution of gender and class. Having lived the connections and ruptures among their social, political, and cultural experiences, black women in Paris were able to critique the meanings of race, gender, and citizenship that anticipated later developments in feminist theory and liberatory black consciousness. The experience of social, psychological, and geographical dislocation and reorientation was a painful but necessary condition for their participation in anticolonial and citizenship rights struggles.

Horth's story maps her protagonist Léa's journeys through three very different geographical spaces: her (unnamed) island home, the school and university classrooms in an (unnamed) metropolitan city, and the public social spaces (from dance halls to drawing rooms) in that city. The story, written like a fairy tale, describes Léa as a smart and imaginative child who had long dreamed of the metropolis, "une ville de cristal et de rêve, un visage énorme, brillant et doux auquel elle donne un nom chantant. . . . [C]e pays lointain est policé, courtois et que les gens qui l'habitent accueillent tous les bons esprits / a phantom city, a cristal dream to which she gave a lyrical name. The residents were polished, courteous, and friendly to all intelligent strangers."[14] Yet the very first paragraph situates her as someone who will never be a full citizen of that city because she cannot express her true identity there. The story opens with her name in a one-word sentence. It is "un nom comme un autre / just a name like any other" (48/118), but it is not the name that she goes by when she eventually sojourns in the city: her white French friends believe that the name does not do justice to the exotic identity that they impose upon her: "Ils la baptisent de quelques onomatopée, évocatrice de fruits étranges, de senteurs inconnus, de danses bizarres et de pays ignorés. / They christened her with some queer nickname full of the aroma of strange fruits, of unknown fragrance, of weird dances and far-off lands" (48/118). By changing her name, they strip her of her identity as her mother's well-loved daughter, as well as "une femme comme toutes les autres / a woman like the others" (50/120). They replicate the rhetorical violence of enslavement by substituting a black person's given name with a new name and thus a new identity.

In its opening, the story alludes to the legacy of African enslavement and sets an epistemological ground-note of the tensions between perceived sameness and difference, the colonial and the metropolitan, being read and misread. Léa is "une enfant comme les autres / a child like the others," though her personality is unique (47–48/118–19). The central marker of difference, though, is Léa's race, her "sang mêlée / mixed blood," "le petit chose sans importance / thing of no importance" that creates a "non-sens/ absurd" and unreadable sign: "âme occidentale vêtue d'une peau scandaleuse / her soul fashioned by Occidental culture but concealed by objectionable skin" (50/120). Though Horth has been emphasizing the tensions between seeing and being seen, being subject and object throughout the brief text, Nardal's decision to translate "non-sens"—which suggests a problem of legibility or making sense to another—with the more philosophical term "absurd"—which implies a state of being—makes Horth's idea a little less dynamic and intersubjective than the original text does. It is also thought-provoking to note Nardal's decision to translate the word "histoire" in the title as "thing," evoking and eliding the title of Oscar Wilde's play *A Woman of No Importance* (1893), given Léa's central lament that she is not perceived and treated as other French women.

Throughout the story, the narrator emphasizes Léa's agency and intelligence. As a girl on a tropical island, she "builds" and "names" the city of her dreams and projects her own ideals of a society where a nonwhite woman's humanity and intelligence are recognized and appreciated. As a student in the metropole she is nurtured by "good-hearted women who formed her intelligence" to prepare her to enter the university (49/119). Léa's "âme viril / intelligence like a man's" affords her access to a world that W. E. B. Du Bois describes in *The Souls of Black Folk* as a kingdom of culture and truth that transcends racial difference.[15] Léa can partake of and contribute to, as an equal, the glorious ideas and art forms of Western civilization "sans aucune distinction de classes et de race / regardless of class or race" and, one might add, without distinction of gender (48/119).

An ironic juxtaposition of images of freedom and bondage permeates this narrative: for example, the BAC school looks like a prison but prepares her to be a full-fledged citizen in the kingdom of culture; the "courtoisie et liberté / courteousness and liberty" that she experiences in the university serve to bind ("liée") her "corps et âme / body and soul" to a nation that nourishes her soul with its cultural riches—described in spiritual terms in Nardal's English translation as "manna"—but denies the emotional and, presumably, sexual satisfaction longed for by her black woman's body, as we see in the closing imagery of the story. In the story, the world of the academy and the culture that it expresses are blind to race and gender; the quality of Léa's mind earns her recognition in academia: "N'a-t-elle pas supris dans le regard de ceux qu'elle essaie de comprendre un lueur de satisfaction? . . . Elle est heureuse . . . heureuse d'un bonheur tout intellectuelle dans ce royaume où les bons esprits se reconnaissent. / Not seldom she caught a glimpse of intellectual delight in the eyes of her professors. . . . She was happy, you will say. Yes, happy with a happiness wholly intellectual, in this environment where intelligent spirits recognized one another, and searched each other out in mutual appreciation" (49/119). Léa is recognized as a citizen of the intellectual realm. However, the city outside the classroom walls is not as welcoming. While she can be accepted and valued as a disembodied "mind" within academia, this mind exists in a black woman's body, which in 1930s Paris evokes the exotic, alluring, and dangerous.

The metropole is a site of bodily pleasures ("le monde et ses plaisirs / the world and its pleasures"), social situations, and sexual relations. Léa, a young woman who loves to creatively follow fashion with an individualistic flair that does not compromise good taste, is an accomplished and vivacious dancer who connects to music in ways that evoke both the conventional characterization of European classical music and dance with white perceptions of the more primal and instinctive qualities of black music: "La musique a pour elle un charme étrange qui réveille en elle un je ne sais quoi venu de la profondeur des âges. Elle en épouse le rythme qui rend sa danse si aérienne. Au bal, elle est toute sensation, toute légèreté, instinctivement. / Music had for her a peculiar charm which awoke in her a certain something that come [*sic*] down from the depths of the ages. She always interpreted the rythm [*sic*] so justly that her dancing was marked by an airy lightness. Instinctively, she was all feeling, all spirit" (50/120).

Despite possessing what would be social assets in any other woman, Léa is not treated like a "femme comme les autres," a woman with feelings and romantic yearnings. Her fashionably adorned body is exoticized as both appealing and threatening: "On la regarde comme on fait d'une belle arme, pièce de cabinet que l'on montre aux curieux / People looked at her as if she were a beautiful weapon, a choice piece to be shown to the curious" (49/119). Her difference is construed as both beautiful and potentially destructive: "Les vues courtes ne peuvent concevoir que dans un gaine si charmante se cache une lame polie et tranchante / Short-sighted people could'not [*sic*] conceive that under such a charming sheath was hidden a weapon, sharp and polished" (49–50/119–20). The irony for the narrator is that it is the most civilized and open-minded French who, while sharing "leur trésor spirituel / their spiritual treasures," can never see her as more than a "fétîche" (a "pagan" religious object) who is invited to receptions as "une poupée qu'on est fier de montrer à ses hôtes, un fruit étrange que l'on est flatté d'avoir découvrir / a doll to be proudly exhibited to guests, a strange fruit that flattered the taste of its discoverer" (50/120). In France she will never be "une femme comme toutes les autres femmes / a woman like the other women" (60/120). The sign of the presence of African "blood" in her woman's body, the "mere" casing for the virile mind and tender heart, the Occidental soul, and scandalous skin, presents a barrier of difference that cannot be surmounted and lowers Léa in the white viewer's estimation.

Nardal noted in an article on Antillean women students in Paris published in *Le soir* in June 1930:

> Par la formation reçue dans la colonie, l'étudiante antillaise est latine. Au fond, elle se sent aussi française que ses camarades métropolitains. . . .

Mais elle est trop fine pour ne pas discerner chez des Français, trop nombreux hélas! le dédain que, suivant leur éducation, ils cachent plus ou moins. Il faut bien le dire que le fait de sa couleur passe toujours avant sa qualité de Française.

Because of the education she received in the colony, the Antillean woman student is Latin [French]. At her core, she feels herself as French as her metropolitan comrades. . . . But she is too clever not to discern among the French, too many, alas! the disdain which, depending upon their training, they hide to varying degrees. It must be said that the fact of her color always counts more than her French attributes.[16]

Color will always trump all other attributes, even individuality, in the eyes of white French people. Yet the woman of color from the overseas territories *is* French because she feels herself French: she has been made French, as she has been made black. Because of her existential intersectionality, she is "both/and," not "either/or."

Léa exists differently in the three different metropolitan spaces: the peripheral island, the classrooms of the metropole, and the public social spaces where she interacts with white members of French society. In each space, different aspects of her identity are valued and recognized by the dominant culture, but she cannot be fully herself in any of the spaces, and she is finally and definitively barred from the metaphorical space of French social relations: "leur coeur" (their heart). There is the suggestion that the heart in this context includes the realm of bourgeois heterosexuality, as Léa's social and geographical exile prevents her from expressing "de vagues rêves de tendresse oubliés, refoulés par des études / vague forgotten dreams of tenderness, repressed by her studies" in more intimate familial spaces. As Sharpley-Whiting notes, "Such isolation gives way to an understanding of certain racial and racist realities in the metropolis, to a crisis in identity that is productively transformed into a desire to create a community and a new identity. She is not a Frenchwoman like other Frenchwomen: she is a racialized Franco-Antillean woman."[17]

This short story represents more than a lament about marginalization, more than an illustration that "black women saw their intellect and their femininity simultaneously denied."[18] It seeks to articulate the "both/and" of a black intellectual woman's lived reality—that she has a vigorous intellect and a body that desires pleasure on her own terms, not those imposed by exoticizing constructions of black women's sexuality.

Navigating Exile: Paulette Nardal's "En exil"

Sadly, we will never know how Horth may have developed her perspective of the black woman navigating the metropole and developing an authentic self in relation to others there. She passed away at age twenty-seven, less than a year after this story was published. But Nardal offered a raw look at an Antillean woman navigating metropolitan spaces in her own short story, "En exil," which was published in the newspaper *La dépêche africaine* in 1929, a year earlier than Horth's tale. Like *La revue du monde noir*, this anticolonial publication focused on current events, politics, and culture throughout the African diaspora and printed stories in both French and English (though not translated). Nardal's brief story follows a domestic worker from her employers' house in the rue Cuvier to her own sixth-floor walkup near the rue Pasteur. Like "Histoire sans importance," this very short story is centered around the tensions between Elisa's subjectivity (her past, her inner life, her intense loneliness in "le mirage de Paris," her desires) and white Parisians' perceptions of her black woman's body as it moves through various metropolitan spaces (particular streets, a public bus, and the shared domestic spaces, hall, and stairway of her apartment building). Though perceived as an odd spectacle, uprooted and "in exile" from her island home, she is the living inscription of the colonial relationships that lie at the heart of Paris and define French culture.

The story is structured around parallel realities: Elisa's "monologue intérieur" and the surrounding white French people's indifference to her humanity, expressed variously in hostility toward, derision of, or curiosity about her exotic appearance. Lost in an interior collage of the voices and sensations of her island home, Elisa passes through spaces at the heart of the Parisian academic neighborhood, whose streets, statues, and monuments memorialize "les grands hommes" of French science and the arts.

The rue Cuvier, where she cleans her employers' "appartement obscur," was named by royal decree after the famed anatomist Georges Cuvier, one of the most influential and toxic developers of French racial theory. Cuvier described Africans as "la plus dégradée des races humaines, dont les formes s'approchent le plus de la brute, et dont l'intelligence ne s'est élevée nulle part au point d'arriver à un gouvernement régulier" (the most degraded of the human race, whose forms are most closely related to brutes and whose intelligence is not high enough to allow them to develop a regular government).[19] Cuvier's violently disrespectful legacy, especially as epitomized by his abuse, in both life and death, of the African woman Saartjie Baartman, is echoed the moment Elisa steps into the rue des Écoles, the main street that runs through the heart of the university: she is attacked physically by wind and rain and emotionally by a white youth's racist taunt.[20] Underdressed for her wet and chilly trip, she reflects, "Ce pays ne convient jamais une vielle negresse" (This country doesn't suit an old negresse).[21] As she makes her way to the bus stop, the surrounding environment is made up of "les visages tendus, les yeux durs, les physionomies fermées et indifférentes des blancs" (the strained faces, the hard eyes, the closed and indifferent physiognomies of whites). Despite the harsh weather, she walks to the rue Racine to save a few pennies of bus fare. The name of this street is resonant as well: Racine is regarded as the master of French tragedy and poetic language, but it is the humanism of his portrayal of characters that has made him so influential to writers the world over. Racine's work epitomizes French civilization and humanism; however, the spectacle of the black woman moving through the street that honors him problematizes French society's view of itself as a standard-bearer of Enlightenment values. The shift in the bus-ticket collector's evolving attitude toward Elisa reflects this dynamic on the level of a black woman's everyday lived experience. Initially, "pendant quelques semaines [il] s'était amusé à la faire enrager" (for a few weeks he amused himself by goading her to anger), but he finally adopts a condescending "protective" attitude toward her, while the other passengers stare at her traditional Martinican knotted madras, "n'avaient pas l'air de se douter que cela pût la gêner" (not suspecting that [their stares] might embarrass her).

While the young, single Léa finds herself vulnerable and thus ravaged by her encounters with French white supremacy, the older Elisa protects herself from this hostile and inhumane environment and behavior by inhabiting a Martinican world inside her head that is completely opposite to the highly regimented, unsocial, and cold (metaphorically and literally) city of Paris. In her mind, she relaxes with friends on a warm evening at home, telling traditional stories ("contes Africaines adaptés à l'âme antillaise" [African tales adapted to the Antillean soul]) introduced by the "formules traditionelles" and eating delicious regional food. The depiction of the scene emphasizes the community's connections to Africa, from the stories to the music of the "noir" whose drumbeats "dans le lointain, retentissent comme un appel angoissant. C'est toute l'âme de la vielle Afrique qui passe, dans ce tomtom antillais, éveilliant chez les causeurs soudain attentifs, un obscure émotion" (in the distance took a hold of them like an agonized call. It was completely the soul of the old Africa that had passed, in the Antillean tomtom, suddenly waking an obscure emotion among the suddenly attentive chatterer). Elisa's reverie is violently interrupted by the conductor calling the stop: rue de Rennes. As she is jolted back to her "réalité"—the hard eyes and indifferent faces of her fellow passengers—she feels "le fardeau de son existence retombe plus lourdement sur ses épaules" (the burden of her existence falling even more heavily over her shoulders).

The only bright spot in Elisa's Parisian life is the hope of her hearing from her son, who has been working for Americans in Colomb; if he is successful there, she will be able to have enough money to return to Martinique. The fact that their small family is dispersed between the French metropole and a colonial periphery where a young Martinican toils for years in hope of recognition by the American enterprise he works for speaks to the power of imperial interests to determine the most intimate domestic relationships.[22] The final paragraph of the story depicts Elisa's return to her apartment on the rue Pasteur. A letter handed to her by the concierge informs her that the Americans have given her son a good price for his leatherworking business, and he will be arriving soon to take his mother back to Martinique. The reader's final image of Elisa is through the eyes and ears of her neighbors. They usually pity her when they hear her heavy footsteps making the six-story climb to her apartment, but on that evening they are perplexed by her voice, "ce refrain étrange, au rythme saccadé, aux syllabes gutturaux et douces" (this strange refrain, with its jolting rhythm and guttural and sweet syllables). Throughout the story, Elisa is a visual rupture of Parisian spaces, an exotic and incomprehensible intrusion on the Parisian cityscape; even the expression of her happiness strikes the Parisians as bizarre, foreign, and primitive. But Elisa has a firm sense of her own identity, even through the pain of displacement to Paris's hostile spaces: she comes from a tradition-rich and community-oriented culture that has survived violent dispersal and maintains, through stories and music, a sense of black humanity that is under constant assault from white imperialism. As Shireen K. Lewis writes in *Race, Culture, and Identity*, "Nardal states categorically that Martinican folklore is based on the adaptation of African tales and she describes the Martinican musical instrument, the tambour, as the Caribbean version of the African tom-tom. Elisa's sense of self is therefore based on a communal black identity rooted in traditional Africa."[23] Even in the sad and lonely conditions of Paris, this elderly domestic worker has preserved her sense of self, hope, and dignity by drawing on her cultural roots, from the wonderful coffee ("dont seules les Antillaises ont la recette" [only Antilleans know the recipe]) that she takes the time to prepare in the morning to the reveries that protect her from the social and epistemological violence of the white people who surround her.

In her essay included in this volume, "Am I My Sister's Keeper? The Politics of Propriety and the Fight for Equality in the Works of French Antillean Women Writers, 1920s–1940s," Jacqueline Couti argues that readings such as Lewis's obscure the class bias in Nardal's "elitist" and misguided use of a working-class woman's suffering to epitomize an unmediated (and unrealistic, because Martinican folk culture is Créole and therefore highly mediated and mixed) African culture. Rather than "focus[ing] on the plight of this underprivileged Martinican *négresse* primarily to denounce racial and socioeconomic inequality," Couti sees Nardal as "mirror[ing] the metropolitan negrophilia of the time" in romanticizing and fetishizing pure Africanness.[24] One might say that "Africa" in this story appears not as "pure" but as appropriated, transformed, and, as Nardal says in this story, "adapted" by Antilleans who, like other enslaved people and their descendants, attempted in brutal conditions to hold on to what they could of their African cultures and ideologies as a survival technique. My own reading, which highlights the epistemological work that this short story is performing in the context of Nardal's interest in and explorations of transnational and intradiasporic constructions of black identity, does not negate Couti's but offers an additional lens through which to view this character. Under this lens, the trajectory of Elisa's aging body as she moves through the metropolitan streets offers an intersectionally informed critique of French imperialist so-called knowledge and white supremacist ideas of what constitutes "civilization."

Paulette Nardal, despite the advantages afforded her by her education, did not come from the class of the mixed-race elite of Martinique, and the experiences of her father, after whom she was named, inflected her view of her class positionality. Emily Musil, in her dissertation, "*La Marianne Noire*: How Gender and Race in the Twentieth Century Atlantic World Reshaped the Debate about Human Rights," states that "because Paul Nardal was categorized as black in Martinique, rather than mixed European-African lineage, he was prevented from moving to the highest ranks in the administration."[25] According to historian Micheline Marlin-Godier, the Nardal family of Paulette's generation, while well educated and relatively well off, were considered "black," not "gens de couleur."[26] Nardal's own personal history as both/and, both elite and black, as well as her Catholic humanism, complicates how readers interpret her relationship to the laboring classes. In its focus on critiquing epistemological violence, her portrayal of Elisa attempts to articulate a theoretical basis from which to disrupt an oppressive system of interlocking ideas and practices that work to erase black humanity, and Nardal was particularly interested in how black women fared in this system. The oscillations of intersecting race and class identities are central to another short story Nardal published seven years later in *L'étudiant noir*, the newspaper founded by Aimé Césaire for Martinican students in Paris that is credited as one of the sites of the first articulations of the concept of diasporic blackness that became negritude.

Nardal explores the survival experience of African diasporic subjects in Paris to interrogate and theorize new and gendered constructions of black identities in her story "Guignol Oulouf," which describes an encounter between a group of educated Antillean women and a Senegalese man in the iconic space of the Parisian café terrace. The narrator is seated at a café in the Latin Quarter for a "quick lunch" under modern lighting that is described as barbaric ("un bariolage barbare des tubes de neon" [a barbaric variegation of neon lights]) when suddenly, dressed in the theatrical costume of an operetta general, "entre la lumière et moi s'interpose la silhouette d'un Noir immense" (the silhouette of an immense Black interposed itself between the light and me).[27] Heightening the grotesque and undignified performance of stereotypical blackness that the black peanut seller portrays is the contrast with a young white cigarette seller on the terrace at the same time, "son collègue métropolitain, éphèbe blond à la sobre livrée marron" (his metropolitan colleague, a young blond man dressed in a somber maroon uniform). The "Noir caricatural" who blocks the artificial light literally and metaphorically sets off a moment of what might be termed "racial panic" in "une Noire antillaise trop occidentallisée" (a too-Westernized black Antillean woman). It is important to note here, given the hierarchical color schemata in Martinican society at the time and Nardal's own both/and racial and class identity, that she identifies herself as "Noire" with a capital *N* after identifying the African as "Noir" when, according to her later self-description, she is a *mulâtresse*. Césaire's generation of Martinican students was the first to try to theorize their relationship to Africa rather than to France: traditionally, the bourgeois *gens de couleur* and *mulâtres* aligned themselves culturally with white French society, rejecting their ties to Africans and Africanness. The narrator's frantic review of her possible behavior toward the African as he approaches her ironically highlights the problems of calibrating Antillaise identity in the metropole: Does she locate herself in alliance with the laughing white customers, does she pretend not to see him (pretending he is invisible to the Westernized black gaze), or does she express her displeasure that he is playing into white stereotypes that undermine the social and political work that assimilated (*évolués*) blacks are trying to do? The narrator decides that she cannot refuse to acknowledge that she and her companions are tied to him at least as much as to the white people on the terrace:

> Il y a cependant, entre nous et lui, à défaut de solidarité réelle. Et puis, rejetant cette mauvaise gêne, pour ne penser qu'à la fraternité réelle qui nous unit aussi bien à ce Noir qu'à ses Blancs pleins d'illusions, nous répondons gentiment au vendeur des cacahouètes.
>
> However, there was between us and him a lack of a real solidarity. And then, rejecting this naughty discomfort, thinking of nothing but of the real brotherhood that united us as much to this Black as the Whites full of illusions, we responded politely to the peanut vendor.

She decides to engage him on a professional level as a journalist by asking him questions. When asked by the narrator why he wears such a degrading costume and performs a caricature of blackness for the white audience, he replies that he had been a stage actor, and his performance now has the dignity of his exercising his profession in a way that allows him to be economically independent: "J'aime autant faire ce métier ridicule, qu'être chomeur ou de vivre des femmes. Les Blancs veulent que l'on fasse rire; moi, je veux bien. . . . [A]u moins, je peux manger" (I'd rather work at this ridiculous job than be unemployed or to live off women. White people want us to make them laugh; me, I say, why not? . . . At least I can eat).

The mutual recognition between the "respectable" Antillaise, who has informed the reader that she, too, has a "profession" (she is a journalist or scholar, or perhaps, if she is Nardal herself, both), and the self-respecting African performing a caricature of black manhood reveals them *both* as performers in a white space. However, black agency and a sense of responsibility lie beneath what looked at first like capitulation to the racist white gaze. The Wolof man sees himself as a professional deploying his disciplinary skills and maintaining, rather than compromising, his autonomy and self-respect. The final paragraph of the story suggests that both the journalist and the former actor are playing roles that enable them to survive with some dignity in a racist society and questions both the "illusions" that the whites have of black humanity and the illusions that bourgeois Antilleans hold on to in order to protect their own humanity and sense of identity. Is the anxious black Antillean woman, well dressed and comporting herself with an air of propriety, any more or less compromised by the white gaze than the peanut seller who engages in antics that allow him to feed himself?[28] Are the Antillean women also engaging in antics, albeit ones that are more discreet and up-to-date, in coming to the metropole to acquire their degrees and certificates?

Horth and Nardal attempted not only to describe but to provide new theoretical tools to analyze black female subjectivity at an important historical moment for those in the African diaspora: the formation and development of anticolonial and citizenship rights movements that emerged after the First World War and that would come to fruition after the Second World War. French women writers of the African diaspora during the interwar period inscribed black female subjectivity into discourses of psychological, cultural, and political liberation. It was a woman writer from another geographical point in the black Atlantic who offered a vision of the transformative presence of the Francophone black woman in Parisian spaces: the African American writer Jessie Fauset. In her essay "The Enigma of the Sorbonne," Fauset inscribes Francophone black women in French history and society by demanding that they be recognized as the latest chapter in a narrative of French civilization and as a sign of modernity itself. This essay was published in the National Association for the Advancement of Colored People (NAACP)'s magazine the *Crisis: A Record of the Darker Races* in 1925, the same year that the U.S. educator and activist Anna Julia Cooper successfully defended her dissertation on the Haitian Revolution and became the first black woman to earn a doctorate at the Sorbonne. Fluent in French, Fauset wrote the article during the year she spent in Paris working on a certificate in French language and culture. Most of the article is a summary of the history of one of the world's most prestigious universities for the bourgeois African American reader, but Fauset ends the essay with a vision of Haitian students she sees in the Place de la Sorbonne: "two absolutely black girls . . . [t]heir hair, stiff, black and fuzzy frames . . . their voices clear . . . and staccato; their movements free and unrestrained" striding beneath the tolerant and indifferent gazes of Louis Pasteur and Victor Hugo.[29] In Fauset's view, the young Haitians whom she inscribes on the Place de la Sorbonne are not the passive beneficiaries of French republican tolerance; they are active agents whose very presence testifies to a historical intervention: "In this atmosphere so completely are they themselves that that tolerance is a quality that they recognize only when they are exercising it towards others."[30] Fauset is careful to emphasize the students' agency and self-possession: "biens dans leurs peaux" (comfortable in their skin), they are the ones who "recognize" and "exercise" tolerance. Fauset herself, as the black American student and tourist mediating and shaping the history of the Sorbonne for her striving black American readers, assumes in turn the power to observe and symbolically deploy the image of the Haitian students. The young women's distinctively black female bodies and hair and the scholarly work that they are engaged in disrupt and reorient the historical narrative of French identities and values, just as Cooper argued that the Haitian Revolution continues to challenge and subvert French national narratives of identity and belonging.

Notes

1. Maryse Condé, "Globalisation et diaspora," *Diogène*, no. 84 (October–November 1998): 30. The translations, except where noted as from *La revue du monde noir*, are my own.
2. W. E. B. Du Bois, "An Essay toward a History of the Black Man in the Great War," *Crisis: A Record of the Darker Races* 18, no. 2 (June 1919): 87.
3. Jeremy Braddock and Jonathan P. Eburne, *Paris, Capital of the Black Atlantic: Literature, Modernity, and Diaspora* (Baltimore MD: Johns Hopkins University Press, 2013), 3.
4. Doreen Massey, *Space, Place, and Gender* (Minneapolis: University of Minnesota Press, 1994), 120.
5. Muriel Descas-Ravoteur, Micheline Marlin-Godier, and Dominique Taffin, *Femmes de la Martinique: Quelle histoire?* (Fort-de-France: Archives départementales de la Martinique, 2008), 60.
6. Paulette Nardal, "L'antillaise étudiante à Paris," *Le soir* 30 (June 1930): n.p.
7. I will use what I assume to be Paulette Nardal's translation of the story. All of the articles in the *La revue du monde noire* appeared bilingually; thus I consider both the English and French versions together as one text. The excerpts from this story and all other citations from *La revue du monde noir* reflect the original translations into English that appeared in the magazine.

8. Paulette Nardal, "L'éveil de la conscience de race / Awakening of Race Consciousness," *La revue du monde noir* (1931): 29/347.
9. Nardal, "L'éveil/Awakening," 29/347, 30/348.
10. Nardal, "L'éveil/Awakening," 29/347.
11. Jennifer Anne Boittin, *Colonial Metropolis: The Urban Grounds of Anti-imperialism and Feminism in Interwar Paris* (Lincoln: University of Nebraska Press, 2010), 156.
12. Paulette Nardal, "Ce que nous voulons faire / Our Aim," *La revue du monde noir* 1 (1930): n.p.
13. Nardal, "Ce que nous voulons faire / Our Aim," n.p.
14. Roberte Horth, "Histoire sans importance / A Thing of No Importance," *La revue du monde noir* 2 (1931): 48/118. Hereafter cited parenthetically in the text.
15. W. E. B. Du Bois, *The Souls of Black Folk* (New York: Signet Classic, 1969), 139.
16. Nardal, "L'antillaise étudiante à Paris," n.p.
17. T. Denean Sharpley-Whiting, *Negritude Women* (Minneapolis: University of Minnesota Press, 2002), 76.
18. Boittin, *Colonial Metropolis*, 154.
19. Georges Cuvier, *Recherches sur les ossements fossiles* (Deterville, Paris, 1812), 1:105.
20. After Saartjie Baartman's death in 1815, Cuvier oversaw her dissection and immortalized his "findings" in *Observations sur le cadavre d'une femme connue à Paris et à Londres sous le nom de Vénus hottentote* (1817), in which he argued that her anatomy proved the eternal inferiority and depraved sexuality of black women. Under his direction, her brain and genitalia were placed on public exhibit in the Musée de l'Homme.
21. Paulette Nardal, "En exil," *La dépêche africaine* 19 (December 1929): 1. All citations in the text to this story are from page 1.
22. There is an interesting disagreement among scholars about where her son has been working his leather business for the last five years. Brent Hayes Edwards locates him in Algeria, presumably the city southwest of Algiers known as Columb-Béchar, which was under French colonization (*The Practice of Diaspora: Literature, Translation, and the Rise of Black Internationalism* [Cambridge MA: Harvard University Press, 2003], 143–44). Tracey Denean Sharpley-Whiting, however, in the translation of the story that she provides in *Negritude Women*, locates Elisa's son in "South America" (117, 118), though perhaps this comes from confusing "Columb" in the original text with "Columbie." There is a third possibility that "Columb" refers to Columbus, Ohio. As Nardal was a Harriet Beecher Stowe scholar, and Elisa's son's company is bought out by "les Américains," this is a possibility as well. Whether Algeria, South America, or the United States, her son is a sojourner in white imperial peripheries.

23. Shireen K. Lewis, *Race, Culture, and Identity: Francophone West African and Caribbean Literature and Theory from Négritude to Créolité* (London: Lexington Books, 2006), 59.
24. Couti, "Am I My Sister's Keeper?"
25. Emily Musil, "*La Marianne Noire*: How Gender and Race in the Twentieth Century Atlantic World Reshaped the Debate about Human Rights" (PhD diss., University of California, Los Angeles, 2007), 17.
26. Conversation with the author, Fort-de-France, May 29, 2015.
27. "Quick lunch" is in English in the original text; the slang is a sign of cosmopolitan modernity. Paulette Nardal, "Guignol Ouolouf," *L'étudiant noir* (1935): 1. All citations in the text to this story are from page 1.
28. A lively of discussion of whether or not Africans and Antilleans should adopt European dress while in the metropole continued through three issues of *La revue du monde noir*.
29. Jessie Redmond Fauset, "The Enigma of the Sorbonne," *Crisis: A Record of the Darker Races* (March 1925): 216–19.
30. Fauset, "The Enigma," 219.

14

Social Imaginaries in Tension?

The Women of Cameroon's Battle for Equal Rights under French Rule at the Turn of the 1940s–50s

ROSE NDENGUE

At the end of World War II, the French government sought to reorganize its relationship with the overseas territories. The French wanted to develop a new legal framework to govern their territories and determine the rights of colonial subjects. Changing the name of the empire from the French Empire to the French Union supposedly embodied this political evolution.[1] The French territories in Cameroon and Togo, which at the time included separate territories under French and British mandates, were thus incorporated into this new union. While allowing for relative liberalization of social and political life, the 1946 reforms also perpetuated, to an extent, the imperial view that structured social relations in the territories. Under articles 80, 81, and 82, the 1946 French Constitution created a two-tier citizenship that would configure the colonies' social and political organization during the following decades. For citizens of the metropole and French nationals overseas, their social and political rights fell under the status of French citizens, but for all others, their rights were determined by the ambiguous status of the French Union.[2] For the latter, access to rights depended on a set of conditions not imposed on French citizens. This was particularly true for the right to vote and social benefits for families.

This situation maintained a form of inequality between local natives and the French. Only a handful of Africans benefited from the colonial reforms. Recognition of these ongoing inequalities, which went against the promises of social and civic equality for all different people within the union, generated frustration and led to numerous demonstrations throughout the French colonies in Africa. To take advantage of the window of opportunity provided by the 1946 reforms, female Cameroonian activists joined together to enlarge this "small opening."[3] They denounced the inadequacies of the "reforms" and demanded equal treatment. While the telling of Cameroonian historiography privileges—with very few exceptions–the male battle for equality through the activist trade unions and nationalist organizations, this chapter takes into account the role that Cameroonian women played in the struggle for equality within the colonial context.[4] Indeed, like their Senegalese and Antillean counterparts, Cameroonian women were important political actors.[5]

Most of these women belonged to the first generation of educated women in Cameroon of the postwar period. The archives provide a wealth of information about educated women in postwar Cameroon, particularly about their organizations. For this reason, I focus on the female organizations that flourished at the dawn of the African independence movements (there are also traces of working-class female experiences in the archives). Essentially, I explore the meaning of the women's struggles for equality during an era when the vast majority of Cameroonians were marginalized.

I draw from documents found at the National Archives of Yaoundé (ANY) in Cameroon, which for the most part consist of petitions addressed to the United Nations from women's organizations, reports of female organizations' activities, and women's correspondences with the colonial administration. In synthesizing and analyzing these documents, I suggest that the battle of educated women for equality was part of a political process. Cameroonian women, I contend, used a new social imaginary to advance their goals and call into question the colonial and patriarchal social order. Here I should note that analyzing this phenomenon relies on the notion of the social imaginary, which Cornelius Castoriadis conceptualized as the origin of social institutions and a means for understanding the permanence or changes of such institutions.[6] Using this concept sheds light on the fact that social institutions are the results of a building process in which "a universe of imaginary significations" not only gives meaning to institutions but also allows individuals to challenge them.[7] Through the intersection of colonial history and gender studies, one can thus begin to understand what seems, at first glance, to be a paradox.

Improving Socioeconomic Rights by Promoting Dominant Colonial Values

The colonizers introduced a new social imaginary in the colonies through schools and clinics. Essentially, they wanted the locals to adopt new social and sanitary norms. Since the beginning of the twentieth century, a few educated African women were involved in the colonial administration's sanitary and social project.[8] In the postwar period, auxiliaries of the colonial project, women also contributed to the "civilizing mission." Indeed, colonial administrators opened new and limited opportunities in public offices to women while simultaneously redefining their role and place in African society by confining them to the private sphere. The women selected for this endeavor were primarily the daughters of prominent local social elites (heads of businesses, community leaders, public officials, the "most civilized"). These girls received an education that prioritized their role as mothers and wives of elite men. Similar to the process that took place in France during the first half of the twentieth century, the objective here was to give African women "the illusion of an education befitting a homemaker" by presenting maternal and domestic work as a "change in educational mores."[9] This approach, based on Western nuclear family settings, introduced a restricted vision of womanhood and domesticity. As stressed by Oyeronke Oyewumi, in African societies "woman" as social category was fluid and situational.[10] In these societies, women were not confined to the private sphere. Instead, they embraced many social roles, held different positions, and participated in different spaces. In many African societies, women were also in charge of farming, crafting, and/or trading. Moreover, as motherhood was recognized as an important social function, some of them (according to their age or class, for example) participated in important political and religious institutions.[11]

The first educated women seized the opportunities resulting from the reforms of 1946, which granted freedom of association and the right to organize. They asked the authorities to fulfill their promises of "modernizing" their values. In particular, the women demanded that all rights involving the welfare state be applied to the African colonies.[12] They worked against the colonial administration, which subjugated the locals based on binary (masculine/feminine, educated/uneducated) and arbitrary (ruling elite / mass) logic. The women fought for equality and insisted that social rights, like family benefits and education, be extended to the entire population.

Denouncing Arbitrary Colonial Power by Promoting Sociosanitary Norms

The archives of the 1950s reveal that there was a certain excitement among the colonized female elites over the question of "developing Cameroonian women." Through organizations like the Evolution de la Femme Camerounaise (EVACAM), educated women became sociopolitical activists.[13] They created associations like the Union of Cameroonian Women (UFC) and the Democratic Union of Cameroonian Women (UDEFEC) to claim social rights for all women and, more generally, for the Cameroonian population. Although they differed over their final objective—the UFC wanted Cameroon to remain in the French Union, while the UDEFEC fought for independence and the reunification of the territory—the two organizations shared a language that wanted to empower Cameroonian mothers and women in general. They endorsed "the model of colonial femininity," which resembled the Western model.[14] In short, the groups' leaders wanted the metropole's legal provisions for social protection to be implemented in Cameroon.

At the start, the two movements' leaders were very close. The UFC was comanaged by a trio of teachers—Julienne Niat, founder and president; Marie-Irène Ngapeth-Biyong, general secretary; and Marthe Ouandié, treasurer—all three of whom were future leaders of the UDEFEC.[15] The UFC's leaders assigned their group the task of teaching African women about their societal functions. As the record states, "This organization's goal is to teach African women about their rights as mothers and wives, especially in social and familial settings, to teach them to conduct themselves well in society and to acquire skills in all domains following the European example."[16] Reading the UDEFEC's statutes reveals the logic behind their objectives; they desired to promote "the organization and education of female citizens, mothers and wives," and "to defend the Cameroonian family in its material, moral, intellectual, and cultural domains."[17]

While this information should be analyzed with some distance, it seems possible to establish a connection between the female activists' involvement in these movements and their marital relations. The administration often adopted this approach, correlating the female activists' involvement in each of the two organizations to their marital ties. In other words, they connected UDEFEC and UFC members to nationalist activists and prominent figures of the colonial administration, respectively. In addition, certain UDEFEC leaders—Marthe Moumié and Marie-Irène Ngapeth Biyong in particular—adopted the same attitude by claiming that their involvement was the result of marital encouragement. One analysis of these testimonies suggests they were an effort to legitimize the women's social behavior by making their motives coincide with male conventions and expectations. After all, educated women were socialized in order to form an "evolved" couple with their spouses.[18] Accordingly, these women adhered to the male conception of white femininity conveyed in colonial institutions and schools. One should note, however, that not all white women endorsed the aforementioned model.[19]

The leaders of the two groups wanted all Cameroonian women to benefit from the new colonial agenda. In order to do so, Julienne Niat submitted requests asking the authorities to offer their financial support for the UFC's women's education program. She presented her approach as complementary to the authorities' "civilizing mission," emphasizing that it gave "basic education of young brides" like childcare and sewing lessons. She also advocated for "domestic training that culminated in an exam," a pedagogical approach that actually struck a favorable chord with the colonial authorities.[20] To demonstrate their interest in the women whose conduct conformed to the marriage and family values the authorities promoted, they instructed the Territorial Assembly of Cameroon

(ATCAM), which had received Niat's subsidy requests, to respond in favor.[21] The UDEFEC also campaigned to extend adult classes for women and create housekeeping schools throughout the territory to teach women "housekeeping and childcare before and after birth."[22] However, far from being content to simply assimilate the colonizers' "model of respectable femininity," the educated female elite used it as a springboard to develop a more or less open criticism of the colonial system.[23]

The UFC's and UDEFEC's requests reveal that the movements' leaders considered access for all Cameroonian women to the domestic ideal an indispensable sign of equality. Carrying out this ideal entailed meeting certain prior requirements, which brought to light the failures of the colonial administration. The two organizations agreed it was necessary to pay special attention to matters concerning children and the related conditions for women; they adopted a critical stance toward the colonial administration's lack of progress in these areas. It is important to highlight that women's grievances are made in a context in which colonial (male) administrators have to deal with the lack of European staff and even fewer women staff in the fields of sanitation and education. As administrators try to handle these shortages by training some African women, they should at the same time pay attention to the reluctance of many African families to send their daughters to school.[24]

Resuming the colonial administration's population and hygienic concerns, inherited from the medical discourse that emerged in the nineteenth century, the leaders of UDEFEC and UFC criticized the lack of social and sanitary infrastructures in the territory, as well as the inadequacies of those that did exist.[25]

In a motion addressed to the UN Field Mission of 1952, the Nkongsamba section of the UFC, which correlated children's health to the health of their mothers, lamented the high rate of infant mortality. They attributed this rate to the administration's failure to organize a health system: "Healthy babies are only born to healthy mothers—protecting children means protecting mothers. Lack of obligatory prenatal care and lack or deficiency of maternity wards everywhere have affected births, resulting in a considerable number of still births and stunted growth. Mothers do not have the skills sufficient for raising their babies."[26] The grievances listed by the UDEFEC in their petition to the same field mission corroborated the UFC's findings: "In Cameroon, the native children have a difficult life. Maternity wards are insufficient to such a point that . . . many pregnant women receive zero care during their pregnancy and give birth far from any medical assistance. In urban centers and places without clinics, the care given to maternity is minimal. . . . [T]he diet is mediocre. All of it contributes to a high rate of infant mortality." The organization denounced the lack of educational infrastructures and the current educational policy (undue dismissals, materials laced with a "colonial spirit"), which caused the low education levels of Cameroonian children. The UDEFEC established a strong correlation between these conditions and those of children who worked in the equally deplorable "colonialist societies."[27] They further condemned the racial discrimination that took place in childcare facilities between children of mixed race and indigenous orphans, where the former received care denied to the latter.[28]

As their final point, the UDEFEC raised the continuing problem of civil status; they lamented the absence of a census for newborns and the population as a whole. A census was very important, because the colonial administration justified restricting Africans from voting by raising the question of individualization. In other words, colonial authorities found it difficult to identify people who could be registered on electoral lists as persons because the colonial system only identified Africans through various social categories like chiefs or elders. Analyzing citizenship boundaries under the French colonial empire, Frédérick Cooper explains that instead of proceeding by nominative registration, French colonial officers used to organize the colonized by vertical channels such as elderly, chieftaincies, or any other authority familiar to the officers.[29] Thus, this claim showed that the organization's leaders were aware of the discriminatory consequences regarding access to social and political rights that this situation created for the local peoples. To change this unacceptable colonial condition, the UFC and UDEFEC proposed solutions to increase Africans' social and political power.

Demanding Greater Social and Political Power for Men and Women

While advocating for training throughout the territory, UFC and UDEFEC leaders were aware that teaching housekeeping and basic skills for health and hygiene were limited when it came to improving people's living conditions, including women. The two organizations thus incorporated into their motions grievances about the social and economic state to empower the colonized. They established a link between equal access to social and economic institutions and the well-being of women and the population as a whole.

The UDEFEC demanded "clean lodgings . . . permitting full physical and mental development" for children and low-income families.[30] In addition, the two organizations recommended making school attendance mandatory for children of both sexes "like in France, Egypt, and many other countries."[31] They further advocated for the creation of more institutions—nurseries, elementary schools, cafeterias, learning centers, orphanages, with school buses and transportation, scholarships, and so on—to manage children's education and recreation "without distinguishing race, . . . social class," or gender.[32] They stipulated that recruiting qualified staff should also accompany the creation of these institutions.

Campaigning for women's economic empowerment, following the approach used by Western feminists of the late nineteenth and early twentieth centuries, while bearing in mind the reforms for social protection and family benefits introduced in France in 1946, the two groups demanded that these measures be expanded to benefit not only French citizens but also the colonies.[33] Due to Cameroon's place as part of the "great family of the French Union," the UFC required "payment for mothers with children, with no exceptions or distinction, for family services to raise and educate their children as in France. [And also] payment for giving birth to encourage childbearing in order to repopulate the territory."[34]

As for the UDEFEC, it considered "instituting a democratic system of social security and family services" in Cameroon and securing a "fair" application of the trusteeship system. Doing so would serve as a starting point to address the "delicate problems" concerning dowries and polygamy.[35]

These practices, which the colonizers (the administration and religious missions) considered social evils and evidence of African women's subordinate status, had become a mounting concern during the 1950s. Therefore, the UDEFEC decided to emancipate these women by developing a legal and social framework to change the practice of child marriages, dowries, and polygamy.[36]

Both organizations wanted to see all women reach social and economic independence. Adopting a moralizing approach, the UFC demanded "the establishment of measures to ensure employment for all women, which will eliminate prostitution. [And put into place] a system of social insurance guaranteeing women sufficient help to ensure a normal life in case they are deprived of their livelihood . . . as it is in France."[37]

Conscious that women throughout the territory had diverse experiences, the UFC and UDEFEC made demands that took into account the specific situation of Cameroonian women; they catered to women of the elite, the popular urban class in the city, and women from rural areas. For example, the UFC denounced the injustices faced by female Cameroonian public servants when compared to their European counterparts in terms of social benefits and health insurance. Equally concerned for the rural communities, the two organizations demanded the modernization of agriculture. In many ways, as a strategy to "liberate Cameroonian women, they echoed the trade-union movement of the 1940s which wanted to improve living conditions and increase agricultural yield."[38] The UDEFEC further condemned the fact that in the Mungo region, the colonial state was robbing widows of their land for the benefit of European agricultural colonization. They also did not forget the plight of female merchants, who demanded the freedom to practice their commerce; the organization's goal was to ensure that all women had an income. Following the same logic, the organization demanded sanitary conditions in marketplaces and an increase in the frequency of market days.

Educated women respected gender hierarchies; they promoted the domestic ideal to get involved in the public arena. Nonetheless, their activism did not promote conventional attitudes. Their presence in the public arena and their claims challenged the colonial male social imaginary, which rested on a binary and conflicting conception of society: educated versus uneducated, ruling elite versus the masses, or public versus private. Questioning this approach, UDEFEC and UFC activists' social imaginary was more inclusive; their definition of political participation expanded far beyond exercising the right to vote. Through their involvement, the activists from the UFC and UDEFEC took political action and initiated a process of subjectivization by "*making the possible* [*sic*]."[39] They effectively became political agents in a system resting upon unequal power relations.[40]

Women's Political Subjectification

For educated women in Cameroon, the roles of mother and wife served as convergent instruments of political action, permitting them to act in the public arena. Whether within the framework of the French Union or by challenging the status quo via nationalism, these women tried to emancipate themselves. Each group of women used the tools at their disposal—the promise of equal citizenship within the French Union or the nationalist movement's inclusive and independent design—to excoriate the dominating force oppressing them.[41] This approach, which took place in two phases in accordance with the changing political atmosphere in Cameroon, allowed women to become "political and moral subjects."[42]

Women's Political Opposition in Its Early Stages (1946–52)

From 1946 to 1952, educated women united their efforts in the Association of Cameroonian Women (ASSOFECAM), then the UFC, to condemn the implicit and explicit discrimination inflicted on women in the political sphere. They wanted to establish a society where women enjoyed equal political rights.

In 1946 Laurence Eteki Maladi, one of Cameroon's first licensed midwives, founded the ASSOFECAM, which Patricia Chamukong describes as one of the first political parties created in Cameroon in the 1940s.[43] The party sought to eliminate the restrictions on women's right to vote.[44] It adopted an approach that called into question the gendered and racist ideas behind the notion of citizens imagined in 1946. At that time, the only colonized subjects with access to citizenship were those "able to prove their personal merit," as well as their civil status.[45] These requirements excluded the majority of the population, and nearly all women, from suffrage. Only a very small minority of women—women with access not only to an education but also to appropriate jobs like nursing, child care, and midwifery—were able to vote. Furthermore, the colonial authorities had an ambiguous attitude toward these women because they had difficulties conceiving of them as citizens. In 1944 Pierre Cournarie, governor of French West Africa (AOF), resorted to familiar arguments to disenfranchise African women when he expressed his reluctance to give Senegalese women from the Four Communes the right to vote, though women in France had just been granted suffrage.[46] Two years later, in 1946, correspondence from the minister of Overseas France addressed to the governor of Cameroon gave an account of the authorities' reluctance to secure women's rights. It revealed that fulfilling certain employment opportunities was exclusive to literate women; in short, the space for feminine action remained essentially domestic.[47]

By fighting for the right to vote for all Cameroonian women, Laurence Dieng undermined the binary logic of the colonial system that created antagonistic categories like "developed" and "behind" to deny the colonized political rights. Dieng's approach assumed all Cameroonian women had equal civic responsibilities and urged literate women to go beyond the domestic skills they had acquired during their training. This organization, which did not receive any support, was banned the year of its creation due to its overly subversive approach.[48]

When the law of May 23, 1951, expanded the electoral body—with a specific clause referencing "mothers of two children, living or dead for France"—and seemed to satisfy at least in part ASSOFECAM's key demand, the UFC then picked up where the fight had left off. Like numerous other Cameroonian organizations, the UFC condemned the law's insufficiencies. In 1952 the UFC wrote a petition criticizing the privilege given to "mothers of two children" and in so doing denounced the fact that women's right to vote was linked to their "reproductive qualities."[49] The UFC therefore demanded the right to vote for all Cameroonian women in a society based on the principles of democracy, freedom, and equal rights.[50] The women who drafted the petition wrote, "We endeavor to obtain equal rights with men in economic, social, and cultural domains."[51] With that in mind, the organization demanded that women have access to all administrative and civil service posts.

It is particularly interesting to note that Julienne Niat created the UFC following her losses in the elections of 1951 and 1952, the results of her male adversaries' sexism.[52] In her description of Niat's journey, Henriette Ekwe reveals that it was riddled with incessant attempts to question the social order.[53] Ekwe states: "Julienne Niat is going to lead a campaign with her baby in her arms to join the ATCAM. She will be the first to lead this type of campaign. We must not forget that women like Mme Niat left for France and earned their baccalaureate degree. She was accepted into the highly selective Paris Institute of Political Studies University, but the colonial administration said no, as women were supposedly destined to be teachers rather than political scientists. So she became a schoolteacher."[54]

While members of ASSOFECAM and UFC seemed to situate the fulfillment of their status as political agents within the colonial framework, the female activists of the UDEFEC felt differently. Allied with the territory's first nationalist groups—the Union of the Peoples of Cameroon (UPC) and the Union of Confederate Cameroonian Trade Unions (USCC)—they envisioned an independent society that would allow them to ensure equality for all.

The Nationalist Movement: Women's Political Opposition Gains Momentum (1952–55)

Created on August 3, 1952, by a group of educated women, including M.-I. Ngapeth Biyong and M. Ouandié, after they had been excluded from the UFC, the UDEFEC invited Cameroonian women to join together and overcome the ethnic, social, and geographical differences dividing their society.[55] Emma Ngom, one of the movement's founders, made this call for action in her speech on May 1, 1952, at a meeting organized by the trade union movement. She urged women to unite under "a national organization of women" and reminded the audience with these words: "Do you think, for example, that the Bassa tribe can save Cameroon? The same goes for any tribe, be it Bamiléké, Boulou, etc. . . . So it would be crazy for a Cameroonian woman to think she could save our country by joining solely with the women of her tribe."[56] She hoped Cameroonian women would unite on the basis of national solidarity and a common struggle for freedom.

This solidarity extended across the continent and internationally. In February 1950 the Cameroonian nationalist women showed their solidarity with "the valiant . . . women of the Ivory Coast who led a historic battle against oppression" by protesting the incarceration of their husbands, nationalist activists within PDCI-RDA, in prison in Bassam.[57] Describing her participation in the Congress of Vienna conference on the Defense of Children in April 1952, E. Ngom describes having been "the only woman from French Black Africa" and thus having been the spokesperson on behalf of all the colonized women in these territories.[58] Similar to other African women's organizations, which were connected to the nationalist parties and their African Democratic Assembly (RDA) affiliations, UDEFEC's approach was transnational. They sought to build relationships with women's organizations sharing this internationalist approach, like the Union of French Women (UFF) and the International Democratic Federation of Women (FDIF), which were close to communist circles. This approach allowed the organization to extend the issues of Cameroon's battle beyond the territory's singular confrontation of the metropole.[59] These organizations described their relationships as both political and amicable, based on their founding principle of "active solidarity," which enabled them to accrue greater visibility for the battles of the colonized and to develop common watchwords.[60]

Reports of the UDEFEC's activities reveal that its leaders wanted women's genuine, indispensable involvement in the nationalist struggle to be recognized. They confirmed the solidarity among female nationalist activists and attested to women's equal capacity for political participation.

The expression of this active nationalist solidarity took on diverse forms.[61] One particular initiative by a female activist "made a space available to the regional trade union" that was unveiled in the presence of four hundred people.[62] Whatever various forms their actions took, the women's position did not imply that the female activists were subservient to the men. And whereas the alliance between female nationalist activists resulted from "an equivocal partnership," women involved in the UDEFEC required equality of the sexes in the political arena.[63] Ngom introduced the movement's first congress by stating that there was "proof that an anticolonialist movement by women exists in Cameroon. . . . Cameroonian women have decided to better organize themselves to take part in the struggle that will bring [their] children closer to happiness and [their] country closer to freedom."[64]

Numerous times since its creation, the organization emphasized being "a movement . . . independent of any political movement."[65] The female nationalist activists thus affirmed their independence from their male comrades, some of whom tried to supervise the women's organization, as well as the international women's organizations.[66] Concerning the latter, they did so in a vain attempt to dissipate suspicions of communism, for throughout the Cold War colonial authorities used the label "communist" to disqualify the nationalist movement and delegitimize its demands.[67]

While the large majority of the colonized were disqualified from taking part in the emerging "modern" political arena, Cameroonian women challenged the colonial and patriarchal social order during the decade following World War II. Having gained access to privileged social circles and, to some extent, embracing the dominant colonial social imaginary, the first educated women joined together based on their common intermediary position. Their model of femininity stressed the inclusion of all women: they demanded that equal rights be instituted between the colonized territories and the metropole, which required granting the colonized greater capacities for social, economic, and political action. Not content merely to spread the dominant norms or asking others to conform, these women used their public position to question the "system of views, duties, and norms" governing their lives.[68] Whether they adopted the reformist attitude—aiming to improve conditions for all, including women, within the French Union—or the more radical position of nationalism, they wanted social, economic, and political equality for people of every background. Through their involvement, these women desired to build alternative identifications by questioning the colonial social imaginary.[69] By inviting the colonized, and women in particular, to deconstruct their place and function in society, the UFC and UDEFEC transformed Cameroonian women and the colonized as a whole into political subjects. In a time and place in which they were denied this status, these women's organizations invited the people to create a new political identity for themselves.

Notes

This essay includes information previously published in Rose Ndengue, "Mobilisations féminines au Cameroun français dans les années 1940–1950: L'ordre du genre et l'ordre colonial fissurés," *Le mouvement social* 2, no. 255 (2016): 71–85.

1. Frédérick Cooper, *Français et africains? Être citoyen au temps de la décolonisation* (Paris: Payot, 2014), 33.
2. Cooper, *Français et africains?*, 134–37.
3. Cooper, *Français et africains?*, 39.
4. For the exceptions, see Ndengue, "Mobilisations féminines," 72. For the trade unions and nationalist organizations, see especially Richard Joseph, *Le mouvement nationaliste au Cameroun* (Paris: Karthala, 1986); Léon Kaptue, *Travail et main-d'oeuvre au Cameroun sous le régime français 1916–1952* (Paris: L'Harmattan, 1986); Achille Mbembe, *La naissance du maquis dans le Sud-Cameroun (1920–1960)* (Paris: Karthala, 1996).
5. For more information, see Cooper, *Français et africains?*, 59–64; Jean Lacroix et Saliou Mbaye, "Le vote des femmes au Sénégal," *Ethiopiques*, no. 6 (1976), http://ethiopiques.refer.sn/spip.php?article413; Clara Palmiste, "Le vote féminin et la transformation des colonies françaises d'Amérique en départements en 1946," *Nuevo mundo mundos nuevos* (2014), doi:10.4000/nuevomundo.66842; Annette K. Joseph-Gabriel, "Gerty Archimède and the Struggle for Decolonial Citizenship in the French Antilles, 1946–51," in this book.
6. See Cornelius Castoriadis, *L'imaginaire comme tel* (Paris: Hermann Editeurs, 2007).
7. Castoriadis, *L'imaginaire,* 52–53.
8. See Pascale Barthélémy, *Africaines et diplômées à l'époque coloniale (1918–1957)* (Rennes: Presses Universitaires de Rennes, 2010).
9. Geneviève Fraisse, *Les femmes et leur histoire* (1998; Paris: Gallimard, 2010), 507.
10. Oyeronke Oyewumi, "Conceptualizing Gender: The Eurocentric Foundation of Feminist Concepts and the Challenge of African Epistemologies," in *African Gender Scholarship: Concepts, Methodologies and Paradigms*, ed. Signe Arnfred et al. (Dakar: CODESRIA, 2004), 1–8.
11. For more information about women's roles in Cameroon society, see "Kaberry Dr. P., Lady Anthropologist. Posting of Cameroons. International African Institute,

'Preliminary report on fieldwork in Bamenda. British Cameroons,'" Aa 4a 3755, National Archives of Buea (NAB), Cameroon; Jean-Claude Barbier, ed., *Femmes du Cameroun: Mères pacifiques, femmes rebelles* (ORSTOM-Karthala, 1985).

12. Gisela Bock, "Pauvreté féminine, droits des mères et États-providence," in *Histoire des femmes en occident: Le XXe siècle*, ed. Françoise Thébaud et al. (Perrin, 2002), 515–17.
13. Subsidy 1952, 2AC 8942, Evolution de la Femme Camerounaise (EVACAM), National Archives of Yaoundé (ANY), Cameroon.
14. Ndengue, "Mobilisations féminines," 75–76; Anne-Marie Sohn, "Entre deux-guerre: Les rôles féminins en France et en Angleterre," in Thébaud et al., *Histoire des femmes*, 169.
15. Ndengue, "Mobilisations féminines," 75.
16. Information note, November 21, 1952, 2, 3AC 3520, UFC 1952, ANY.
17. Marie-Irène Ngapeth Biyong, *Cameroun: Combats pour l'indépendance* (L'Harmattan, 2009), 82–83.
18. Ndengue, "Mobilisations féminines," 76, among others.
19. See, for example, Irène Jami, "La France entre les deux guerre," in *La place des femmes dans l'histoire: Une histoire mixte*, ed. Geneviève Dermenjian et al. (Paris: Belin Éditions, 2010), 299–310.
20. Subsidy request made by Mme Ngoumou Félix (née Niat Julienne), May 16, 1953, letter no. 109, 1AC 4755, ANY.
21. Ndengue, "Mobilisations féminines," 76–77.
22. Information note, October 31, 1952, in UDEFEC, "Motion à présenter à l'ONU," 3, and information note, Congrès de l'UDEFEC of August 6, 7, and 8, 1954, September 4, 1954, in UDEFEC, "Résolutions sur les revendications," 1, 2AC 7035, Activités 1952–56, UDEFEC, ANY.
23. Laure Bereni and Anne Revillard, "Un mouvement social paradigmatique? Ce que le mouvement des femmes fait à la sociologie des mouvements sociaux," *Sociétés contemporaines* 85 (2012): 21.
24. See Barthélémy, *Africaines*.
25. Sohn, "Entre deux-guerre," 168.
26. Information note, November 21, 1952, 3.
27. UDEFEC, "Motion," 1, 2.
28. For more on this subject, see Emmanuelle Saada, *Les enfants de la colonie: Les métis de l'Empire français entre sujétion et citoyenneté* (Paris: La Découverte, 2007).
29. Cooper, *Français et africains?*, 74–75, 152–54.
30. UDEFEC, "Motion," 3.
31. Information note, November 21, 1952, 3.
32. Note, 4–5; UDEFEC, "Motion," 3; "Premier congrès," 6, 2AC 7035, ANY; UDEFEC, "Résolutions," 1–2.
33. Bock, "Pauvreté féminine," 515–54.

34. Information note, November 21, 1952, 4.
35. UDEFEC, "Motion," 3; UDEFEC, "Résolutions," 2.
36. For more on this subject, see Ayesha M. Iman, Amina Mama, and Fatou Sow, *Sexe, genre et société : Engendrer les sciences sociales africaines* (Paris: Karthala, 2004); Oyeronke Oyewumi, *African Women and Feminism: Reflecting on the Politics of Sisterhood* (Trenton NJ: Africa Research & Publications, 2003).
37. Information note, November 21, 1952, 4.
38. Ndengue, "Mobilisations féminines," 78–80.
39. Castoriadis, *L'imaginaire*, 99.
40. Romain Bertrand, "Chroniques d'une guerre morale: Subjectivation par l'ascèse et formation de l'État à Java," in *Matière à politique: Le pouvoir, les corps et les choses*, ed. Jean-François Bayart and Jean-Pierre Warnier (Paris: Karthala, 2004), 58.
41. Federico Tarragoni, "Du rapport de la subjectivation politique au monde social: Les raisons d'une mésentente entre sociologie et philosophie politique," *Raisons politiques* 62 (2016): 123–24.
42. Tarragoni, "Du rapport," 125.
43. Patricia B. Chamukong, "The Evolution of Cameroonian Women in Politics" (MA thesis, University of Yaoundé, 1990), 81.
44. Chamukong, "The Evolution," 74.
45. Cooper, *Français et africains?*, 41.
46. Cooper, *Français et africains?*, 59–60.
47. Ndengue, "Mobilisations féminines," 74–75.
48. Chamukong, "The Evolution," 82.
49. Odile Goerg, "Femmes africaines et politique: Les colonisées au féminin en Afrique occidentale," *Clio: Histoire, femmes et sociétés* 6 (1997): 7, accessed January 25, 2015, doi: 10.4000/clio.378.
50. Ndengue, "Mobilisations feminines," 78.
51. Information note, November 21, 1952, 4.
52. Ndengue, "Mobilisations féminines," 77–78.
53. Henriette Ekwe was one of the nationalist female activists in Cameroon who joined the cause in France in the 1970s while a university student.
54. Interview by the author with Henriette Ekwe in her home in Douala, July 8, 2011.
55. Ndengue, "Mobilisations féminines," 75, 79.
56. "Premier congrès," 2.
57. "Résolution: Comité féminin de l'UPC, Section du Rassemblement démocratique africain, réunie le 5 février 1950," Activités UPC, 1950–1954: Union des populations du Cameroun, 1AC 19/10, ANY. The Democratic Party of Ivory Coast (PDCI) was affiliated with the RDA, like many African nationalist parties from French colonial territories.

58. "Résolution: Comité féminin de l'UPC," 2; Ndengue, "Mobilisations féminines," 84.
59. Emmanuelle Bouilly and Ophélie Rillon, "Relire les décolonisations d'Afrique francophone au prisme du genre," *Le mouvement social* 2, no. 255 (2016): 10.
60. Ndengue, "Mobilisations féminines," 84; Pascale Barthélémy, "Macoucou à Pékin: L'arène internationale, une ressource politique pour les Africaines dans les années 1940–1950," *Le mouvement social* 2, no. 255 (2016): 17–33.
61. See Ndengue, "Mobilisations féminines," 81.
62. "Premier congrès," 4.
63. Ndengue, "Mobilisations féminines," 81.
64. "Premier congrès," 1.
65. UDEFEC, "Motion," 1.
66. Ndengue, "Mobilisations féminines," 83–84.
67. Information note, a/s UDEFEC, October 14, 1952, 2AC 7035, ANY.
68. Tarragoni, "Du rapport," 126.
69. Castoriadis, *L'imaginaire*, 55–85.

Contributors

Jacqueline Couti is an associate professor of French and Francophone studies at the University of Kentucky. Her first book project, *Dangerous Creole Liaisons*, considers the ways in which white and black French Caribbean writers represent sexed female bodies and sexual difference to advance their political ideologies, often hoping to vindicate one outlook over others. Her second book project, *Sex, Sea, and Self*, offers a rereading of the relevance of black authors at the beginning of the twentieth century. This revaluation covers male and female authors of color who, for their own political, cultural, and personal ends, reject or reproduce the (largely white) metropolitan and Creole exotic colonial mythology that surrounds Creole women and Creole sexual stereotypes such as the *doudou* (mulatto women as tantalizing objects of desire). Professor Couti has also published numerous articles in highly respected academic journals.

Joseph Diémé earned his PhD at the University of Iowa in 2006 and subsequently joined the Department of World Languages and Cultures at Humboldt State University, northern California. He is currently associate professor and director of the French and Francophone Studies Program. He teaches languages, cinema, literatures, and cultures of the French-speaking world. His research focuses on the inscription of law, history, and cultures in French and Francophone colonial and postcolonial literature. He is the author of *De la plantation coloniale aux* *banlieues: La négritude dans le discours postcolonial francophone* (2012). He is currently completing a book manuscript on postcolonial discourses and tribal language under President Barack Obama.

Sarah Fila-Bakabadio is an associate professor in American and African American studies at the University Cergy–Pontoise (France). Her work first explored black nationalisms in the United States and now examines the Black Atlantic through the intellectual, cultural, and visual connections between Afrodescendants in the United States, Africa, and Europe from the nineteenth century to the present. She has published articles on Black Atlantic historiography, Afrocentrisms, black populations in France, and the black body. Her study of African American Afrocentrisms, *Africa on My Mind: Histoire sociale de l'afrocentrisme aux États-Unis*, was published in 2016 (Les indes savantes).

Claire Oberon Garcia is a professor of English at Colorado College. Her research and teaching interests are focused on gender and the Black Atlantic. She was lead editor on *From "Uncle Tom's Cabin" to "The Help": Critical Perspectives on White-Authored Narratives of Black Life* (Palgrave Macmillan, 2014) and has contributed chapters to *Paris, Capital of the Black Atlantic: Literature, Modernity and Diaspora* (Johns Hopkins University Press, 2013), *Henry James's Europe: Inheritance and Transfer* (Open University Press, 2011), *From Bourgeois to Boujie: Black Middle-Class Performances* (Wayne State University Press, 2010), and *The Harlem Renaissance Revisited* (Johns Hopkins University Press, 2010). She has also authored several articles in journals such as the *International Journal for Francophone Studies* and *Palimpsest: A Journal on Women, Gender and the Black International.* She feels strongly about bringing black studies scholarship to communities outside of academia and is currently collaborating with the Jamaican writer Alecia McKenzie on a study of how the experiences of enslaved Africans are being curated and commemorated in museums throughout the Black Atlantic.

Félix Germain received his PhD in African diaspora studies from the University of California at Berkeley. He is currently an assistant professor of Africana studies at the University of Pittsburgh. His research interests include black social movements and gender relations in France, the United States, and the French Caribbean. He has published numerous articles and is the author of *Decolonizing the Republic: African and Caribbean Migrants in Postwar Paris, 1946–1974* (Michigan State University Press, 2016).

Stéphanie Guyon is an assistant professor of political science in the Department of Law and Political Science of the University of Picardie Jules Verne. She is a member of the Centre Universitaire de Recherches sur l'Action Publique et le Politique, Épistémologie et Sciences Sociales (Centre National de la Recherche Scientifique). She has been working on French Guiana for fifteen years. Her PhD dissertation dealt with the colonial legacy in French Guiana contemporary politics, in particular, the politicization process of minoritized groups (Amerindians and Maroons). She published the special issues "L'état outre-mer" (with Violaine Girard and Audrey Célestine), *Politix*, no. 114 (2016) and "Outre-mers indigènes" (with Benoît Trépied), *Genèses* 91 (2013). Among various articles, she published "L'engagement des transfuges coloniaux: Les mobilités sociales au prisme du genre, de la classe et des hiérarchies coloniales," *Politix*, no. 111 (2016); "Des 'primitifs' aux 'autochtones': Savoirs ethnologiques et politiques publiques en Guyane de 1946 à nos jours," *Genèses* 91 (2013); "Politisation et hiérarchies coloniales: Amérindiens et Noirs-marrons en Guyane française (1946–1990)," *Critique internationale* 50 (2011). She is also the coauthor of *Sexes, genre et politique*, Economica, "Études Politiques" (2007).

Hilary Jones is an associate professor of history and African and African diaspora studies at Florida International University. Her book, *The Métis of Senegal: Urban Life and Politics in French West Africa* (Indiana University Press, 2013), examines the making of a multiracial community in Senegal's colonial capital. She has published in the *Journal of African History*, *Slavery and Abolition*, and the *International Journal of African Historical Studies*. Her work also appears in several edited collections and research works. Jones received research awards from Fulbright-Hays and the Social Science Research Council. She is an associate editor of the *Journal of West African History* and serves on the board of directors of the West African Research Association.

Annette K. Joseph-Gabriel is a scholar of contemporary Francophone Caribbean and African literature with interdisciplinary specializations in black transnational feminisms, Afrodiasporic literary movements, and slavery in the Atlantic world. She is currently an assistant professor of French and Francophone studies at the University of Michigan, Ann Arbor. Her forthcoming book, *Decolonial Citizenship: Black Women's Resistance in the Francophone World*, examines black women's articulations of citizenship through their work in anticolonial movements in Francophone Africa and the Antilles. Her articles have appeared in *Small Axe*,

Nouvelles études francophones, *Slavery and Abolition*, *Eighteenth-Century Studies*, and the *French Review*. She is a recipient of the Carrie Chapman Catt Prize for Research on Women and Politics and is the managing editor of *Palimpsest: A Journal on Women, Gender, and the Black International*.

Silyane Larcher is a historical and political sociologist and research fellow at the Centre National de la Recherche Scientifique. She specializes in the history of citizenship in the French Atlantic (metropole and colonies), with a particular interest on the tensions between race and universalism. Her first book, *L'autre citoyen: L'idéal républicain et les Antilles après l'esclavage* (Armand Colin, 2014), examines from the perspectives of political philosophy and historical sociology the relationship between French citizenship and the making of race and colonial exclusion in postslavery French Caribbean societies, from the second abolition of slavery to the end of the nineteenth century. She has also published scholarly articles in *Sociologie*, *Le mouvement social*, *L'homme et la société*, *La vie des idées (Books and Ideas)*, and *Palimpsest: A Journal on Women, Gender, and the Black International*. Her current book project focuses on the sociohistorical and political context that led to the rise of Afrofeminism in contemporary France.

Nadine Lefaucheur is a retired sociologist of Centre National de la Recherche Scientifique and an associate member of the LC2S (Laboratoire Caribéen de Sciences Sociales) of the Université des Antilles. She worked for years on the family and gender in France and particularly on single-parent families. She is the coauthor with Georges Falconnet of *La fabrication des mâles* (Le Seuil, 1975) and a contributor to *L'histoire des femmes*, edited by Georges Duby and Michelle Perrot (Plon, 1991–92). She has published many articles on gender and family, eugenics, and the history of public policies with regard to "abnormal" families, especially single mothers. She also published issue number 17 of *Pouvoirs locaux dans la Caraïbe* (articles analyzing the statistical data on gender and interpersonal violence in Martinique and some life stories about women's barriers and resources to escape domestic violence). Among various articles published by Nadine Lefaucheur on gender and family in Martinique, see, in particular, with Stéphanie Mulot, "La construction et les coûts de l'injonction de virilité en Martinique," in *Boys Don't Cry! Les coûts de la domination masculine*, ed. D. Dulong, C. Guionnet, and E. Neveu (Presses Universitaires de Rennes, 2012) and, with Joëlle Kabile, "Sociology of Gender in the French Caribbean: A Slow and Fragile Process," *American Sociologist* 48, no. 3–4 (2017).

Robin Mitchell is an award-winning assistant professor of history; she currently teaches at the California State University Channel Islands. She received her doctorate in late modern European history from the University of California, Berkeley, with a designated emphasis in women, gender, and sexuality. Her scholarship includes the forthcoming book project *Vénus noire: Black Women, Colonial Fantasies, and the Production of Gender & Race in France, 1804–1848* with the University of Georgia Press; the articles "Ourika Mania: Interrogating Race, Class, Space, and Place in Early 19th-Century France," in "Black Paris: Circulation and the Mapping of Black Experience," special issue of *African and Black Diaspora: An International Journal* (2015 online; 2017 in print) and "L'Affaire de la Négresse Henriette Lucille: Race, Gender, and Social Status in Eighteenth-Century France," *Transnational Subjects: History, Society and Culture* 2, no. 2 (April 2012); and the chapter "Another Means of Understanding the Gaze: Sarah Bartmann in the Development of Nineteenth-Century French National Identity," in *Black Venus, 2010: They Called Her "Hottentot,"* ed. Deborah Willis and Carla Williams (Temple University Press, 2010).

Monique Milia-Marie-Luce is an assistant professor in contemporary history at the University of the French West Indies, campus of Schoelcher. She is a member of the research laboratory AIHP-GEODE EA927 (Archéologie Industrielle, Histoire, Patrimoine / Géographie-Développement Environnement de la Caraïbe) and an associate member of the LC2S (Laboratoire Caribéen de Sciences Sociales). Her publications include "Puerto Rican in the United States and French West Indian Immigrants in France," in *Migration to Western Europe and the United States*, ed. Ana Maragarita Cervantes-Rodriguez (Temple University Press, 2009); "La grande migration des Antillais en France, ou les années BUMIDOM," in *Terres d'Amérique*, ed. André Calmont and Cédric Audebert (Karthala / Géode Caraïbes, 2007); and "Une tentative avortée d'immigration de travail: L'affaire des bonnes antillaises 1922–1924," in *Empire et engagés*, ed. E. Guerassimoff and I. Mandé (Riveneuve, 2016). Her research about the connection between the state, colonies, and overseas departments is also featured in the book published by the Archives of CTM (new name of the Departmental Archives) that examines the history of the General Council of Martinique (*Le Conseil Général de la Martinique 1827–2015, pour le pays, par le pays*, Fort-de-France, Archives Départementales de la Martinique, Conseil Général de la Martinique, 2015).

Stéphanie Mulot is a professor of sociology at the Université Toulouse Jean Jaurès. Her research interests include social and medical anthropology, chronic disease, citizenship and discrimination, gender and health, family studies, domestic violence and patriarchy, black feminism, intersectionality, and the memory and representation of slavery. Professor Mulot edited the special issues of *Anthropologie et santé*, no. 5, "En quête de soins: Soignants et malades dans la globalisation," and no. 3, "Médecines, mobilités et globalisation." She has also authored more than twenty articles in various academic journals.

Rose Ndengue is a PhD candidate in African history at CESSMA (Centre d'Études en Sciences Sociales sur les Mondes Africains, Américains et Asiatiques) at Université Paris Diderot. She has worked on sexism and racism in France, exploring, in particular, the Collectif des Féministes Indigènes (CFI). She is currently working on women in Cameroonian politics since 1945. She is the author of "Mobilisations féminines au Cameroun français dans les années 1940–1950: L'ordre du genre et l'ordre colonial fissures," *Le mouvement social*, no. 255 (2016).

T. Denean Sharpley-Whiting is the Gertrude Conaway Vanderbilt Distinguished Professor of African American and Diaspora Studies at Vanderbilt University, where she directs the Callie House Center for the Study of Global Black Cultures and Politics. She is the author or editor of twelve books and three novels. She is currently at work on the monograph *Men I'd Like to Have Known: The Adventurous Lives of a Revolutionary Romantic, a Contraband Soldier, a Peripatetic Painter, and an Africanist Documentarian*.

Tyler Stovall is distinguished professor of history at the University of California, Santa Cruz, where he is also dean of the Humanities Division. He is currently serving as president of the American Historical Association. He specializes in the history of modern France, in particular, the study of labor, urban history, social history, race, and postcolonialism. Professor Stovall has written and edited several books on the subject, including *The Rise of the Paris Red Belt* (1990); *Paris Noir: African Americans in the City of Light* (1996); *The Color of Liberty: Histories of Race in France* (2003, coedited with Sue Peabody); and *Transnational France: The Modern History of a Universal Nation* (2015). He is currently completing a global history of the relationship between freedom and race tentatively titled *White Freedom: The Racial History of an Idea*, forthcoming from Princeton University Press.

Index

IN THE FRANCE OVERSEAS SERIES

Regeneration through Empire: French Pronatalists and Colonial Settlement in the Third Republic
Margaret Cook Andersen

To Hell and Back: The Life of Samira Bellil
Samira Bellil
Translated by Lucy R. McNair
Introduction by Alec G. Hargreaves

Colonial Metropolis: The Urban Grounds of Anti-Imperialism and Feminism in Interwar Paris
Jennifer Anne Boittin

Paradise Destroyed: Catastrophe and Citizenship in the French Caribbean
Christopher M. Church

The French Navy and the Seven Years' War
Jonathan R. Dull

I, Nadia, Wife of a Terrorist
Baya Gacemi

Transnational Spaces and Identities in the Francophone World
Edited by Hafid Gafaïti, Patricia M. E. Lorcin, and David G. Troyansky

Contesting French West Africa: Battles over Schools and the Colonial Order, 1900–1950
Harry Gamble

Black French Women and the Struggle for Equality, 1848–2016
Edited and with an introduction by Félix Germain and Silyane Larcher

The French Army and Its African Soldiers: The Years of Decolonization
Ruth Ginio

French Colonialism Unmasked: The Vichy Years in French West Africa
Ruth Ginio

Bourdieu in Algeria: Colonial Politics, Ethnographic Practices, Theoretical Developments
Edited and with an introduction by Jane E. Goodman and Paul A. Silverstein

Franco America in the Making: The Creole Nation Within
Jonathan K. Gosnell

Endgame 1758: The Promise, the Glory, and the Despair of Louisbourg's Last Decade
A. J. B. Johnston

Colonial Suspects: Suspicion, Imperial Rule, and Colonial Society in Interwar French West Africa
Kathleen Keller

French Mediterraneans: Transnational and Imperial Histories
Edited and with an introduction by Patricia M. E. Lorcin and Todd Shepard

The Cult of the Modern: Trans-Mediterranean France and the Construction of French Modernity
Gavin Murray-Miller

Cinema in an Age of Terror: North Africa, Victimization, and Colonial History
Michael F. O'Riley

Medical Imperialism in French North Africa: Regenerating the Jewish Community of Colonial Tunis
Richard C. Parks

Making the Voyageur World: Travelers and Traders in the North American Fur Trade
Carolyn Podruchny

A Workman Is Worthy of His Meat: Food and Colonialism in Gabon
Jeremy Rich

The Moroccan Soul: French Education, Colonial Ethnology, and Muslim Resistance, 1912–1956
Spencer D. Segalla

Silence Is Death: The Life and Work of Tahar Djaout
Julija Šukys

The French Colonial Mind, Volume 1: Mental Maps of Empire and Colonial Encounters
Edited and with an introduction by Martin Thomas

The French Colonial Mind, Volume 2: Violence, Military Encounters, and Colonialism
Edited and with an introduction by Martin Thomas

Beyond Papillon: The French Overseas Penal Colonies, 1854–1952
Stephen A. Toth

Madah-Sartre: The Kidnapping, Trial, and Conver(sat/s)ion of Jean-Paul Sartre and Simone de Beauvoir
Written and translated by Alek Baylee Toumi
With an introduction by James D. Le Sueur

Lightning Source UK Ltd.
Milton Keynes UK
UKHW040710041222
413176UK00015B/109

9 781496 201270